Praise for

"What I loved about this book is that not only did it open my eyes to angels I'd not met before, it also suggests practical tools to use in communication with the angels, including mandalas, letter writing and specific affirmations. What you use depends on your need and the angel you are communicating with. A great go-to book for your spiritual library."

—Dr. Georgina Cannon, author of *The Third Circle Protocol* and instructor at the School of Continuing Studies, University of Toronto

"A wonderful new book by author Crystal Pomeroy, *Angels and Goddesses*. In this book, the author brings together her extensive knowledge of the archangels and goddesses and how they are linked in a new way. This book is very well researched and well written. Included in the pages are easy-to-follow steps for anyone on any level. Crystal shows how the angels and goddesses can help you and how to connect with them at any time, any place, and in many ways."

—Lynn Andrews, *New York Times* bestselling author of the Medicine Woman series

ANGELS

and

GODDESSES

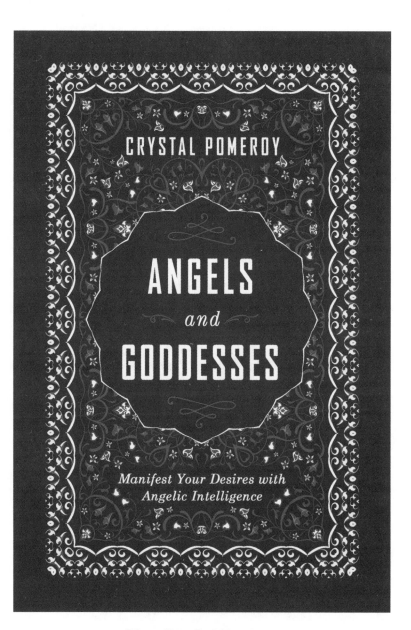

CRYSTAL POMEROY

ANGELS

and

GODDESSES

*Manifest Your Desires with
Angelic Intelligence*

Llewellyn Publications
Woodbury, Minnesota

FIRST EDITION
First Printing, 2022

Book design by Colleen McLaren
Cover design by Shira Atakpu

Llewellyn Publications is a registered trademark of Llewellyn Worldwide Ltd.

Library of Congress Cataloging-in-Publication Data
Names: Pomeroy, Crystal, 1969- author.
Title: Angels and goddesses : manifest your desires with angelic
    intelligence / Crystal Pomeroy.
Description: First edition. | Woodbury, Minnesota : Llewellyn Publications,
    2022. | Includes bibliographical references. | Summary: "Practical and
    energy-based practices to connect spiritually with angels and goddesses
    for manifestation, healing, prosperity, and other desires"-- Provided by
    publisher.
Identifiers: LCCN 2021044289 (print) | LCCN 2021044290 (ebook) | ISBN
    9780738764894 (paperback) | ISBN 9780738765020 (ebook)
Subjects: LCSH: Spiritual life. | Spirituality. | Goddess religion. |
    Goddesses. | Angels.
Classification: LCC BL624 .P643 2022 (print) | LCC BL624 (ebook) | DDC
    204/.4--dc23/eng/20211117
LC record available at https://lccn.loc.gov/2021044289
LC ebook record available at https://lccn.loc.gov/2021044290

Llewellyn Worldwide Ltd. does not participate in, endorse, or have any authority or responsibility concerning private business transactions between our authors and the public.

All mail addressed to the author is forwarded but the publisher cannot, unless specifically instructed by the author, give out an address or phone number.

Any internet references contained in this work are current at publication time, but the publisher cannot guarantee that a specific location will continue to be maintained. Please refer to the publisher's website for links to authors' websites and other sources.

Llewellyn Publications
A Division of Llewellyn Worldwide Ltd.
2143 Wooddale Drive
Woodbury, MN 55125-2989
www.llewellyn.com

Printed in the United States of America

Disclaimer

The information shared in this book is not designed as a replacement for your doctor's or psychologist's recommendations, but as a complement. If you apply any information in this book, the results are your own responsibility. Neither the author or publisher assume responsibility for your results in health, angel connections, or any other area.

© Lucero Guerrero

About the Author

After a college education in Spanish and Latin American Studies, Crystal was led home to the spiritual world she had been introduced to as a child. Her mother, an erudite scientist, teacher, activist, and astrologer, had sparked Crystal's interest in the esoteric arts and fueled her knowledge since childhood. By the time she was eleven, adults were consulting Crystal to interpret their dreams.

At age fourteen, she was calculating and interpreting astrological charts and studying with several renowned teachers, including the likes of Dorothy McClean and Joseph Campbell. Under the tutelage of Reverend Pearl Shannon, she began her intensive practice of affirmative prayer at age sixteen.

When, after college, she realized that her calling was to help others through sharing universal laws and angel connections, Crystal ended up reaching millions through writing, media, courses, groups, and personal treatments whose potency has garnered an extensive international client base.

The reader will find guided meditations and videos with angelic mudras and other tools in this book at www. crystalpomeroy.com. Follow the author by her name on Facebook and YouTube, and on Instagram at @crystal_clearalways.

Dedication

To the light beings who guide,
empower and work with me and other healers.

To Maya, angel-mother, shining among the stars.

Acknowledgments

To my mother Maya, who long before I did, foresaw and nurtured my interest in divine laws, angels, and the sacred feminine. She's in every healing I give and every prayer I say. To my agent and publicist, Devra Ann Jacobs, who's faith, guidance, and promotional skills were absolutely decisive to this book and with it, my life. To the enthusiastic, luminous and loving participants in my Divine Empowerment group. To my fifth generation of healers: Tere Vicente, Gala Rodríguez, María Luisa Rodríguez, Angy Navarrete, Norma Ramírez and Blanca Rebollar. To my dear Mayan elder Tere Arteaga. To Claudia Schimmer, Carmen Lorrabaquio, George Rosales and Lucy Aspra, angel-friends. To Amy Glazer, Anna Levine, Kat Neff, Laura Kurtz, Aundrea Foster, and everyone at Llewellyn International who applied their talents, bringing new beauty and light to these angels and goddesses.

Contents

Introduction / 1

CHAPTER 1:
Zadkiel and Amethyst:
Forgiveness and Alchemy / 7

CHAPTER 2:
Michael and Faith:
Protection and Miracles / 31

CHAPTER 3:
Raphael and Mary: Healing Your Beliefs,
Body, and Situations / 79

CHAPTER 4:
Hophiel and Constance:
Beauty, Brilliance, and Intuition /115

CHAPTER 5:
Chamuel and Charity:
Love, Happiness, and Self-Esteem / 159

CHAPTER 6:
Uriel and Grace:
Codes for Angelic Abundance / 199

CHAPTER 7:
Gabriel and Hope: Birth, Blessing,
Spiritual Rebirth / 243

Conclusion / 269
Pronunciation of Deity Names / 273
Bibliography / 275

INTRODUCTION

Several millennia ago, before the onset of patriarchy, the divine feminine had a central role in worship. Different goddesses had different symbols, colors, and specialties. The seven archangels identified by Pseudo-Dionysius in his classic and highly influential *Hierarchy of Angels* are closely connected to these goddesses. Archangel Michael is inextricably entwined with the Tibetan spiritual-warrior goddess Simhamukha, Zadkiel with Isis and Ixchel, and Gabriel with Guadalupe-Tonantzin (the Mexican name for the Virgin).

Besides their connection with archangels, goddess-centered cultures worldwide shared a system of spiritual technology whose remnants shine through the shards of archeology and myth. They include magical mandalas, angel-flower connections, and—beyond invocation—*fusion* with light beings. I have adapted these and other lost treasures as part of the unique offering of Angelic Intelligence.

To speak of angels is to speak of goddesses, to connect with them and reignite our feminine powers independently of our gender identification. These powers were put on hold with the onset of patriarchy, which downgraded women and all but excluded them from their once vital role as healers, spiritual leaders, and magic makers. In fact, through its emphasis on domination, the patriarchy has repressed not only women but the individual in general. Although toxic masculinity has grown, the sacred masculine was buried along with the sacred feminine. It's time for us for us to bring them both back to the surface. Angels help all of us retrieve our hidden gifts: healing, compassion, transmutation, co-creation, abundance, faith, courage, focus, and authority.

Like a magical tree, the roots of Angelic Intelligence reach into humanity's ancient past to a time when masculine and feminine were more balanced. As for its branches, they spread upward into a realm of light beings that healers and alchemists once worked with closely. Over milennia, these connections faded from view. But the realm is timeless, and the angels and their goddess companions are waiting to collaborate and restore our confidence and power.

Angels and Goddesses: Divine Co-workers

Besides its connection to angels, the spiritual technology of goddess-centered cultures included contemporary keys like the creative use of thoughts, words, feelings, and imagination. Yet other dynamic elements remain largely forgotten. For instance, colors were not only used for decoration but for vibrational purposes as well. Diverse shades were known to affect one's energy in different ways and were used to awaken specific inner powers and activate connections with certain light beings.

As opposed to today's more passive meditation and prayer, wise ones applied their minds to magical actions. They would open and close portals, move energy, cleanse, sweep, dissolve, cut, and travel through time in order to select desirable futures. Besides invoking and visualizing light beings, they fused with them. Their technology also included mandalas and connections with flower and tree angels and with the earth herself. With Angelic Intelligence, I retrieve and update these lost treasures.

My term "vibrational science" refers to the application of higher laws such as faith, gratitude, creative imagination, forgiveness, and love—laws that help us reconnect with Source and manifest our desires. Today, knowledge of these principles has expanded; millions apply positive thinking, visualization, affirmations, and related tools to change their lives and raise their vibration, crossing over for the first time into the mainstream. The results often seem magical yet can be inconsistent. Sooner or later people tend to experience some sort of block: they don't get the sense of peace they once did, manifestation seems to take too long, or things go great for a time only to reach a plateau. Then frustration sets in. Most people are not aware that in a world parallel to our own, light beings actively seek to help us move through those blocks and precipitate new levels of mastery. This book is designed to open the door and let the light beings in.

Although the concept and many of the methods proposed in this book are original, the idea of collective awakening is not exactly new. Toward the end of the nineteenth century, Ralph Waldo Emerson and his colleagues spoke of a new, transcendental kind of thought that was beginning to emerge, one which surpassed the power of everyday mind.[1] In the mid-1900's, Teilhard de Chardin said that a fresh kind of life was appearing in human consciousness that was changing its very structure.[2]

When I began developing this field, I had been teaching metaphysical and Pagan wisdom for two decades. I was reaching hundreds of thousands through my conferences, classes, guided meditations,

---

1. Ferguson, Marilyn, *The Aquarian Conspiracy* (New York: Penguin, 1987), 29.
2. Ibid., 33.

healings, publications, and radio and television appearances mainly in Mexico where I'd been living. My knowledge was part of a legacy received since childhood, when my mother had taken me to study with renowned teachers and authors, including Joseph Campbell, Dorothy Maclean, and Reverend Pearl Shannon, who initiated me in the practice of divine science in San Francisco where I grew up. I had learned to heal and precipitate miraculous outcomes for myself and others; teaching had come as an outgrowth of this work.

How to Use This Book

Each chapter focuses on one archangel and his feminine complement, exploring their particular gifts. For instance, chapter 6 centers on Uriel and Grace, who help us deepen our gratitude and also manifest material prosperity as we activate the secret powers of our hands. Like the rainbow whose beauty includes a range of colors, the archangels and their divine complements cover a full spectrum of inner work and other areas of life. For support on pronunciation, you will find a guide at the end of the book.

If you choose to follow each chapter in the order it appears, you can climb the angelic rainbow, a spectrum that takes us through the purple of transmutation to the white of spiritual rebirth. I would love for you to spend several weeks exploring its offerings and applying its keys before moving onto the next one. If you have a need to work on some particular area such as forgiveness, healing, finances, or your love life, you may prefer to focus on that related archangel. You can also use the book as an oracle, opening the pages randomly to see what messages the angels have for you on any given day. Whatever your inclination, I suggest that at some point you give special focus to the first two chapters on Zadkiel and Michael and devote at least one month working with each as your time allows.

Finding Your Light Network

Besides facilitating contact with angels, this book optimizes the results of your inner work, such as forgiveness, manifestation, healing, and positive prayer. And as we will see a bit further on, it does something more by teaching you to use your Angelic Intelligence.

As I followed the dots revealed in my research, it often seemed like an invisible force was guiding me to uncover a worldwide web of pre-patriarchal wisdom. With the revelation came a particular series of symbols, including butterflies (representing our light body), cocoons, rainbows, mandalas, weaving, and flowers. When I began to give my first course on Angelic Intelligence, I discovered that these very symbols had been appearing on the paths of a high number of participants, before they had taken the first session. Have butterflies, cocoons, rainbows, mandalas, weaving, or flowers been appearing on your path? What angelicities—my name for angelic synchronicities—led you to this book?

I had been studying, applying, and teaching metaphysics for most of my life when in 2011 I began to deepen my research of the seven archangels. I became fascinated at how each of them relates to a certain set of metaphysical principles. Zadkiel rules forgiveness and release; Michael, faith and courage; Raphael, healing truth; and Uriel, prosperity and gratitude; to name only a few. As I studied their symbols, colors, and attributes, I was even more amazed to find to find their roots in traditions that pre-date institutionalized religion by thousands of years. The methods I share include techniques adapted from those traditions, making a new offering to the field, one that improves your contact with each archangel along with their companion deities and nature spirits. As you embark on the journey through the pages that follow, angels, goddesses, and related light beings will be guiding you to activate your personal Angelic Intelligence.

Chapter 1

ZADKIEL AND AMETHYST: FORGIVENESS AND ALCHEMY

If you're attracted to forgiveness, releasing negative emotions and conditions, and increasing your feelings of self-worth, then you'll love Zadkiel and his twin flame, Amethyst. Sharing these gifts, the purple archangels lead our way onto the angelic rainbow. Like its counterpart in the visible sky, this rainbow shines in the subtle realm. Each of its colors relates to a certain archangel and his powers. Each is a door that opens onto a unique sphere of magic, which we explore in the chapters of this book. The gold at the end of the rainbow is not just a fairy tale. It describes the magical results that come from following the path of the seven archangels, each of them connected to certain colors, symbols, and powers.

Besides radiating in the purple spectrum, Zadkiel and Amethyst relate to the entire rainbow. The first archangel is a radiant youth who wears purple robes and has great, gold wings. His symbols also include a cross to cross out low-vibration attitudes and conditions, and a chalice to direct us to the place of true change, which is within. Besides relating to rainbows, Zadkiel is the angelic regent of transmutation, elimination, justice, service, devotion,

7

forgiveness, self-worth, and alchemy. He rules Sahasrara, the violet and golden crown chakra whose lotus has a thousand rainbow petals.

As for black-haired Amethyst, she's known to be quite tall and wear purple dresses and shawls. Of the seven divine complements, only she bears the name of a material object. A little-known fact about amethysts reveals their unusual properties and symbolic connection with Zadkiel. This stone symbolizes our physical incarnation that, with the help of angels, can be transmuted into a portal of higher existence.

A look at the properties of the amethyst confirms its special magic. Evolving from plain quartz crystals, purple and violet hues appear when the crystals are exposed to radiation from surrounding stones, triggering the iron traces within the crystal to produce their deep colors. If subjected to heat, amethyst's colors fade, reappearing when irradiated with gamma or X-rays. This same method is even used to turn common quartz crystals into amethysts. Amethyst's name signals the ultimate goal of the purple archangels. The plain crystal symbolizes our physical body: when in contact with inner work and connections with angels, like an amethyst taking on magical colors, it becomes a portal of higher existence. Just as amethysts can be revived by the right radiation, Zadkiel and Amethyst reignite our magic.

Transmuting Love: Door to the Angelic Rainbow

Shining at the top of the rainbow, purple has the highest frequency of the visible light spectrum. The purple archangel connects us with the sublime vibration of alchemical love, preparing us for fusion with the rest of the angels. Of Zadkiel's gifts, this is the most magical.

When it comes to transmuting, not all loves are equal. The most common kind comes easily, when pleasant feelings arise in response to certain people, animals, and situations. And then there is love that takes work. Zadkiel rules this power and helps us generate it in three important ways: forgiveness, heartfelt service, and a sense of worthiness. If you've ever worked with these attitudes, you've discovered that they're powerful but not necessarily easy to sustain or even to achieve in the first place. The purple and their companion deities support this shift.

Forgiveness: The Highest Alchemy

Over the last twenty years, I've enjoyed the magical results of these attitudes firsthand and witnessed them in the lives of thousands of others. When we transmute resentment, guilt, indifference, and unworthiness, we precipitate miraculous changes: harmony in relationships, new inner peace, accelerated healing, and financial abundance.

One of my first experiences with this magic was after my initial and prolonged resistance, when I finally began to forgive my father. I had been in my teens when a renowned psychic and metaphysical teacher said I needed to do this. Her advice surprised me—I wasn't a vengeful person, and although he had been abusive, I didn't walk around nursing my wounds or fuming about it.

My dad was a cultured, talented man and a good provider. He also had an explosive temper, a stinging belt, and addictions to alcohol and to fondling his daughters.

When my parents got divorced, I stayed with my wonderful mother and my life took off. I was focused on academic goals, activism, and esoteric studies. As for the situation with my dad, my sister and I eventually confronted him about the sexual abuse. I felt empowered and generally enthused about my life, not stuck or paralyzed by memories, not consciously at least.

When my teacher later mentioned forgiveness, it seemed like a nice idea but didn't really grab me. "Why send good intentions to people who do bad things?" I wondered. It wasn't until some years later when I felt blocked in several areas that I was willing to actually get down to the inner work it requires, setting aside ten minutes daily to look within, perceiving my own judgmental thoughts toward my father, and repeating affirmations such as: "I bless you and release you in peace" and "I release you to the loving hands of Spirit and move into my true good now."

After many years without contact, my father suddenly sought me out and came to visit me in Mexico. He was supportive, respectful, and for the first time in my life, it seemed as though he was interested in me as a person.

I then broadened this daily practice, releasing my hard thoughts toward everyone, including myself. Cultivating harmony, I avoided unnecessary arguments (a big change for me!) and applied other keys shared in this chapter. My prayers became more powerful. Unexpected doors began to open. I was guided to start a business and everything just fell into place. A few years later, I felt called to share metaphysical principles with others, and soon after that—through a series of unplanned events—I received a flood of invitations to give paid conferences and appear on national radio and television.

Since then, my work has given me the opportunity to see the results of forgiveness in the lives of thousands of others. As did I, many people experience some initial resistance to doing the work. Yet when they actually apply this universal law, they experience inner peace, their relationships and bodies heal, and their finances are unblocked.

What Forgiveness Is and Is Not

I came to understand that forgiveness isn't only for vengeful people. Neither does it mean accepting abuse or injustice. Far from being passive, it's a brave choice to free ourselves. The root of the word "resentment" means "to go over a feeling." When we resent people and situations, we unconsciously accumulate negative attachments to them. These links lodge in our auras and block the flow of good. When we forgive, we release the blocks.

In his book *Desert Wisdom*, philosopher and linguist Neil Douglas-Klotz translates the immortal Lord's Prayer: "Forgive us our trespasses as we forgive those who trespass against us." In Aramaic it meant: "Untie the knots of failure binding us, as we release the strands we hold of others' faults."[3] To forgive is to untie the knots, let go of the past, and move forward in a greater radiation of love.

The results are magical, but the process isn't always easy. Like other forms of intentional love, it can seem elusive or almost impossible. It takes work to let go of hard feelings toward people who have hurt us or others. Personally, at times I've experienced unconditional love, only to feel myself once slipping again into judgmental attitudes. The alchemy of forgiveness cannot be explained in worldly terms. As a woman in one of my classes argued with me, "It's only natural to resent what I've gone through." I answered, "You're right, and if you want supernatural results, you need to make a supernatural effort." Fortunately, there are supernatural beings who facilitate this and other positive changes and support lasting harmony. A bit further on, we will see original, fun ways of opening to their assistance.

---

3. Neil Douglas-Klotz, *Desert Wisdom: Sacred Middle-Eastern Writings from the Goddess to the Sufis* (San Francisco: HarperSanFrancisco, 1995), 249.

Transmuting Love Has Been Used in Many Goddess Traditions

A look at two such traditions from different continents sheds light on this kind of alchemy.

The better known of the two is *Ubuntu,* a Bantu doctrine deriving from various oral traditions in sub-Saharan Africa. Meaning "a person is a person through other persons," or "I am myself through you," Ubuntu focuses on connectedness, including kindness, respect for others, helpfulness, and forgiveness. Ubuntu's origins are rooted in a prebiblical practice connected to Ma'at, the Egyptian goddess of truth, righteousness, and cosmic order.

On the other side of the world, ancient Incans practiced *munay* (pronounced moon-eye), a principle still used by native medicine men and women. Also known as the art of love, munay is a state of intentional kindness that overcomes the impulses of our lower nature. As it does so, it connects us with the gold. Considered a powerful healing force, munay includes forgiveness, reconciliation with our personal and family stories, and loving feelings and actions for ourselves, for others, for Pachamana—the Peruvian creator goddess—and for every living thing. Forgiveness, loving service, and self-worth are Zadkiel's themes—once again, we discover their ancestral connection with the sacred feminine.

The alchemy light body—Zadkiel's crown jewel—is also part of munay: to live in this deeply loving way leads to spiritual awakening and prepares our energy vehicle so that when we pass on from the physical, we can ascend to a higher realm known as *hanak pacha.*

Zadkiel and the Goddesses of Transmutation

In a post-industrial society, we are told to create, manifest, and make things happen. Pre-patriarchal cultures had a more holistic view. They knew that endings must precede beginnings, and they honored a Great Mother whose power—both to create and to dissolve—permeated nature and the cosmos. This force is in each of us, and Zadkiel helps awaken it and dissolve undesirable attitudes and conditions at their root in the quantum realm of possibilities.

We will now look at four goddesses of transmutation who work with Zadkiel: the Toltec Xochiquetzal, Coatlicue, Tlazolteotl, and the Celtic Samhain.

Xochiquetzal: Purple Goddess of Renewal and the Light Body

Like Zadkiel, Xochiquetzal rules rainbows. She has a special valley where weavers work incessantly, making bright garments for the afterlife—a reference to the light body. She is said to have emerged as the first woman from a purple pool, emphasizing her powers of rebirth and also the goddess presence in humans.

Connect with Purple

Purple, violet, and related shades comprise a force field that connects us with the angels of alchemy. You can feel the difference from the moment you begin your prayers, meditation, or journaling. Take a moment to close your eyes and imagine that Zadkiel and Amethyst are right there in front of you: large, majestic, and shining in a lovely tone of amethyst, as you repeat one of the following invocations, depending on your intent.

You can use a purple pen to write affirmations of forgiveness, change, and self-worth, and light a purple candle while working with these attitudes and energies. For intensity, you could even use purple paper and a gold ink pen.

In the exercise section of this chapter, you will find more ways to integrate the magic of purple.

Invocations to Empower Your Inner Work

"Zadkiel and Amethyst, please center my attention and empower my prayers (meditation, mantras, journaling)."

"Angels and goddesses, please direct my inner work and help me release unloving attitudes toward myself and others."

"Angels of alchemy, please help me release my mental noise and connect my emotions as I pray."

After these invocations, spend six minutes or more (six being a goddess number) applying some of the many affirmations and techniques described throughout this book (or your own preferred practice).

If your intention is one of Zadkiel's specialties (forgiveness, release, enforcing your sense of self-worth, dissolving resistance to change or reigniting the flame of loving service), hold to the vision of the purple archangels before you and choose from the following affirmations. Repeat the words aloud and make sure to connect your emotions. For an even deeper effect, write out the affirmation 6, 9, 18, or 24 times, affirming aloud and with feeling.

Invocations and Affirmations to Transmute Unworthiness

"I invoke Archangel Amethyst and the goddesses of change to remove any conscious or unconscious blocks to success and happiness now."

"Zadkiel and Amethyst, please dissolve any programming that could block me receiving my good (success, wellness, prosperity, happiness)."

"I give thanks for the energy of angels that pours through my being, dissolving any unconscious rejection of my divine good now."

"The angels and goddesses support me in releasing feelings of unworthiness that I have absorbed or inherited, so I may receive my complete good now."

"Zadkiel and Amethyst, please shine your transmuting rays in my deep mind and dissolve the tendency to doubt my worth."

Note: Self-love is vital to Angelic Intelligence, and you'll find more keys to turn it on throughout this book.

Invocations and Affirmations for Forgiveness

"Angels send me forgiving love, and I send forgiving love to others now."

"I am not alone in my intention to forgive, the angels of alchemy are with me, helping me release hard thoughts and radiate the love that I am now."

"The forgiving love of angels pours into this situation, producing perfect results for all involved, here and now."

"Zadkiel and Amethyst, as leaves turn purple and fall, shine your violet light into my mind and cause resentments and toxic guilt to fall away now."

Invocation to Open to Positive Change

"I invoke the angels of transmutation to dissolve my resistance to change and I give thanks for the new doors of good that open for me now."

Invocation to Release Attachments

"Angels of release, with your purple light, please dissolve my impulse to control people and situations, and help me let go and let God, now and always."

Invocations to Fuel the Flame of Loving Service

To connect with angels, it's vital to keep the flame of service burning in our hearts. Angels are here to assist other beings and will work more closely with people who persist in this resonance. Choose from the following invocations to repeat as you begin your day or before you start your work:

"Thank you, angels, for connecting me with the joy of service now."

"Zadkiel and Amethyst, please guide me to serve with love, in balanced, effective ways, now and always."

"I invite the angelic forces to serve and prosper through me now."

Begin to Ignite Your Light Body

This simple key will allow you to use the energy generated by your inner work to turn on your light body. Right after a session of prayer, meditation, journaling, or affirmations, say out loud three times and with mindfulness: "Zadkiel and Xochiquetzal, please weave this energy of love (and/or awareness, faith, peace, or wellness), into my light body so that it may shine brightly, sustaining my connection with higher realms, now and always." As you repeat the words, remember to visualize and *feel* the scene they describe.

Keep paper and pen handy as you continue to work with these angelic affirmations and invocations, because the angels will inspire you to come up with your own.

Sweeping a Clear Path: Coatlicue and Samhain

Witches, brooms, and autumn go farther back than Halloween storefronts, deriving from the forgotten magic of cleansing, a practice that was central to native traditions.

At the beginning of November, when nature's work of decomposition is well underway, the goddess of rebirth, Samhain, brings forth the Celtic New Year.

In ancient Mexico, Fall Equinox was called the Day of the Dead and considered the most important quarter of the year. Violet, Zadkiel's color, prevailed on altars, and purple flowers were set on them to help the departed with their transmuting light. As we will see further on, flowers are active promoters of Angelic Intelligence. For numerous "Pagan" cultures, the fall season—and death in general—were not associated with demise, but rebirth and awakening instead.

Brushing, sweeping, and cleansing are not just physical actions. Consider Coatlicue, a Toltec goddess of life and death. She gives birth to Huitzilopochtli, a spiritual warrior hero who, like Jesus, is symbolically reborn at Winter Solstice as the new sun. Her story is revealing:

The widow Coatlicue was sweeping her temple, when a ball of brightly colored feathers fell from the sky and impregnated her. Her 400 previous children conspired to kill their brother as soon as he was born. The goddess warned the developing infant, who sprang from her womb fully armed, immediately vanquishing his hostile siblings[4].

---

4. "Leyenda de Coatlicue y Coyolxauhqui," Inside Mexico website: https://www.inside-mexico.com/leyenda-de-coatlicue-y-coyolxauhqui/.

That her previous children were ashamed of the widow's pregnancy indicates that she was older: the archetypal wise woman in the phase of life most related to transmutation.

In the native cultures where these goddesses emerged, brooms aren't only used to clean floors but also to brush away obsolete attachments, habits, and energies.

Coatlicue's sanctuary represents that sacred space within; her sweeping is the freedom that comes as we care for that space. This act leads to connections with angels—the ball of colored feathers—who seed the discovery of our true identity, the divine conception in this story. The incipient awakening upsets our previous limited creations—the angry siblings.

In the Exercises with Zadkiel and his Goddess Colleagues section of this chapter, you'll find ways to turn chores and even personal hygiene into angelic acts of power.

Tlazoteotl and the Magic of the Magnetic Earth

The ancients recognized a kind of transmutation that is neglected in our times and that the angels help us recover. We find it exemplified in the ancient earth goddesses who are colleagues of Zadkiel and Amethyst. Besides dissolving and cleansing undesirable situations, these feminine forces were invoked to literally pull undesirable emotions and tendencies out of humans.

A striking example is the ancient Mexican goddess, Tlazolteotl. Like Zadkiel, she ruled cleansing, change, and forgiveness. Like damp soil, her lips were black, a goddess color connected to purple. They could absorb and dissolve whatever needed to be cleansed: from illness, garbage, and waste to guilt and blame. Her feast day was in autumn, season of transmutation.

Although Tlazolteotl's cult has been practically erased, her essence lingers and continues to heal through purple angels, purple flowers, and the earth herself. Some of these powers have even been proven by science, albeit indirectly. For instance, it's been shown that physical contact with the earth absorbs our excess of positive ions. It restores the electrical balance that underlies all the body's chemical, cellular, and healing processes,[5] normalizing brain waves,[6] sustaining cognitive function,[7] improving sleep,[8] and shielding the body from electromagnetic pollution.[9] To this day, descendants of Mayans lie naked on the ground to connect with Mother Earth's energies. Similar knowledge existed around the ancient world. It is said that when the Buddha was in deep meditation under the Bodhi tree, a demon named Mara repeatedly tried to distract and weaken him. It was only after touching the ground and invoking assistance from the earth goddess that Buddha was able to overcome the attack and achieve enlightenment.

Exercises with Zadkiel and His Goddess Colleagues

We will now see keys to turn common activities and situations into angelic acts of magic. Your personal care, cleaning, list-writing, earth connections, and full moon rituals can unblock you in new ways.

---

5. Cinton Ober, with Steven Sinatra, and Martin Zucker, *Earthing: The Most Important Health Discovery Ever* (Laguna Beach, CA: Basic Health Publications, 2010), 11.

6. Ibid, 82.

7. Ibid, 95.

8. Ibid, 45.

9. Ibid, 78.

Magical Cleaning

The angels of alchemy make enlightenment easier and turn chores into acts of magic. We find echoes of this wisdom in a modern Japanese monastery practice that derives from ancient goddess traditions. Monks begin their day with cleaning and spend a third of their time on chores, not because the monastery is dirty but to keep their minds cleared of shadows. In his book, *Cleaning Manual of a Buddhist Monk*, Keisuke Matsumoto shares "a story of a disciple of Buddha who achieved nirvana while sweeping incessantly and chanting over and over, 'Sweep the dust, remove the dirt.'"[10] A tradition of Kuan Yin evokes earlier roots of this practice. While the goddess was working to clean the temple, animals appeared to assist her. The peacock used his tail—symbol of the heavenly rainbow—to sweep the floor.[11]

A client of mine calls her Sunday housecleaning her experience of going to church. Taking a bath, washing clothes, or even dusting can be acts of magic.

Angelic Cleaning Rituals

As you make your bed and put your room, home, or office in order, you can repeat aloud: "I call on Amethyst and Zadkiel, to clear and brighten my space, life, and mind now."

While sweeping the floor or organizing your desk, you might affirm: "Angelic energies pour through my world and sweep out stale attachments and conditions now."

10. Keisuke Matsumoto, *Manual de limpieza de un monje budista*, trans. Crystal Pomeroy, Kindle version, 55–56.
11. Merlin Stone, *Ancient Mirrors of Womanhood* (Boston: Beacon Press, 1990), 29.

While taking a shower, visualize the water cleansing your aura as you affirm: "The love of angels pours over me, and I am freed and renewed, here and now."

Even brushing or washing your hair can be an act of magic. While brushing, repeat the affirmation: "The angels of transmutation sweep my aura and mind, and I am clear and free now." When you wash your hair, visualize the angels touching your head and affirm: "The love of angels frees me from mental limitations now."

When you have to do something that requires physical exertion, such as cleaning out your car or moving boxes or furniture, put fire into the effort and repeat: "I am firm in releasing whatever needs to go now."

When Dirt is Cleansing

The angels of transmutation work closely with the earth herself. There are simple yet powerful ways to receive their energy, improve your inner work, and even free you during those times when you feel your own best efforts to forgive, release, and transmute just aren't enough.

Put your bare feet on the ground, or simply touch it while affirming: "I am one with the angelic energies of the Mother, and they draw from me resentments, guilt, and attachments now."

The earth emanates transmuting powers, and turned soil has a special charge. People plow or dig it for planting and hollow it out for burial. Receive this potency in your garden or another place where you can dig or touch freshly turned earth. Get on your knees, bend over, and press the soil with your forearms and hands, as you say, "Thank you, Sacred Mother, for your loving embrace. Please draw these knots of resentment from me (confusion, pain, or another state you wish to release). Transmute them and use the energy to create new good."

Apply this special key that I discovered on my own while work-ing personally with the subtle essence of Tlazoteotl: as you touch the earth, feel her loving power in the soil, feel how it absorbs toxic emotions, drawing them from you in response to your request.

Emergency Contact

At those times when touching the ground is inconvenient or impos-sible, you can still use affirmations like those above to invoke the Earth Mother. Just as gravity is exerted all over the planet, her mind and powers are present and will respond. To quicken the connec-tion, imagine you are touching the soil.

Angelic Transmutation List to Dissolve Challenging Attitudes and Conditions

- At the top of a sheet of purple paper or a fresh page in your journal, write these words: "Angelic energies pour through my life and dissolve all situations and influences that are no longer for my highest good."

- Below this affirmation, make a list describing the things you'd like to erase from your life as though you were already free.

- As you write each line, optimize it by imagining that you're actually writing a letter to a confidante, sharing the good news of your freedom. Then, before writing the next intention, pause to imagine the situation dissolving into a field of purple.

- After finishing your list, write across it diagonally: "Trans-muted by Zadkiel and Amethyst."

Every day, set aside a few minutes to review your list. Notice the changes related to your intentions, and pause to thank the angels for their assistance. When something has been dissolved, cross it off. Once again, visualize the remaining situations disappearing into a field of purple. You can redo your list as needed.

Full Moon Transmutation Ritual

- Light a purple candle.
- Invoke and visualize Zadkiel, Amethyst, and Xochiquetzal or other goddess colleagues named in this chapter.
- Repeat aloud three times: "Please dissolve whatever attitudes and conditions block my divine good."
- Write your transmutation list as described above.
- Light a gold candle, repeating aloud three times: "I give thanks for the wealth of new good that the angels bring forth for me now."
- Leave the purple and gold candles burning in sight for an hour.

Zadkiel's Flowers

As mentioned earlier, flowers are powerful allies of angels and goddesses. Violets and other purple flowers support forgiveness, transmutation, and release.

Of all blooms, dark purple and black roses are particularly effective. They are emissaries of feminine transmutation, and their spirit will literally draw out attachments, false guilt, and other attitudes you can't release by yourself.

Invoke the Angel of the Dark Rose

1. Choose an attitude you want to be free from. It may be guilt that doesn't belong to you, toxic shame, a disempow-

ering attachment, a persistent resentment, a fixation for the approval of others, or whatever else you wish to work on.

2. Sit or lie in a comfortable position with your eyes closed.

3. Visualize a large, black rose before you (if you prefer, see it as dark purple).

4. Say aloud and mentally, "Dark Flower Spirit, please pull from me any false guilt (or whatever attitude or feeling you wish to release)."

5. Spend 6 minutes feeling how the flower's magnetic force draws that attitude from you.

6. Thank the Dark Flower Spirit for her help.

Besides asking for specific assistance, you may prefer to alternately ask the Flower Spirit to heal you as it sees fit. Repeat: "Dark Flower Spirit, please draw from me whatever I need to release now." These light beings are sentient and savvy at unblocking. Before I researched them, they had been appearing to offer me their assistance, drawing out attitudes I hadn't even recognized, such as guilt for the karma of others who have created systems that damage the environment, and confusion after separating from my husband.

Zadkiel's Mandalas for Forgiveness and Unblocking

Since ancient times, mandalas have been associated with the sacred feminine and used as portals to healing and awareness.

Inspired in this tradition, I've designed angel-flower mandalas as an effective key to awaken your powers and connect with light beings. Let me show you how to make your own mandala with simple materials you have around your house or things you can easily acquire from the stationery section in your local grocery store.

1. Before gathering and/or purchasing your materials, choose from the following Zadkiel specializations so you may focus on:

   - forgiveness

   - dissolving resistance to change

   - releasing attachments to situations, people, or a concern with the approval of others

   - awakening your spirit of loving service and directing it successfully

   - transmuting feelings of unworthiness and allowing yourself to receive success, wellness, riches

   - freedom from whatever blocks the angels wish to lift from you.

2. Take a moment to quiet your mind, focus on your intention and ask the angels, flowers, and cosmic essences to help you achieve it. Hold to your purpose as you get the following items:

   - purple paper or poster board and a gold or blue pen, crayons and/or paints; or, alternately, cream or white paper and purple pen and coloring implements

   - your favorite adhesive stick or glue

   - depending on the size of your mandala, 20–30 small images of violets or other purple flowers

   - one large (1½") and three or more small (½") images of Archangel Zadkiel with twin flame Amethyst. (You can download, cut out, and paste; if you prefer, draw the images onto the poster board.)

Make Your Forgiveness Mandala

1. Trace a large (10" or more) circle, and then line it evenly with violets. (As described above for the angel images, choose your favorite way to fill the circle with flowers.)

2. Draw or paste the image of the angels in the middle, and the smaller images around the inside of the circle to taste.

3. At the top of your mandala, write an affirmation, such as:

   "Zadkiel and Amethyst, please surround me with the trans-muting light of myriad purple flowers, and dissolve my hard attitudes as I release all to God's forgiving love."

   "I surround myself with the violets and purple flowers of the planet and ask that they touch my heart and help me radiate love toward myself and all others."

4. Inside the circle, write the names of anyone you can remember that you have ever felt resentment or offense toward. Be sincere with yourself and go deep. To receive the complete results of forgiveness, we have to go completely within.

Center Your Attention in Your Mandala

At night before going to bed, spend ten minutes gazing at your mandala. Imagine the energy of all the violets of the planet surrounding you, touching your aura and dissolving resentments as you repeat the affirmation and send loving thoughts to everyone on your list.

Zadkiel's Unblocking Mandala

Use the materials described above, exchanging the violets for black roses. If you like, exchange the center image for that of a black or dark purple rose.

The writing on this mandala consists of an invocation like one of these:

"Zadkiel and Amethyst, please apply your magnetic powers to draw from me whatever attitudes, attachments, or influences I can't release on my own."

"Dark Rose Angel, please draw out of me any attachments and attitudes that may block my good."

"Angels and flowers of transmutation, please embrace me with your presence and draw from me feelings of unworthiness." (Adapt to include any attitude you wish to release.)

Observe your unblocking mandala; as you invoke the roses, mentally experience their presence. Then close your eyes and visualize their image and magnetism drawing out unwanted energies and attitudes. This method is particularly effective if used before fusing with Archangel Michael's force field, as we will see in the next chapter.

Write to Zadkiel

One of the most miraculous forms of positive prayer is to write to an archangel. Besides being a lost art form, handwritten letters are an archetypal method of contact that breaks through even the hardest blocks to answered prayer. When you write to an angel, a special door opens that lifts your affirmations and invocations to a higher degree of potency.

Write to Zadkiel when other methods of forgiveness or healing your sense of self-worth haven't worked.

Here is an example of an angel letter for forgiveness.

To Archangels Zadkiel and Amethyst

Dear angels,
I love you and bless you. Please help transmute my conscious
and subconscious resentments to forgiveness, bring peace to my
soul, and harmonize my connections with (name of person or
people).
I send up these words for your work of guidance and healing:

(Write your favorite forgiveness affirmation six, nine, or twenty-one
times. Choose or adapt from those shared on pages 14–15 or 25–26.)

Without your help I couldn't have done it.
With love,
Sign your name

Write the letter daily during three or four weeks, as needed until
peace fills your heart and the situation is healed.

Angel letters are particularly effective if done before dawn, or
whenever the others involved are sleeping.

Letter to Release Feelings of Unworthiness

Adapt the above example, requesting that Zadkiel and Amethyst
help dissolve any unconscious blocks to your success and happiness.

Choose or adapt your favorite affirmation of worthiness (pages
14–15) and write it in the letter six, nine, eighteen, or twenty-four
times.

After writing them, hide or destroy the letters. Talking about or
showing them to someone brings their vibration down to the level
of common mind, thus blocking transmutation.

Real Gold

The angels are guiding you to choose from the many keys shared in this chapter: visualizations, affirmations, invocations, Zadkiel's transmutation list and forgiveness letter, angelic grounding, sweeping and cleansing, and angel-flower mandalas. Some of these can be easily integrated into your current daily habits. As for the others, I suggest you begin with one or two methods, and persist in them for twenty-eight days (a complete lunar cycle). Give thanks for your progress, and try a different combination for the next four weeks.

The pot at the end of the rainbow is not a cartoon fantasy—it really exists. Its gold is not from earthly diggings, although it is magical.

Ancient wise ones knew that power doesn't come from the world of appearances. For them, resentment was an invitation to higher love, death to a new life, and release—not a form of loss, but an empowerment.

There's a Native American prophecy of a time when the esoteric teachings of the world would be revealed, the Rainbow Bridge would reappear and we would walk it.[12]

Zadkiel, Amethyst, and their network of sacred essences are radiating in a purple realm, ready to lift us onto the bridge. To contact them, the first step is to make a place for transmuting love: forgiveness, heartfelt service, and self-worth. By invoking their alchemical colors, vibrations, and activities, they will fill our lives with the gold of peace, wellness, and prosperity. The shadows of our energy body will be transmuted so that our golden body can begin to shine. And humanity's golden road will be paved with new light.

---

12. Steven McFadden, *Legend of the Rainbow Warriors* (Bloomington, IN: iUniverse Publishers), 13.

Chapter 2

MICHAEL AND FAITH: PROTECTION AND MIRACLES

The divine commander of the angelic host, Michael is earthlings' protector. He supports us to master our thoughts, accomplish spiritual goals, shake off psychic parasites, and unleash our potential as miracle workers.

Michael's beautiful face is surrounded by waves of long hair. His color is bright blue. Usually depicted with a lance or sword and a shield, he often wears armor and carries a chalice or grail. He's sometimes shown with a dragon, serpent, or demon at his feet. The blue archangel removes negative entities and guards over portals of all kinds, from the doors and windows in our homes, to the doorways of our minds and the portals between dimensions, which he can open and close. When nothing short of a miracle will do, Michael makes the difference.

Michael facilitates the retrieval of our sacred masculine energies of strength, focus, will, and determination, which in turn support our inner feminine attributes of love and faith—symbolized by the grail. His divine complement is Faith. Hers is one of the most important of angelic missions: to fuel the flame of faith in our hearts, deepening our prayer powers and opening the way for spiritual victory. Her outer robe is blue, signifying protection, and under it she wears a white garment, reflecting her luminous awareness and force.

Related to Vishuddha, the throat chakra, Michael empowers our speech and self-expression and breaks through blocks to answered prayer. Through the blue ribbon of the angelic rainbow, he and Faith vanquish negative energies of all kinds. Of all the archangels, they are the most concerned with awakening our angelic light body. This is the quickest and most significant way we can lift our vibration and ensure direct passage to the highest possible realm on transition from the physical.

Michael's Mysteries

The Prince of Archangels may seem enigmatic, even paradoxical. Angels are beings of love, so why does their chief appear in full armor and brandishing weapons? Why do his images include a devil or dragon? Even Michael's name is a mystery: it translates as a question, "Who can be like God?" These questions are divine riddles; to explore them reveals Michael's connections to goddess traditions. It also opens our understanding in ways that go beyond conventional knowledge about him. Just reading this chapter will stimulate your Angelic Intelligence. As you apply its tools, you will achieve a new level of freedom and mastery.

Michael and the Warrior Goddesses

As Prince of the Archangels, Michael has a special role in awakening our Angelic Intelligence, and it stands to reason that his connection to the sacred feminine would run deep. There are many goddesses who resonate with his heroic energy, including the Hindu Durga and Mesoamerican Jaguar Woman.

His connections with Tantra goddess Simhamukha are particularly striking. Like Michael, Simhamukha's principle color is blue, associated with divine protection. She brandishes a sharp knife—akin to the archangel's sword—carries a staff reminiscent of his lance and a skullcap that resonates with his shield and chalice. She has the face of lion, her version of Michael's dragon, and she dances blissfully over a human corpse, reminiscent of the demon or serpent at Michael's feet, on "cremation ground," the Hindu equivalent of a graveyard, one of the portals Michael guards.

To the Western mind, these images seem to oppose a loving, harmonious divinity, as may an angel in armor. The contrast brings into relief the role of power, protection, and strength on the spiritual path. Such forces recur in the earliest worship of a Divine Mother who was not only sweet and omnipresent but also had sacred masculine powers of action, intervention, and conquest, which she applied to support her beloved humanity and rescue it from the negative forces of the world. Simhamukha's roots can be traced to that same Divine Mother. In our times, Archangel Michael has come with his hosts to act on behalf of the sacred feminine, restoring our spiritual power and paving humanity's golden pathway.

Simhamukha: Spiritual Warfare, Goddess-style

In many ancient traditions there are important goddesses whose connections with Michael have gone unnoticed. As I developed Angelic Intelligence, I discovered these corollaries, their importance, and how they support Michael's mission with humanity.

Known as "Mother of All Conquerors," the blue goddess carries her knife in the right, masculine hand, showing her readiness to wield dominion. With it, she averts psychic attacks, vanquishes demons and other destructive influences, and transmutes negative mental states into compassion.

The staff she hugs embodies her consort, reiterating the embrace of her own masculine force. Simhamukha's skullcap or bowl is symbol of the sacred feminine. This receptacle is made of the bone that protects the brain, showing the head-connection she shares with Archangel Michael. As for the corpse beneath her feet, it represents the ego or lower self that has died in her dance of mastery, as well as her freedom from the low-vibrational forces that lodge in the physical body. Having vanquished death, she now oversees cemeteries, portals of transcendence. There she keeps guard, preventing negative entities from invading her adepts on either side of the doorway.

In various ancient traditions, lion-faced Simhamukha is the leader of Tantric leonine goddesses. She appears accompanied by two fierce dakinis (feminine light beings): *Bear-face* and *Tiger-face*. Do ferocious animals seem an odd match for a goddess? To master the challenges inherent to the spiritual path, we need strength, protection, and divine support. This need was understood by the ancients, whose earliest representations of the Great Mother Goddess portray her as either part lion or as a lion-master. She is ubiquitous, beautiful, and blissful but also has another, more intense facet. Like a lioness prowling through the night, this goddess hunts down negative energies that lurk in the unseen and applies her martial prowess to vanquish them.

It was this prowess that empowered Egyptian Isis, enabling her to rescue her beloved Osiris. Her myth is intrinsic to the archetype of the warrior goddess. After Osiris had been dismembered in a death that symbolizes humanity's fall from the light realm into matter, Isis searched across the land for the pieces of his body, which she reassembled. Like Isis' resurrection of Osiris, the Divine Mother enters our fallen world and intervenes to reassemble our true, luminous nature. She shares this essential task with Archangel Michael, Simhamukha, and their warrior colleagues in the subtle dimensions.

Lions appear with goddesses around the globe, including the Roman Cybele, Babylonian Astarte, and Egyptian Sekhmet. The word *sphynx* originally referred to a winged figure with a lion's body and a woman's face. The tarot card Strength, from the Rider-Waite-Smith deck, shows a woman with an infinity symbol over her head—representing the divine female—peaceably controlling the mouth of a lion.

By no means cute, shrinking, or passive, these imposing feminine archetypes resonate with Michael's strength and power in defense of all that's good.

The Dragon Connection

This mythical beast offers more connections between the warrior angel and the ferocious goddess. Simhamukha's goddess-follower Palden Lhamo also has two supporting dakinis, one of them called *Dragon-face*. Texts describing Simhamukha and her entourage often use the Sanskrit word *drag-po,* meaning "ferocious."[13] According to the Webster dictionary, the etymology of "dragon" includes the Sanskrit word *darsayati*, meaning "he causes to see." Both Simhamukha and Michael are divine awakeners. Their lion and dragon energies give them the edge they need to free humanity from the forces that hold us in slumber.

---

13. Camille Simon and Nathan W. Hill, Edinburgh Handbook of Evaluative Morphology, (Edinburgh, UK: Edinburgh University Press, 2015), 384.

In China, the dragon is associated with enlightenment. Known for its superpowers, it can move between heaven and earth. There is a Chinese teaching about another, negative dragon force that works to sabotage our higher path.[14] A similar duality is seen in feathered serpent gods like Incan *Viracocha*, Mayan *Kukulkan* and Toltec *Quetzalcoatl*. Their reptile nature has been transmuted and lifted off the ground, acquiring the ability to fly.

Supernatural Protectors

In my work as a speaker, I've noticed that novices tend to relegate Michael's support to the physical dimension. Simhamukha specializes in spiritual and psychic protection, and Michael also defends these subtle gifts. It's true, there are many testimonies of his intervention to prevent accidents, violence, and similar threats. In fact, he assists in positive breakthroughs of all kinds, including miracles. But his greatest work is the protection of our minds, souls, and energy, improving the results of our spiritual work and restoring our condition as free, victorious light beings, and our connection to the Divine.

Like Simhamukha with her knife, Michael carries his sword and alternately his lance in the right hand. Whereas the goddess integrates masculine powers, the archangel embodies them. He wields his weapons to overcome inner and outer blockage, transmuting it to divine good.

Simhamukha's skullcap resonates with Michael's helmet, grail, and shield. The helmet symbolizes protection of our mind. The grail is a feminine vessel that receives the bliss of divine connection, a connection he works to protect. He usually carries a shield, an

---

14. Pangeas, Revista Interdisciplinar de Ecocrítica Vol. 1 (núm. 1) (2019), https://rua.ua.es/dspace/bitstream/10045/100508/6/Pangeas_1_04.pdf.

instrument of angelic technology that shines in the invisible realm of Spirit, waiting for us to use it, as we will see further on.

Like the corpse that Simhamukha dances on, the snake or demon at Michael's feet refers to the conquest of the lower self and the entities attached to it. The blue angel and goddess both guide souls to the next plane of existence and protect the living and the dead from the energy parasites that tend to gather around the portal called death and, for that matter, all other portals.

It's no coincidence that the helmet and skullcap both relate to the head. There's a connection between our biological brain and the light body that ancients understood. They knew that higher thought patterns activate electrochemical circuits and neuropeptides, triggering processes throughout the body that lead to the activation of our light body. This higher vehicle is the opus magnum of both Simhamukha and Archangel Michael.

This knowledge, which shines through myths worldwide, was inspired in the belief in an omnipresent Mother Goddess, who works for us, in us and with us to assist our higher birth. In a golden age before the onset of patriarchy, the human condition was thought to be "larval," comparable to a caterpillar before it begins to become a butterfly (the latter was a universal symbol of the light body).[15] Within its cocoon, the caterpillar brain secretes certain substances that trigger its metamorphosis. This secretion comes from an area akin to the thalamus and hypothalamus in higher animals.

Warrior goddesses Innana and Artemis are also connected to Michael. Mysterious, ancient representations of them are similar to parts of the brain. In the exercise section of this chapter, you'll find methods to activate the goddess-angel portal in your head.

---

15. Musaios, *The Lion's Path: The Big Picture and What It Means to You* (Sardis, Canada: Golden Scepter, 1988), 35.

Chapter 2

Protection from Extraneous Forces

Michael and Simhamukha support victory over the lower self, but also over extraneous forces that tend to hold us down. These include: collective beliefs (in illness, scarcity, and other forms of limitation), group memories that are specific to a species, family, or a community, mind control technology, low-vibrational media, programs inherited from our ancestors, and the labels or negative intentions that others direct at us.

Perhaps the most important influence they overcome is that of negative entities. Although the idea may sound too religious or superstitious for some, most traditions have teachings about invisible, intrusive beings. They have been diversely called egregores, phantoms, fallen angels, demons, and disincarnate souls. Dense thoughts and emotions actually gather together, taking on a life of their own and turning into a kind of entity. In *Fringe Knowledge for Beginners*, author Tom Montauk says that the forces of negativity know which humans have come into this world with a mission to help and conspire to block them. He calls these entities "permanent agents."[16] One of the most formidable types are what the Gnostics called "archons," powerful parasites that lodge in our energy field and hold us in negative mind states, on which they feed.

You may have heard that all your problems and limitations are really caused by what's going on inside you. It's true, the power is in you and yet is often sequestered or weakened by an extraneous presence. This idea enjoys increasing acceptance, even among numerous psychologists and psychiatrists-turned-authors whose patients have experienced remarkable healings after low-vibrational entities have been released from them. Such entities fuel many syndromes including depression, neurosis, psychosis, phobias, obsessions, sui-

16. Tom Montauk, *Fringe Knowledge For Beginners* (Kindle version, 2012), 88.

cidal tendencies, addictions, arrogance, and the compulsion to control people and circumstances. They even contribute to physical problems such as illness and scarcity.

If our true nature is divine and unlimited, why do we live in a world of pain, injustice, and death? This is a not a real world. Nirvana or Heaven, places of bliss, love, and Infinite Good, are more real. What holds us in the shadow world are low-vibrational beings.

Archangel Michael, his twin flame Faith, and their warrior-goddess colleagues release the pawns and connect us with a network of angelic beings. Although this freedom culminates on transition from the physical, with their support we begin to experience vast improvement in our spiritual work and circumstances.

Some eschew the idea of identifying with a warrior in the belief that this way of thinking can intensify our challenges, causing us to have something to fight. It's true that in an absolute sense, negative forces cannot prevail over the power of Infinite Good. However, in this world of appearances, the path of progress often seems slow, difficult, and frustrating. Warrior-goddess archetypes show us the shadows that hold us back and complement our feminine powers of love, intentionality, and co-creation with masculine forces of determination, courage, and strength. This combination accelerates our progress and gives us the edge we long for.

They also remind us that we are not alone. Michael, Faith, and their spiritual warrior colleagues can and do intervene, ensuring our victory. They cut away and shield us from negative forces of all kinds and strengthen us to develop our own warrior powers of faith, focus, and authority. And by fueling our light body, the blue archangels will precipitate our latent wings, lifting us beyond the shadow worlds—and when the time comes to abandon our physical bodies—to fly unhindered to the joyous realms of love.

Take Your Weapon

The archetypes of Michael's weapons—in particular his sword and shield—connect us with his divine energy and help block, cut away, and dispel negative forces. Although we think of them as physical implements, they have been historically connected to magic. In ancient times, shields and swords were often inscribed with runes or words of power, reflecting the common belief in their metaphysical properties.

Power Shields

Today, this millenary wisdom has found resonance in the laboratory. At Stanford University and the Mind Science Foundation in San Antonio, Texas, Dr. William Braud designed and directed studies on the power of human intention. As shared throughout the pages of his book, *Distant Mental Influence,* his experiments confirmed that our minds, dreams, and health can be affected by the negative intentions of others[17]. They also show that we can block undesirable influences through what he calls "psychological shielding strategies." For instance, we can "visualize a safe or protective shield, barrier or screen,"[18] to "prevent penetration of the influence."[19]

When we enrich our visualization with angelic images, it becomes high spiritual technology. The following keys are designed to connect you with Michael's shield energy, to strengthen your faith and focus and access physical, psychic, and spiritual protection for yourself and others.

---

17. William Braud, PhD, *Distant Mental Influence: Its Contributions to Science, Healing, and Human Interactions* (Charlottesville, VA: Hampton Roads, 2003), xxxi.

18. Ibid, 19.

19. Lynne McTaggart, *The Field: The Quest for the Secret Force of the Universe* (New York: HarperCollins, 2002), 136.

Depending on your needs and preferences, you may choose, adapt, and apply these keys for six, nine, or twelve minutes daily. As you affirm, visualize the angels, the shield, and the sword.

Decrees for General Protection

Visualize a shield around yourself or others and hold on to that image as you affirm:

> *"I am not alone or without protection. The Divine Guardian is with me, watching over me and shielding me on all levels of my being, now and always."*

> *"We are not alone or without protection. The Divine Guardian is with us, watching over and shielding us always and on all levels of being, now and always."*

Affirmation to Protect Others in Dangerous, Uncertain, or Toxic Surroundings

> *"There's no place God's light cannot shine, and God's light shines around (name of person) and fills their path, while Archangel Michael shields them with his hosts, and with the sword of divine authority frees them from any influence unlike the divine good that surrounds them now."*

Affirmation to Protect Your Home

> *"Michael, Faith, and their hosts surround our home with a blue mantle of protection into which nothing negative can penetrate and out of which only good will come, now and always."*

Affirmation to Strengthen Focus and Shield Against Distraction

"Archangel Michael and his force field fill my life and touch my mind. With divine authority, he shields me from distraction, strengthening my focus to move ahead on my true priorities. Thank you, Michael; thank you, Mother and Father."

Decrees and Visualizations for Psychic Protection

"In the name of Free Will, I reject any influence except divine good, which shines directly into all the levels of my mind and emotions. This decision shields my subconscious from overt and covert suggestions or vibrations that are not in tune with divinity now."

"I am not open to induction, manipulation, or sabotage. Michael's blue light shields me, now and always."

"I fill my subconscious with Michael's blue light, and it naturally rejects any influences that are not for my highest good, now and always."

Affirmations to Call on the Shield of Your Accumulated Prayer Work

Thought patterns of faith and love surround you with a vibrant energy shield. The effects are cumulative: every prayer, every kind and positive idea you have ever held, has strengthened the field of power that surrounds you on the invisible plane of Spirit, and you can call it up.

"My accumulated, conscious thoughts of faith shine around me, fusing with Saint Michael's shield to block out any negative influences and intentions now."

"My accumulated thoughts of love have connected me to the Source, whose power shields me, now and always."

"My accumulated, conscious connection to Spirit (Goddess, God, the angels, Infinite Good, or your own preferred term) shines through me and around me, increasing the force of my prayers and shielding me with Its power, now and always."

Affirmation to Close a Session of Personal or Group Prayer

"The power of these prayers is used by angels to strengthen the divine shield of faith and love that surrounds the planet and covers all those who seek it consciously or unconsciously, now and always."

Physical Shields

In the exercise section of this chapter, you'll find simple instructions to make physical angel shields to protect your space, energy, and communications.

Enforce the Power of Your Words

Archangel Michael is related to the throat chakra, a center of self-expression, confidence, and power. It's also a portal of confidence. Throat problems are often a sign of fearfulness. Confidence is essential for effective communication. In fact, the two are inextricably entwined. Our confidence grows when we're able to express ourselves. With empowered words, we can connect with others, communicate successfully, set limits, and defend our ideas. With words of faith, we can attain mastery over our thoughts and circumstances. Such words are not just ideas—they are themselves a kind of portal. Spirit acts through them to close doorways to lower dimensions and open the way for divine manifestation.

This is verbal magic, a skill connected to the sacred feminine. The name of the goddess Hecate derived from the ancient Egyptian term for wise matriarch, *hek*, who used *hekau*, words of power. Barbara Walker says she could:

> "...*make things happen just by speaking—as witches, centuries later. Logos power was usurped by male gods such as Yahweh, who claimed to bring things into being by saying them. But long before the Bible, hekau were the material of all creative word magic, spells, charms, prayers, invocations, exorcisms, chants, liturgies, and every other mystic verbal practice... Shakespeare's three Weird Sisters in Macbeth are late versions of ... Wyrd, the Triple Goddess of Fate, whose name also meant "word" because she had the creative power of the logos."*[20]

There is growing interest in decrees, mantras, and affirmations, and it's fueling the retrieval of a sacred feminine art within your reach. This art was blocked by institutional religions that tried to sequester a universal gift and limit it to a small clique of male "authorities." In a pattern repeated in many creeds, they would dictate which prayers were holy and persecute as witches those who used their words to heal and manifest outside official strictures. These events were part of a historic tendency in which colonizers or dominant groups have reprimanded, publicly and with violence, those who have spoken

---

20. Barbara G. Walker, *Man Made God: A Collection of Essays* (Seattle: Stellar House Publishing, 2010), 277.

out, stood up for their rights, or named their native gods. Much of the repression has been toward women, not only by authorities but by parents and husbands. As recently as the eighteenth century, many European men would physically punish and publicly humiliate their wives for being outspoken.

Though many of us haven't been directly exposed to such trauma, it has left an impression on the collective psyche. Studies in the field of biogeneology show that our generation's challenges are recorded in our genes and passed on to our descendants. Nor has the patriarchal scheme entirely disappeared. The family, school, and social dynamics of our times tend to suppress or downplay the self-expression of more vulnerable members. When it comes to words, on the one hand we love them, and on the other we have been genetically and socially conditioned to hold back.

Archangel Michael and his female light-colleagues support the retrieval of our verbal power. They work to build our confidence and faith and direct them in our words. With their support, speech becomes a vehicle to exercise our free will and reclaim dominion over our awareness, life, and circumstances.

Invocations to Free and Retrieve the Power of Your Words

"Michael and Faith, please dissolve the effects of personal or collective memories that have limited my self-expression. Unblock the power of my words, now and evermore."

"Archangel Michael, master of subtle dimensions, please remove any energies that may keep me from using my verbal powers entirely, now."

"Angels and Goddess of Words, dissolve my fears and retrieve my voice of power, here and now."

Affirmation to Shield Your Interactions with Others

"By the power of Michael's shield, I now seal my communications under the law of good. I shield my throat from words that clash with my divine heart of love, I shield my attention from distraction and false appearances. Only good can come through my interactions, has come through them, and will come through them, now and always."

Shield Your Throat Chakra

Besides repeating invocations and affirmations, we can reconnect the energy centers related to our throat chakra. This chakra's main aspects are communication and self-expression. Its goddess is Sakini-Shakti; her five heads facilitate mastery—Michael's power—over the physical and psychic realms.

The resonance with Archangel Michael is reiterated in systems around the ancient world. According to the Cherokee tradition, the energy doorway of the throat is blue and rules the manifesting power of the voice. In ancient Egypt and other parts of Africa, the throat chakra was related to the creative power of words. The Incan equivalent of these energy centers are *pukios*. The throat *pukio* is blue, connected to manifesting, communication, personal power, faith, and will—all of which relate to Michael.

In the exercise section of this chapter, you'll find various special keys to shield this center, unblock your self-expression, and empower your voice for public speaking, one-on-one encounters, affirmations, decrees, and other modalities.

Michael's Sword: Cut Away Insecurity and Unleash Your Prayer Power

Like that of his goddess counterpart, Michael's sword is an archetype of divine might and authority. It cuts through low-vibrational energies, strengthens our confidence, and intensifies the force of our prayers.

You connect with this weapon when you pray with determination and hold firmly to the truth that you're not a victim of circumstances. You also connect to it in the face of limiting appearances when you persist in radiating the energy and intentions you want to manifest. I shared these insights on forceful prayer with author and health activist Pauline Bondonno. She said that this perspective "challenges what I was taught in church as a child, that spirituality meant being meek."

I had an experience that brought this type of power into relief. I'm not usually nervous or impressionable. But one day I was driving down a narrow street in a city known for a high incidence of violence toward women, when a large truck blocked my way. As I sat there stuck behind the wheel, it came to me that this could be a trap. Fearful, I wondered if the truck was blocking me on purpose. I then realized that I was succumbing to the mass hysteria around danger for women. There in the narrow, blocked street, I shook off the fear. I began to affirm, "I am powerful." Suddenly, a wave of confidence flowed over me. The truck moved, and more importantly, I felt as though the waters before me had parted. Once again I was the master of my destiny; my way was as clear as I have felt it in my most confident moments.

In today's society, women often feel vulnerable or at risk on some level or another. The insecurity can radiate into our homes and families, leaking insidiously into the social fabric. Even as we apply common sense to care for ourselves, we may wield the sword of prayer to defend our inner security. Of course, this doesn't mean that men can't benefit from applying their archetypal sword energy. One of the healers I have trained is a man who has applied the suggestions in this chapter to improve his confidence, his ability to stand up for himself, professional success, and prayer power. But these keys may be particularly timely for women, through our exerting a healing, freeing effect on all humanity. The following affirmations and tips will help imbue your affirmations and decrees with victorious force.

Affirmation for Self-Empowerment

"I am powerful, I am empowered, I am power. The Goddess roars through my words, here and now."

Affirmation to Banish Negative Influences and Dissolve Blocks to Your Good

Pray with force, then close your session by repeating three times: "Like Michael's sword, my words of power have cut through apparent limitation and allowed Infinite Good to manifest (as peace, protection, wellness, success), here and now."

Invocation to Cut Through Collective Mind Fields of Apathy, Fear, and Toxic Aggression

"Michael and Simhamukha, please fill this place (city, country, planet) with your blue, protective force fields. Cut through low vibrations and transmute them into compassion now."

Invocation to Cut through Inner and Outer Resistance

"Archangel Michael, please enter my mind and life. With your sword, cut me free from inner and outer resistance, and restore my conscious connection with Divine Omnipresence now."

Invocation to Free Humanity from Negative Entities and Intentions

"Archangel Michael, please cut through any intention to lower our vibration and hold us in a divine frequency, now and always!"

The Fortress of Your Prayer

The archetype of spiritual protection is deeply embedded in the human psyche. When using hallucinogenic plants, people worldwide have reported seeing medieval-type fortresses, a symbol closely connected to prayer. While participating in a Toltec ceremony in Mexico, I entered a vision state in which I saw a fortress of light built of all the prayers and faith-filled intentions generated by people everywhere. I watched as these prayers and intentions became luminous ribbons that floated toward the fortress, winding their way into its walls, which turned ever more luminous. In a dimension beyond time, their accumulated light was available to strengthen anyone who needed and sought out the energy of faith. Other prayer ribbons floated into a road of golden light, paving its surface. I was told that this was the true "Golden Path of Humanity." Although I had read esoteric traditions about our species moving toward such a path, I had wondered how this could be: a look at the current direction of civilization seemed anything but golden. Suddenly, I understood that the path is not cemented in the world of appearances but in higher dimensions into which we are moving, paved with the light of our inner work.

Tips to Increase Your Prayer Powers

- Say them with force.

- Invoke Michael's cutting energy and that of the warrior goddess.

- As you affirm or request assistance, visualize myriad angels filling your space and touching your being. This will lift your vibration and that of your space beyond the reach of any undesirable influence.

- Do your affirmations in a quiet place without interruption, and in a physically relaxed position. This combination frees your mind to focus completely on ideas and feelings, and puts your subconscious into a more receptive mode. (If you are physically tired, choose a position that is comfortable but not conducive to nodding off.)

- Write out your affirmations by hand. With our body and nervous system more involved, our attention gets more fully engaged. Studies with college students prove that handwriting, compared to computer writing, favors retention and understanding. When it comes to affirmations, just as your pen breaks through tiny fibers on the paper's surface, writing words of truth cuts through layers of doubt and distraction, printing Spirit's patterns directly on a deeper level of your mind.

- Pray and affirm for others. Michael and his hosts work to serve humanity. When affirming for yourself or a dear one, intersperse your prayers with prayers to help the planet, a certain region, or a group with special needs. If praying for protection and defense, you might adapt the words and use them for children in situations of abandonment, danger, or abuse. While working on healing, devote some prayers to support someone else's recovery, or those who are in hospitals around the world. Prayer is one of the most powerful ways of supporting others and also lifts the vibration of our prayers to that of selfless love, which is the frequency of angels.

- Pay attention and remember to repeat the words with strength and determination. Don't cower in a corner meekly. Like a lioness or bear defending her cubs, when you defend your mind from doubt, do it with force. As I say to my groups, affirm like a wild woman, a wild man. Project authority and your affirmations will break through limiting beliefs and force fields.

- Walk with firm, rhythmic steps around your space, repeating your prayers in a commanding voice. As you do so, visualize and hear Michael and his myriad hosts accompanying you, feet stamping and wings rustling. To claim mastery over your attitude and surroundings, walk and speak like this throughout your house, room, or workplace.

Exercises with Michael and His Goddess Colleagues

The following keys combine the power of your imagination with color, images and other materials to empower your mind, energy, and voice, and clear your aura, space, and situations.

Shields for Empowerment and Protection

Simply cut out four- to six-inch circles of blue paper or cardboard. On them, write: "Archangel Michael's Shield." Hide paper shields in key places such as behind a picture near your door, under your computer, in your glove compartment, in your pillowcase, under your mattress, under the mattress of your child or another family member, or under an object on your desk.

The shield image offers psychic protection and can cut through negative energies. After attending my classes, numerous mothers have placed them under their children's mattresses with positive results in their behavior, happiness, and sleep patterns. On one occasion, I had a banking executive studying with me who longed to have an office of her own. It looked unlikely, since everyone on her floor was stuck in a cubicle and there was only one nice, private office that was soon to become available. A coworker seemed intent on competing with my client for it. The latter avoided getting into a power struggle and with the help of Uriel's mandala (see chapter 6), she visualized her dream office. After several weeks, she used the shield method, making the circle and putting it under her computer. Within a matter of days, things began to shift at work until suddenly she was informed that she would be getting the nice, private office.

We can invoke Michael's sword to cut through low vibrational thoughts that drain our energy, resolve, and concentration, and cause depression, nightmares, and a general sense of being blocked.

Shield Your Words

The following options can be used to unblock your self-expression, empower your communication skills, or increase the force of your decrees and affirmations. Read through them and begin to work with those most suited to your needs and priorities.

Throat Chakra Shield to Overcome Blocks to Self-Expression

Use this key to remove blocks like the fear of speaking out, shame about expressing yourself, or feelings of unworthiness to receive attention. Since these psychological patterns are embedded in the subconscious mind, apply this method daily for twenty-eight days or longer until you perceive a lasting improvement in your ease of expression.

1. Before going to sleep, tape or draw a small image of Michael's shield (described on the previous page) over your throat chakra. (If you prefer, you may skip this step and simply visualize and affirm as suggested below.)

2. Visualize Michael drawing near, surrounding you with his blue wings or force field, passing his sword over the front of your throat and placing his shield over that chakra.

3. Hold to this image as you repeat the following invocation: "Archangel Michael, please cut away doubts, shame, or fears that have limited my self-expression. Shield me from influences that might suppress my voice, and restore my word of power now."

4. Continue to visualize and repeat the request to Michael for six minutes.

5. Have paper and a pen on hand to write down the dreams or ideas that come into your mind as soon as you wake up.

Throat Chakra Shield for Public Speaking and Other Meetings or Encounters

Use this key to prepare for a speaking engagement, a negotiation, a meeting for work, a date with family, a class or a presentation you are going to give, or any situation requiring confidence and clarity. Apply it for up to seven nights before the occasion:

1. Apply step 1 of the previous exercise.

2. Visualize Michael drawing near, surrounding you with his blue wings or force field and placing his shield over your throat chakra.

3. As you hold to this image, repeat the following invocation: "Archangel Michael, please strengthen my confidence and shield my mind and throat in your blue light so that divine words flow through me with love, clarity, and power."

4. Continue to visualize and repeat the invocation for six minutes.

5. During those minutes, visualize yourself speaking (in your conference, meeting, etc.) with confidence, strength, and joy while those present watch you with enthusiasm.

6. Have paper and a pen on hand to write down the dreams or ideas that come into your mind as soon as you wake up.

Throat Chakra Shield to Increase the Power of Your Affirmations, Invocations, Decrees, and Prayers

1. Apply step 1 as described in the previous exercise.

2. Visualize Michael and Faith coming near, surrounding you with their blue wings and force field.

3. See Michael passing his sword near your throat, cutting away shadows.

4. Visualize Faith, Michael's blue companion, touching your throat and placing a shield over your throat chakra.

5. Repeat: "Archangels Michael and Faith, please remove any weakening influence, strengthen my faith, and shield my

throat in your blue light so my words be charged with divine authority and magic, now and always."

6. Repeat the request three times.

7. You can also use this shield before going to sleep at night. In that case, have paper and a pen on hand to write down the dreams or ideas that come into your mind as soon as you wake up.

Goddess Shield

When the lion roars, the jungle trembles. When the Lion Goddess roars, the jungle of the world bows to her power. The ancients were familiar with this special force. It can give our prayers a unique power to dissolve blocks and precipitate divine manifestation. Use it just before beginning a session of your favorite affirmations.

1. Repeat: "Under the protection of Simhamukha, I call on the Divine Lioness forces to draw near and fill my space."

2. Visualize yourself surrounded by lioness goddesses. They may appear as lions, women with leonine features and attributes, or beautiful women accompanied by lions.

3. Hold to this image as you repeat: "Sacred Lioness, please touch my throat chakra and fill my words with your courage and power."

4. Visualize the Lion Goddess and feel her hand or a large, soft paw gently touching your throat.

5. Repeat the invocation three times or more.

6. Write and/or repeat positive affirmations as usual.

The above keys will open the doorway for empowered communication, working directly on your deep mind and personal energy. The support is likely to surge from within, as new confidence, faith, and clarity. Support may also appear in the form of ideas that come into your mind, guidance from your dreams, angelicities (synchronicities of angelic guidance), or opportunities that appear on your path. You may be inspired to share your thoughts or ideas in new ways. You could feel guided to take a course in public speaking; teach a class; work with a therapist, coach, or support group; purchase and apply the advice of a self-help book; explore a new avenue of work; or exercise your speaking or prayer skills in new ways. Ask Simhamukha and Michael to make you aware of new ideas and pathways and to imbue you with initiative and courage to act on them.

Angelic Sword Technology

Besides its connection to self-expression and prayer, Michael's sword is a living tool of power. Swords, lances, and sticks have been used by shamans throughout the ancient world not for physical battle but to overcome negative force fields.

The following technique banishes psychic vampires that bring down our vibration, causing depression and nightmares as well as a general sense of being blocked.

Remove Psychic Parasites in Three Steps

As mentioned above, negative entities are involved with many of life's challenges. Overcoming their influence is an ongoing part of our path of power. The tools of Angelic Intelligence shared in this chapter and throughout this book give us an edge in that path. As we apply them, our inner magic becomes increasingly evident.

However, in life there are times when we feel overwhelmed. For instance, you may be a positive, loving person with a regular spiritual practice, and you can still feel barraged by negative thoughts. Or you may repeatedly have unpleasant dreams that don't seem to come from your own mind or offer helpful guidance. Or despite persistent efforts in prayer and visualization and despite calling on the angels for support, you may be plagued by a condition or situation that won't go away. Such times indicate a prevalence of psychic parasites. To remove them, the following method is surprisingly effective.

1. Affirm: "Michael, please come before me and with your sword of power cut away any influence that is trying to feed on my energy or bring down my vibration."

2. For three to six minutes, visualize the blue archangel before you, passing his sword at about an inch distance around every part of your body, from the top of your head to the soles of your feet. Feel how threads of energy are being cut as he does this.

3. While visualizing, repeat: "Michael, please open your interdimensional door and guide these energies to their present place in the evolutionary path of love. Please seal the door so they may not return."

Repeat the steps daily for twenty-eight days, and use them periodically as needed. If you're experiencing recurrent, negative dreams that defy interpretation, apply them before going to sleep at night.

My dear friend, author Lucy Aspra, suggests wearing a sword pendant (I often do) or carrying one in our wallets. You can draw a sword on a small card or piece of paper, color it blue, and write Archangel Michael's name on it. Keep it with you and when you feel a need, touch it and make a mental request such as, "Give me faith in this situation," "Strengthen my confidence," or "Help me not criticize others."

Toltec Spiritual Warriors

Michael resonates with the hero or heroine who appears in mythologies throughout the ancient world. Not only are they capable of rising to a challenge, but actually require opposition in order to exert their identity, and are present within each of us as a force of willpower, audacity, and resilience.

In Mexico, where I've studied and taught for many years, the native Toltec tradition is called the Path of the Warrior. Its symbolism speaks clearly to a higher meaning of battle. The key Toltec fighter is Sacred Hummingbird, born with the baby sun at Winter Solstice. When I first heard of him, I wondered how such a delicate being could be called a warrior. Eventually, I understood that his strength is of an inner sort, enabling Hummingbird to remain suspended in the air by incessantly beating his tiny wings. As for the word "warrior," in Toltec vocabulary it means "one who knows how to fight in life and to overcome the lower self." The presiding higher power, Ometeotl, (translated as "Father-Mother Divine One") has imbued Hummingbird with achieving willpower, the cosmic and human strength expressed through the sun, a sentient being who works perpetually to share its light and warmth. On the first morning of winter, adherents of native Mexican teachings stand facing the sunrise, and welcome Hummingbird in the following manner, which you can use by yourself or with a friend, family member, or group:

Toltec Winter Solstice Blessing

1. At or shortly after sunrise on the day of Winter Solstice, stand facing east (the direction of the rising sun).
2. Lift your arms straight out before you and spread your fingers open, imagining the rays of the rising sun enter-

ing the space between them and shining into your bloodstream.

3. Hold to the above image, feeling the sunlight flowing through your entire body as you repeat the following words and compatible ones that come to you for six minutes: "You have come here, Precious Child, sun-ray that ascends, Lord Who Gives Us Willpower in Spite of Adversity. Fill us with your essence so that we may be our best selves in the cycle now beginning. Precious Hummingbird, as you hold yourself in the air with your tiny wings, strengthen us to hold to the highest vibration of thought, word, and action."

As you may have noted, this Mesoamerican warrior resonates with the divine Son of Judeo-Christian lineage, who is also symbolically born around Winter Solstice. The connection between them doesn't stop there. In his book *The Aquarian Gospel of Jesus the Christ*, Levi Dowler describes the Messiah as, "The Prince of Peace, [who] went forth in battle ... not a drop of blood was shed ... His sword is truth, his shield is faith, his helmet innocence, his breath is love, his watchword peace... this is not a carnal war; it is not man at war with man, but it is right against the wrong ... love is warrior, love is armor, love is all and love shall win."[21]

The Sun of God

It is interesting to note that like the Toltec Hummingbird, Jesus was considered in mystery schools to have come from the sun. So were the archangels, among whom the largest and most radiant is Michael. It's even more intriguing that throughout Mesoamerica,

---

21. Levi H. Dowling, *The Aquarian Gospel of Jesus the Christ* (New York: Penguin Group 2009), 145.

sunlight was understood to be more than a physical kind of energy. The Mayans, for instance, would (and still do) invoke different solar blessings depending on both the season and the hour. For example, the sunrise imparts willpower to be true to one's purpose throughout the day, whereas sunset awakens intuition.

Similar solar practices were widespread throughout the ancient world. The sun was considered a sentient being, a portal of Angelic Intelligence. From the perspective of left brain, or physical science, ideas like these may appear to be primitive superstition. But there are other types of science whose laws are intuitive, spiritual, or angelic. From their standpoint, everything in creation has a consciousness of some type, including the sun. In both astrology and solar-centric traditions around the globe, the attitudinal correspondences of our local star happen to coincide with Archangel Michael's gifts of free and divine will, initiative, confidence, and strength.

Receive Angelic Sunlight

Willpower, focus, courage—whatever strengths you need to fulfill your life purpose, be true to your ideals, and reach your goals will be fortified by repeating the following sun prayers. The ideal time to do this is at sunrise or in the morning as you stand facing the sun. If you live in a place with dark winters or can't go outside or look through a window, do this upon rising: Face east and imagine the sun rising as you affirm for six minutes:

> *"Solar angels touch my being with their rays, clarifying my true priorities and strengthening my focus to apply my talents in tangible results today and always. Thank you angels, thank you, Mother-Father."*

"The Sun of Divine Will empowers my being with rays of diligence, and I feel these rays penetrate and lift me up now. Thank you, Mother-Father."

"Solar angels, please bring to light my true purpose, and strengthen me to act on it effectively during the divine window of this day."

"I stop waiting for circumstances or people to support my ideals. Solar angels are with me and they empower me to feel, speak, and move in the highest and best ways, and I act on their angelic direction now."

"I stop waiting for circumstances or people to support my ideals. Archangel Michael and his hosts are with me, and they empower me to think, speak, and move in congruence with my highest self. I act on their angelic direction now."

"Archangel Michael, give me clarity to know what I need to do, and fill me with the strength to do it now."

The Angels of Sunflowers

Because of their special relationship with the sun, sunflowers have been considered sacred since ancient times. Incan priestesses called sun maidens wore large sunflowers made of gold. Associated with Archangel Michael, sunflowers are a floral incarnation of the warrior essence. No delicate bloom, these flowers' growth is an act of power. Their long, fleshy stems—which can reach more than twenty feet—enclose an elaborate hydraulic system that allows young flowers to turn and continually face the sun in its daily path across the sky. When mature, the stems become fixed, facing only the east, the direction of Michael and the rising sun.

Sunflower angels are glad to share their strength with us, to hold our attention in the light, in Source, in happiness, in devotion to the Divine.

Invoke the Sunflower Angels

1. Imagine a Sunflower standing before you, firmly planted in the earth with its great flower above your head.

2. Sense its angelic essence: you may actually see a tall, golden angel standing with the flower, or simply capture its bright, golden aura.

3. Place your attention on your body as you affirm: "My body isn't solid, it's made of tiny particles of light. Sunflower Angel, please merge your essence with mine and fill me with your strength to hold to the good (to divinity, to Omnipresent Light, to your devotion, or whatever you wish to focus on)."

4. Feel the sunflower merge with your body.

5. For six minutes, see golden rays stream from your body. Imagine they take the form of sunflower petals. As though your face were a sunflower, see yourself looking toward the divine light that glows above you like a sun. As you visualize, repeat the following affirmation: "I am one with the Sunflower Angel, I am one with the strength to stand firm in the light (in self-esteem, in love, in divine connection, etc.)."

Michael's Mandala: Strengthen Your Faith, Lift Your Vibration, Awaken Your Willpower, and Work with Your Quantum Twin

The Prince of Archangels has a very special mission: to strengthen our light body. His force field is blue, the color of protection. Like a clear sky lifts your spirits, Michael's energy lifts your being onto a higher frequency.

The shift is not just only mental. Biologists say that each cell of our bodies is like a battery,[22] with negative charge in its core and a positive charge on the outside. Measurements done with nanoscale voltmeters[23] reveal that the human body is equivalent to "a package of electrical storms,"[24] a power source unto itself. However, we're used to thinking of ourselves as solid, inert matter. Since our perception manifests conditions, this belief traps our energy potential into a limited, material form. When we fuse with Michael's blue radiance, we are moved beyond the reach of low-vibrational energies that tend to occupy our minds and physical body. Our energy becomes sealed and shielded, and our vibration rises much more quickly than it can with merely mental practices such as affirmations, prayer, meditation, and visualization. Suddenly, we are boosted beyond linear thought with its limitations and distractions. Our warrior spirit finds a new level of empowerment.

Our Michael body connects us with Sirius, the blue star inhabited by helpful spirits who were recognized in ancient Egypt as facilitators of awakening and divine transcendence.

For the first time in print, I share my original method that combines ancient practices with modern-day knowledge of what I call vibrational science. It will facilitate a close connection with the Prince of Archangels, lifting your vibration like few practices can and bringing victory in this life and beyond.

---

22. https://www.brucelipton.com/blog/what-are-the-volts-electricity-your-human-body.

23. Ibid.

24. https://knowingneurons.com/2012/12/14/brain-battery/.

1. Before gathering and/or purchasing your materials, choose one of Michael's specializations to focus on, such as: determination, decision, willpower, sustained attention to the good, persistence in spiritual awareness, unconditional love, or freedom from low vibrational influences from within and without.

2. Take a moment to quiet your mind, focus on your intention, and ask the angels, flowers, and cosmic essences to help you achieve it. Hold to your purpose as you gather the following items:

   - bright blue paper or poster board and a gold pen; or, alternately, white paper and blue pen and coloring implements.

   - depending on the size of your mandala, 20 to 50 ½ inch images of sunflowers

   - 1 large (1½") and 3 or more small (½") images of Archangel Michael with twin flame Faith. (You can download, cut out, and paste; or if you prefer, draw the images onto the poster board).

Make Your Michael Mandala

- Trace a large (10" or more) circle, and then line it evenly with sunflowers. (As described above for the angel images, choose your favorite way to fill the circle with flowers.)

- Draw or paste the image of the angels in the middle, and the smaller images around the inside of the circle.

- At the top of your mandala, write two affirmations, one referring to Michael and another for the sunflowers.

Choose from the following affirmations to connect with Michael and his companions:

"Michael's blue light fills my body and mind, and my focus is clear, now and always."

"I am one with Archangel Michael and his twin flame, I am imbued with the vibration of faith now."

"I am joined to Archangel Michael, and his strength fills me now."

"I am one with Archangel Michael, I am one with unconditional love, which I now radiate toward all, including those who have bothered or upset me."

"I am one with Archangel Michael, and I am filled with the highest angelic vibration now."

"I am one with Michael and Faith, and I shine through-and-through with their blue light now."

Adapt the following affirmation according to your intent, and write it on your mandala:

"I surround myself with the sunflowers of the world, who fill me with strength to stand firm in the light (in self-esteem, in the awareness of Omnipresent Good, in divine connection, in faith, or your own preferred intention)."

Using Michael's Mandala

At night, before going to bed, spend twelve minutes working with your mandala in the following way:

1. Ask Archangels Michael and Faith to fill your house with their presence and that of their hosts.

2. Mentally go through the rooms of your house, imagining Michael and his myriad blue angels filling each space

completely with their presence and ending up in your own bedroom. (You may perceive them as winged beings or simply as an intense field of blue light.)

3. Ask Michael to come before you and visualize him and Faith however you can imagine them, floating over you.

4. For a couple of minutes, imagine the energy of all the sunflowers of the planet surrounding you, touching your aura, and imbuing you with their light and willpower as you repeat the sunflower affirmation you wrote on your mandala.

5. Repeat once, slowly and with attention: "My body isn't solid, it's made of light particles, which are porous. Michael and Faith, please come and merge your blue, shining essence with mine."

6. Once again, focus on these two, blue angels floating over you, and feel how they move through and into your porous light-body until it glows bright blue.

7. Holding to the sensation of being fused with Michael's blue force field, repeat the invocation you wrote on your mandala for six minutes.

Your Time-Travel Twin: Send Yourself the Future You Choose

Among our different energy bodies, there is a part of ourselves I call the time-traveling twin. Unlike our physical body, it's not confined to space or time. In fact, it's continually slipping out of the present and into the future, where it connects us with the outcomes that are preprogrammed by our accumulated beliefs, actions, and vibration.

I had the opportunity to study with French author and physicist Jan Pierre Garnier-Mallet in Mexico City and was fascinated by the explanation of our ability to send part of ourselves into the future so that it may bring back the outcomes we program or intend for.

He mentioned in the seminar that what he calls our quantum double is particularly active at night. While our physical body sleeps, it moves more freely through time. He said that before going to sleep, we can ask our double to go into the future and send us a certain outcome. My classmates and I applied the suggestion and discovered that it did indeed work—sometimes. However, the results weren't always so great.

The physicist explained that preexisting potentialities, or futures we have chosen inadvertently with our negative thoughts, could sometimes prevent our twin from going where we send it. He said that it helps to send thoughts of love to someone who got on your nerves during the day. It occurred to me that the variances in the twin's results could also be caused by negative entities that tend to hang out around humans. So I began to connect with Archangel Michael, the great protector, to lift up my love vibration in a more inclusive manner and also clear out entities before sending my twin on her nighttime journey.

Since then, I've been sharing the method in one of my workshops, and it has proven amazingly effective for numerous participants.

Clear Your Space for Your Time-Traveling Twin

1. Follow the instructions on pages 64–65 to make Michael's mandala, writing this affirmation on it: "I am one with Archangel Michael, I am one with unconditional love, which I now radiate toward all, including those who have made me angry or upset."

2. Before going to bed at night, apply the steps on pages 65–66 to use your mandala. Say aloud, "Archangel Michael, please appear above me," imagining that you see him (or his blue force field) floating there.

3. Repeat, "My body isn't solid, my body is a mass of light particles that are porous, and I ask that Michael fuse with my light body now."

4. Visualize and feel how Michael moves into your body until it glows bright blue.

5. Spend 6 minutes repeating the following words: "I am one with Archangel Michael, I am one with unconditional love, which I now radiate to all." Send this kind intention to everyone you can think of, including those who have bothered you or made you angry.

(Optionally, you can prepare to send your twin by applying the parasite-cutting methods shared on pages 56–57.)

Call on Your Time-Traveling Twin

After using your mandala or invoking the power of Michael's sword, repeat the following request three times:

> *"Archangel Michael and Guardian Angel, please accompany my time-traveling twin in its journeys tonight. Time-traveling twin, accompanied and protected by Archangel Michael and my Guardian Angel, please go to the future where (name your intention) has manifested, and send this or something better to me tonight while I sleep."*

One of many examples of results is that of Marcela, a saleswoman who was taking my courses and had decided to start her own baked-goods company. She had landed a hefty order from a nationwide restaurant chain, but she just couldn't get the funds together to finance the ingredients and equipment she would need to produce it. The restaurants urgently needed the desserts, and if Marcela couldn't deliver, her clients would cancel the order and give it to a competitor.

The night after learning this technique, Marcela followed the above steps, asking her twin to go "to the future in which I am able to cover this order quickly and successfully."

The very next day, an acquaintance offered to lend Marcela the money needed to finance the order, and the restaurant told her they would wait for her until she could deliver the baked goods.

Garnier Mallet suggests we avoid calling on our quantum twin to help others unless they expressly request it. A cousin called to tell me she had been diagnosed with advanced breast cancer and was scheduled for surgery. She asked me for prayer support for a successful outcome. I told her about the quantum twin method and she agreed to being helped. When using this method to help another, we can do it through our own twin. After making the mandala connection as described above, my request was, "Time-traveling twin, under the protection of Archangel Michael, please work with my cousin's twin. Go to the future where she has been completely cured, and send this or something better to her while she sleeps." Her doctor turned out to be excellent, the operation a complete success, and she has been free of recurrence since then.

There's an important exception to the rule about not programming for others unless they expressly want you to, and that's when it comes to one's mother or offspring. Mallet says there is a very strong quantum connection in this particular relationship that makes it a natural exchange. In chapter 7, we'll see more about the long-reaching influence of matrilineage, which optimizes the prayers and visualization we do for them.

Light Up the Goddess-Angel Portal in Your Brain

1. Sit in a comfortable position. To make sure you stay awake during this exercise, it's probably better not to lie down.

2. Begin to breathe deeply, slowly, inhaling through your nose, pausing after each inhalation, and exhaling completely through your mouth.

3. Repeat: "I call on the forces of divine protection to surround and shield me now."

4. Sense a blue, luminous mist enfolding you.

5. Repeat three times: "I call on the goddess and angel forces to activate their portal in my mind."

6. Focus on the point between your eyebrows and then move your attention from there straight back into the center of your head.

7. Imagine the goddess figure on pages 32–35, and visualize that it glows in that same point in the center of your brain.

8. See her figure in bright blue light. With each breath, hold to this image for 3 to 6 minutes. She becomes brighter as you hold to this image for 3 to 6 minutes.

Alternately, apply the above keys, substituting the goddess figure for Michael and Faith in steps 7 and 8.

This exercise can be done before going to bed at night or at another time if you prefer.

Repeat it daily for at least twenty-eight days (a lunar month), and periodically thereafter as desired.

Letters to Michael

When you really need a breakthrough, when someone is doing something unfair like withholding your documents, belongings, or payment, or when you wish to guide or get through to a dear one who doesn't respond to reason—when nothing short of a miracle will do, write to Archangel Michael.

I have written many of these letters and frequently recommend them to others, with outstanding results.

Letters for the Guidance of Loved Ones

An architect named Cecily came to see me about her teenage son, Benny. Tears streamed down her face as she sat on a stone bench outside my door and explained that the situation had become untenable. He had dropped out of school, refused to work or help around the house, was taking drugs, and had become rude and aggressive. She had reasoned, pleaded, threatened, and made every possible effort to get through to him. Nothing had worked. Cecily was desperate.

I suggested she write the following letter:

To Archangel Michael

Dear Prince of Archangels,

I love you and bless you. Please work with my son's guardian angel so that he may find sobriety, reconnect with his motivation to live, take initiative in his studies and help at home, be more communicative, and treat me with respect.

I send up these words for your work of guidance and healing: Benny is not alone or limited to his own dark thoughts. There's a great light with him and in him, and it shows him everything he needs to see for his success, happiness, sobriety, responsibility, attitude toward me and toward life; and this light blesses him with love and with intuitive understanding now.

(I told her to write the affirmation three times in the letter.)

Thank you for your labor of guidance for my son.

With love,

Cecily

Two weeks after she had come crying to see me, Benny's mother returned. With a big smile, she told me that her son had made a 180-degree turn for the better. He had decided "on his own" to go back to school. He was helping around the house, treating her respectfully, and talking about his plans and feelings.

Use or adapt the above letter for a child, grandchild, sibling, friend, or anyone who seems to be in special need of guidance.

Letters for Collecting Accounts Due or When Someone Reneges on a Commitment

Adapt the above example, requesting that Michael and Faith intervene with the guardian angel of a person who owes you money.

Write the following affirmation six times in this letter:

"There's good in (name of client). The good in him is moving him and will not let him rest until he pays the full amount he owes."

This letter can be adapted if someone reneges on a commitment to return something they've borrowed or deliver documents or work, or even to achieve a fair agreement or receive a proper outcome to a legal case.

Write the following affirmation six times in the letter:

"There's good in (name of person). The good in her is moving her and will not let her rest until she returns my book (or finishes the work she promised, returns my necklace, passes a fair sentence, etc).*"*

Letters to Fulfill Our Own Commitments and Intentions

Write to Michael and the goddesses of strength. Ask them to support your focus, will, and determination and facilitate propitious circumstances so you can follow through on your intent and your own promises and goals. In this letter, write the following affirmation six to eighteen times:

> "I am not alone or without support to follow through on my intention. I have a Divine Companion who is with me always, strengthening me, directing me and supporting me within and without, now and always."

Letter for a Case of Dire Need

Rebecca was a businesswoman who came to see me after her cousin had been kidnapped. At first, the kidnappers would call the family and put the cousin on the phone so that they would know he was alright. They demanded a hefty ransom and said that if it wasn't paid by a certain date, they would eliminate him. The family did what they could but weren't able to gather such a high sum. By the time she consulted me, three months had gone by since the kidnappers' last call.

I suggested Rebecca write to Michael, requesting intervention from the guardian angels of her cousin's captors so that they would release him quickly and in good health, including the following affirmation twelve to eighteen times:

> "There is no place that God's light can't shine, and God's light shines in my cousin and on his path. Archangel Michael surrounds him with his hosts, and with his sword of divine authority, cuts away any situation or influence unlike the all-powerful divine good that surrounds him now."

Two weeks after she began to write this letter, Rebecca's cousin was found inside an empty rooftop water tank. Although dirty and exhausted, he was happy to be alive and rescued.

You can write to Michael to support healing or any other situation that needs a miracle. If someone has a grave health issue, I recommend they write to both Michael (for a miracle) and Raphael (for healing), choosing an affirmation from those shared in chapter 3, and writing it in the letter eighteen times or more.

Special considerations when writing to Michael:

Write the letter daily during three or four weeks, or as needed until peace fills your heart and the situation is healed.

If you write to get through to a person or people, try doing it before dawn or when you think those involved are sleeping. It's been scientifically proven that we have a strong telepathic link to others[25] that is particularly strong during sleep[26]. Angel letters lift this connection to its highest level. Archangel Michael breaks through negative energies or resistance, empowering our connection to the guardian angels of others. For several months, I wrote to him for help with my son, among other things, to release his fixation on digital screens. One day my son remarked that he had dreamt he needed to spend less time on screens. He also became more responsible, studious, happy, helpful around the house, and discerning about certain negative "friends."

Sometimes people ask if they can write their letters or affirmations on the computer. Any sort of positive application with words is valuable, but you can't compare the impact of hand-written messages.

As said in the previous chapter, hide or destroy your letters. Secrecy is vital for the outstanding results they tend to precipitate.

As seen in the example of Sara, who desperately needed healing, you can include Michael as a recipient in letters to Raphael for healing, Chamuel for self-esteem or relationship concerns, Uriel for abun-

25. William Braud, PhD, *Distant Mental Influence* (Charlottesville, VA: Hampton Roads, 2003).

26. Russell Targ and Jane Katra, PhD, *Miracles of Mind* (Novato, CA: New World Library, 1999), 96–99.

dance, Jophiel for pressing intellectual or academic projects, and so on. You'll find these letters in each archangel's chapter in this book.

The Magical Prayer of Michael's Name

In the light of goddess traditions, Michael's enigmas expand our understanding. The snake at his feet reveals the shadows encountered in our hero's journey. His warrior nature strengthens us to overcome those shadows, and the dragon enforces his might.

We have one more mystery to explore: Why does his name translate as the question: Who is like God? This is not just any name. When spoken, the words "Archangel Michael" radiate throughout the subtle world, bringing order to the invisible realms and sending each type of force to its right place in the vibrational scheme of things. Bradshaw notes that in spiritual release therapy, the entities depart when told to do so in Archangel Michael's name, whether or not the host believes in angels or a higher power.

This name's meaning, "Who is like God?," is a trap for the lower mind. Ancestral traditions used myth, story, and often seemingly absurd, paradoxical questions to precipitate new cognitive processes. An example of this practice is the *koan* used in Zen Buddhism. Meditating on questions such as, "What's the sound of one hand clapping?", or, "How would you drink in a single sip the entire Atlantic Ocean?", are used to snap the adept's mind out of linear reasoning and, as they do, precipitate enlightenment.

Like divine crossword puzzles, enigmas and riddles get our minds in gear and can lead to deeper levels of faith. This is the idea behind the practice of "ask-firmations." Rather than simply affirming, "I'm doing great," we're told to ask, "How could this possibly get better?" The query provokes a positive answer from within.

Like an angelic *koan*, Michael's name directs our questioning in the highest possible way. Unlock this ancient secret and experience a new level of faith and results by repeating the following decrees:

"Archangel Michael, who is like God? Who is like God in this situation? No one and nothing like God is present and working in this situation, and only good can come from it."

"Archangel Michael, who is like the Divine Mother? Who is like the Divine Mother in my spiritual path? There's no power like the Divine Mother on my path, and only good is coming from it now."

"Archangel Michael, who is like Spirit? No one is like Spirit in my mind, life, and circumstances."

You may of course substitute your own preferred name for divinity:

"Archangel Michael, who is like Omnipotent Good? Who is like Omnipotent Good to direct my healing? No force can prevail over Spirit's power that directs the healing processes in my body (in my emotions, for my sobriety, etc.), *here and now."*

"Archangel Michael, who is like the Goddess? Who could prevail over the might she has unleashed in my child's life, opening his way for success and happiness now?"

Adapt these words, apply them to your own concerns and situations, and repeat them daily for six minutes or more, as you savor their meaning.

Our Celestial Portal

Michael and Faith are the prince and princess of the archangels. Their goddess colleagues are some of the strongest and most ancient of deities. Together, they combine sacred masculine and feminine forces to protect the earth. Like great felines in the night, they roam the shadows of negativity, breaking up dense energies and removing entities. They restore our voice and empower our words. They lift our prayers to a miraculous potency. They strengthen our courage, our confidence and our faith—not a faith of pleading and grasping, but of divine understanding and certainty. As we invoke, visualize, write to, and fuse with them, using the technology of their spiritual weapons, we discover a new level of freedom and mastery. We can work with our time-traveling twin, sending ourselves more desirable futures. Most importantly, we can turn on our blue angel body, freeing ourselves from the vibrations of the lower world, preparing for flight to a higher dimension.

Chapter 3

RAPHAEL AND MARY: HEALING YOUR BELIEFS, BODY, AND SITUATIONS

This pair are the angelic agents of life on Earth who renew our capacity to heal ourselves, others, and the planet. In our times, their gifts are increasingly crucial. As the second decade of a new millennium came to a close just when humanity was experiencing a renaissance of holistic practices, a global pandemic seems to have deprived us of our divine birthright of wellness. Remember that the principles of angelic healing are immortal, and Raphael works to help us retrieve them, optimizing our powers in the face of any appearance.

Raphael's color is vibrant green. He's often depicted with a staff to symbolize the energy of trees and a fish, a representation of our connection to the natural kingdom. His twin flame is Mary. Her name derives from *mar*, meaning ocean, source of earthly life, alluding to her ability to renew our life force and wellness. From her crystal heart temple on the etheric plane, she works to activate healing love in hearts around the planet. Raphael and Mary relate

79

to Anahata, the heart chakra, and sometimes to the third eye, both gateways to divine perception.

Raphael and Mary's presence shines in the emerald ribbon in Earth's rainbow body. Their helpers on the ground include green and growing flora in forests, meadows, gardens, cracks in city sidewalks, anywhere sunlight meets water and life sprouts in its never-ending work to beautify and renew the planet. Their verdant essence also touches us through people: nurses, doctors, therapists, shamans, and all involved in the labor of healing. From their force field, Raphael and Mary call us back to our power to manifest wellness. As you turn to them and apply their keys, you activate the healing energy in your physical and rainbow bodies.

In ancient times, healers around the planet would connect with angelic forces, collaborating with Raphael and Mary and their colleagues in the subtle realms. Then, for thousands of years, the light workers faded from popular view. With the arrival of the age of angels, their powers have resurfaced, facilitating your connection with the cosmic and natural worlds and precipitating your inherent gifts as a healer. These keys include science—both physical and spiritual—in addition to divine truth, plant energies, angelic tantra, the healing powers of love and wrath, and the angelic spirits that enliven them.

Their ancient roots can be seen in the Emerald Tablet, a slab of green stone inscribed with the precept "As above, so below," attributed to Hermes. The mysterious Hermes, also known as Angelus, is the so-called "father" of esoteric healing, often called a god or king. The tablet hails from an era when healers and custodians of sacred knowledge were usually women. They worked with healing laws and would inscribe their methods on green stone (green being associated with wellness). The Hermetic law described above finds an intriguing parallel with the string theory of quantum physics. Above the four tangible dimensions—width, depth, height, and time—there are a series of higher dimensions that scientists describe being rolled into strings. It is believed that the four lower dimensions precede from these higher levels. From a metaphysical standpoint, when we connect our perception to higher truths, the appearances of the tangible world can be healed or made whole.

What happened to the women who wrote on these ancient tablets? Around the world, warring tribes of mysterious origin surfaced and conquered relatively peaceful societies in which women had been equal to men, suppressing feminine power.

Much knowledge was lost, and activities led by women were taken over by men, including the healing arts. Thousands of years later, we've become accustomed to projecting our power onto specialists, machines, and products in little boxes. This is not to belittle the wonders of allopathic medicine. Discoveries such as public hygiene and penicillin offer prevention and treatment for most illnesses today. Western technology, with blood transfusions and surgery, can save lives after an accident or even transplant a body part. The problem is that we confuse these methods with the source of our wellness, when they are really divine channels. The projection can actually sabotage recovery. As Dr. Jacob Liberman notes: "Many doctors look upon the patient as having something wrong with them, which the doctors then think or hope they can 'fix.' By the same token, people have been habituated to think there is something wrong that can only be 'fixed' by doctors...most patients [end up] having a helpless feeling about their health."[27] From their radiant garden in the subtle world, Raphael and Mary shine through, guiding and assisting us to rediscover our healing powers.

---

27. Jacob Liberman, OD, PhD, *Light Medicine of the Future* (Rochester, VT: Bear & Co., 1991), 167.

Their reappearance in the collective mind is inseparable from feminine empowerment. A key link in their return was the Truth movement that began in the nineteenth century, in which women have been particularly active. Raphael's domain includes physical and spiritual science, and the latter was espoused by groups (Science of Mind, Unity, Divine Science) that have since emerged. Over the years, the legacy of these teachings has found its way into popular culture, including the now common knowledge that thoughts and words can heal our bodies, emotions, and lives, knowledge that seems to particularly attract women. In the twenty-first century, therapeutic modalities continue to multiply.

Healing is a particularly angelic activity, and as you work with the affirmations and keys shared in this chapter, your personal access to the presence and gifts of angels will be strengthened. If they haven't already done so, sooner or later they will make themselves seen, heard, or somehow perceived, assisting you and others through you. The invisible allies of wellness will also restore your conscious connection with all of life and revive your true nature of love and power.

Over twenty years of work as a healer and trainer of healers has allowed me to experience these gifts firsthand.

Besides facilitating healing and increasing your perception of angelic dimensions, your Raphael powers will enable you to precipitate divine solutions in whatever might cross your path. You can begin to connect them now, right where you are. You don't have to go live in the Amazon, time-travel to ancient Egypt, or climb Mt. Kilimanjaro on your knees at Summer Solstice. You don't even have to cross the street. The only sacred site you need to visit is the diamond field within you.

Your Healing Heart

Wellness emanates from love, and the angels of healing operate through the heart portal. Both spiritual and physical science teach the healing properties of this energy center. Connecting with light beings can increase your heart power.

Raphael and the Goddesses of Healing Love

As it has with Raphael, healing love has long been associated with goddesses around the world, and the following technique connects us with their magical heart energy that is shining in the invisible plane of Spirit.

Fuse with the Heart of the Goddess

Ancient adepts would not only apply their minds, they would ignite the powers of the energy body by absorbing or fusing with light beings. The following keys are designed to ignite your divine healing heart. Choose those who attract you most and apply them.

Isis

In your mind's eye, see her before you with black hair, dark skin, and great, green wings. Imagine that your heart is made of light rather than matter, and then experience it fusing with hers as you repeat:

> *"Beloved Isis, you whose wings embrace humanity, radiate your healing love through me."*

Kuan Yin

Best known for her love of people of all stations and status, the Chinese goddess of compassion and healing is depicted with her hair in a bun, a radiant white gown, and strands of jade and pearls. Her heart is described as a sacred orchid. Visualize, invoke her image, and imagine her response as you say:

"Kuan Yin, you who behold all beings with love and empathy, please put your orchid flower heart in me."

Ixchel

Besides healing and midwifery, the Mayan goddess Ixchel (pronounced EE-shull) relates to love and rainbows. Her hair and skin are dark, and her dress is woven of brightly colored cotton. Feel her chest chakra fusing with yours as you say:

"Dear Ixchel, you who lovingly minister to those in need, radiate your rainbow heart through mine."

Green Tara

This Tibetan goddess embodies the healing compassion of all buddhas. Seated in the lotus position and dressed in flowing, regal clothing, she emanates the green light of growing things. To connect with her, use the following words and visualization:

"Green Tara, you who radiate the compassion of all buddhi, open your lotus heart of love in me."

Fuse with the Hearts of Your Favorite Healers

We can visualize the heart energy of past healers fusing with ours while we affirm: "Great women healers of the past, you who have channeled the love of the Divine Mother, put your healing heart power in me."

You can adapt the above suggestions to fuse with the heart of a human healer who has moved on to the light realm, such as Emma Curtis Hopkins, Florence Nightingale, Louise Hay, or your own favorite. Since this is a free exchange, remember to first request their help respectfully. Repeat, "If it's for the greatest good of all concerned, I request that through my guardian angel in connection with your guardian angel (name of the person you're calling on from the other side), that you share your healing heart vibration with me."

Apply the above keys for nine minutes daily, nine being a goddess number.

In the exercise section of this chapter, you'll find a method to empower your heart's healing vibration with angelic tantra.

Raphael and the Wrathful Goddesses of Healing

From the warm, white sands of the Caribbean to the cool, green forests of the Himalayas, we find traces of Raphael's goddess colleagues. Their dual powers of love and wrath enrich our angelic healing.

Mayan goddess Chac Chel, whose name translates as "Great Rainbow" and even resembles that of Raphael, was both an oracle and a healer. As a seer, she could perceive the hidden forces—emotions, thoughts, and entities—behind disease, and with her jaguar claws, destroy them. On parchment codices and in stone carvings, she appears with a wrinkled face. One of her most ancient facets was that of an elderly women. This resonates with the Mayan people's respect for older people, for their wisdom and their special powers. Chac Chel's archetype was eventually absorbed by Ixchel.

Chac Chel's dual powers of kindness and ferocity are shared by other goddesses of healing. For instance, in the secluded mountains of Tibet, where ancient ways are still in practice, primarily women healers worship Parnasavari. Among her many parallels to Raphael, her main color is green. She's connected to foliage, wearing a dress of leaves. She carries a noose for trapping demons and a scepter to shatter illness. Mantras mention her dual nature: a peaceful heart that pacifies epidemics, and wrathful speech that destroys poisonous spirits.

The methods of savara healers clearly resonate with Raphael. Savaras consider illness to be an interruption in the flow of energy that stems from negativity "embedded in the patient's psyche ..., toxic substances, harmful psychological forces or malevolent supernatural agency."[28] Savaras have been trained to see the "insubstantiality of a disease."[29] Whether treating an individual or an entire village, savaras apply their inner powers in combination with plant and goddess energies. Their millenary technology confirms our healing work and guides us to enrich its love, magical wrath, hand movements, and plant-spirit energies.

Connect with the Healing Truth

Just as Parnasavari helps her healers see the insubstantiality of illness and envision wellness, Raphael and Mary facilitate our access to the good that abides beyond challenging appearances. Spirit is omnipotent, or absolutely powerful, omniscient—all-knowing, omnipresent—in all places at once, and what I call *omnilovent*—infinitely kind. Situations that seem oppressive, painful, or limiting have no basis in the force of love that sustains reality.

In its infinite kindness, divinity did not create us to be victims of circumstance, but rather as the image and likeness of power. And it has given us the freedom to choose wellness as often as we need to.

When we're faced with illness or other challenging situations, they seem very real. Yet they exist only in the world of appear-

28. Miranda Shaw, *Buddhist Goddesses of India* (Princeton, NJ: Princeton University Press, 2006), 190.

29. Ibid., 189.

ances. By redirecting our attention from the apparent problem and generating a mental picture of wellness, we open a door to a universe of possibilities. The effect is not merely a placebo or mood booster, it's a power of mind that's been scientifically proven. The late, great astrophysicist, John Wheeler, said that in the light of quantum mechanics, "in a strict sense, the term observer no longer exists. In some mysterious manner, we participate in everything we observe."[30]

For many physicists, the idea of creative perception sounds too mystical or New Age, so they tend to publicly deny what has become a sort of family secret, "the skeleton in the physicists' closet.'"[31] Since the 1920s, when the influence our perception exerts on matter was first discovered, more than a thousand experiments have been applied to test it, and it has been consistently demonstrated.

We will now see examples of this law in action and how the angels can help us apply it. One basic yet decisive way is to persistently visualize wellness. This opens a door in the quantum field that surrounds us and in fact sustains our outer reality. New outcomes become possible. Sometimes the results take time, and at others they can be instantaneous.

Mind Over Medicine

The experience of Cynthia exemplifies this power, and also illustrates the importance of persistence. A businesswoman and mother of three adult children who has since become a healer in my group, she explains: "I was driving my compact car through an intersection on the way to get a facial, when a Cadillac came flying through the

---

30. Abelardo Hernandez, trans. Crystal Pomeroy, *El Corazón de la materia* (Madrid, Spain: Ediciones Contraste, S.A., 1995), 101.

31. Bruce Rosenblum and Fred Kuttner, *Quantum Enigma, Physics Encounters Consciousness* (New York: Oxford University Press, 2008), 3.

stop light. The next thing I knew, I woke up in an ambulance. I felt a tube in my mouth and saw a paramedic over me, and I figured there had been an accident. From the expression on the paramedic's face, I knew I looked bad.

"As it turned out, my head had a deep gash, seven vertebrae had been pulverized, fourteen ribs and both kneecaps were broken, and my left arm almost cut off. When they moved me around I could hear the pieces of my bones crackling. The doctors told my family that I might not make it through the night. When the nurses would come to attend and bathe me, they couldn't hide their shock at my appearance and continually commented on how terrible my case was.

"I never accepted their opinions. The whole time I kept telling myself I would be alright. Lying there I would close my eyes and imagine I was doing what I loved: dancing, working out, gardening, calling my clients. Repeatedly, they told me that I would never look normal or walk well. But I would look at myself in the mirror, thinking I have a beautiful face behind this face, and I would hold to the image of a pretty reflection.

"The doctors said that my vertebrae would be crooked if I didn't get an operation. And if I did, there was a high likelihood that I would die or end up crippled. One way or another, my neck and legs would almost surely be paralyzed.

"I didn't go for surgery or even a neck brace. After a couple of weeks, they sent me home to rest my deformed body. While I lay there in bed I used my mind. I repeated positive affirmations. I sent forgiving thoughts to the students who had crashed into me, and to myself because at the time of the accident I was on my way for a facial, when I could have been doing inner work. Most of all I visualized. I imagined myself at the gym lifting weights, dancing with my boyfriend, visiting my friends.

"Since the only part of my body that wasn't injured was my midsection, I began doing sit-ups in bed. Against doctors' orders, I would move my legs and, little by little, get up and walk to the window. There I would look down to the garden and imagine myself cutting the roses. I felt the hard, spiny stems in my fingers, the soft petals on my face and a sweet fragrance filling my nose. I would look down at the path where I used to run and imagine I was jogging alongside the other runners. As for my business, I continued working by phone, never telling my clients or anyone except my family and closest friends about the accident."

When challenging appearances overwhelm our senses as in the case of Cynthia's accident, persistence can be decisive. Except for having some tissue removed from her knees and an eyebrow straightened out, she never did get surgery. One by one, she resumed her work and social activities. On a certain occasion, a friend asked her, "Why are you crooked?" With an amused smile, Cynthia says, "It was true...I could walk, work, and do a lot of things, but I couldn't move my neck and I had to turn my whole body."

She continued her exercises and visualization. Few people ever heard about the accident. She wasn't putting on a front; she simply didn't want to attract more energy to the problem.

Today, at a stage of life when most people are retired, she works out at the gym for two to three hours daily, manages a successful business in the construction industry, and is active socially with volunteer work and spiritual studies. Her family doctor told her that he has another patient, a man less than half her age who had a similar accident years ago and is still confined to a wheelchair.

In the eyes of the Divine, behind every crooked face is a beautiful one, behind fear is joy, behind pain is complete wellness, and behind bad news is a perfect outcome. If we persistently pause to behold it, the good ends up emerging.

Prayers to See Beyond Appearances

Not everybody has Cynthia's fortitude or conviction. When faced with a challenge, our anxiety buttons get pushed. The angels of wellness will help us remember and behold the truth behind the appearances.

"Archangel Raphael, please help me behold the divine truth behind this appearance and allow it to manifest now."

"Dear angels of healing, please help me see the good in this situation."

"Raphael and Mary fill this situation with their light, bringing the healing truth into view, here and now."

In the exercise section beginning on page 108, you'll find keys to find out the truth in special situations.

The Power of Denial

Love and creative imagination are powerful, but they are often not enough. Before beginning her visualization and forgiving those involved, Cynthia mentally refused to accept the sentences that were passed on her health and appearance as definitive. This was not just a positive affirmation; it was a form of denial.

Healing isn't so much about creating wellness as it is about removing the blocks in our beliefs and emotions. If someone suffers a knee injury and the doctor tells them they will never be able to run again, it can be quite challenging for the patient to believe a positive affirmation like, "I am perfectly healthy." Denials are a form of intervention that immediately help neutralize the limiting belief. For instance, to heal your knees you can affirm:

> *"No occurrence or condition of the past or present can keep Spirit from expressing its perfect life through my knees now."*

In treating for pain, I use affirmations like the following:

> *"There is no power to hurt, there is only God's loving power that never hurts but always frees us and lifts us up.*

> *"There can be no painful process going on in you because the only real processes are divine processes, and they never block you or hurt you but free you and lift you up to complete wellness now and always."*

When giving classes and conferences on angels, prayer, healing, or abundance, I usually start by treating those in pain so that they'll be able to enjoy our session: I ask that anyone experiencing pain at that moment raise their hands. I spend five to fifteen minutes repeating affirmations similar to those above and apply related techniques shared in this chapter until everyone present confirms that they are completely or almost completely free of pain.

Affirmative denial is a controversial topic. Promoters of neurolinguistics say that the subconscious doesn't pick up the word no.[32] If you say, "I can't be sick," it skips the denial and just gets, "I can be sick." Furthermore, they affirm that the subconscious goes into a sort of paralysis when we hear words of negation. That's why it's more effective to tell a child, "keep your room nice," than "don't be messy." The mind has many levels, and in some situations this could apply. If a person who grew up in poverty rejects their condition in fear, saying to

---

32. "Your Unconscious Mind Does Not Process Negatives: Replace Don't…with what you WANT," Life Puzzle website: https://lifepuzzle.com.au/your-unconscious-mind-does-not-process-negatives-replace-dont-with-what-you-want.

themselves, "I won't be poor," with anxiety and stress, their thoughts may attach them to the idea of lack. And then there are those who think that to deny contagion is irresponsible and might lead to a lack of physical care. These practices are not designed to replace physical treatment or prevention but rather to dissolve the beliefs that uphold negative conditions. After years of studying the mind-body connection in the laboratory, biologist and best-selling author Bruce Lipton says that beliefs control biology. He cites the results of certain Christian groups in the southern United States who have put their faith to the test by drinking poison and with medical documentation, successfully praying to resist the effects.[33] Of course, we're not suggesting anyone do this test. However, when it comes to mind power, affirmative denials can undo the beliefs that—on the quantum level of reality—underlie illness, optimizing the body's healing processes to an extraordinary degree. This approach doesn't ignore a condition in the hope that it will somehow go away. It takes the belief by its shirt collar, looks it in the eye, and dissolves it. As Ernest Holmes wrote, "The practitioner's mind is not in a dream state. Quite the reverse," it's "coming out of a dream state into a higher reality."[34]

As discussed in chapter 1, your angelic powers not only help you create the energy and experiences that you want, but also dissolve undesirable conditions. Denial is a way of expressing divine wrath: our authority to wipe out blocks to wellness, success, and every kind of good. In the late 1800s, it was author and teacher Emma Curtis Hopkins who coined the term "affirmation." Along with teaching positive decrees, she taught the use of denials: "When the right negations are stated, our affirmations are exceedingly effective."[35]

---

33. Bruce Lipton, *Spontaneous Evolution* (Carlsbad, CA: Hay House, 2010), 12.

34. Ernest Holmes, *How to Use the Science of Mind* (Los Angeles: Science of Mind Publishing, 2002), 58.

35. Ruth Miller, PhD, *Unveiling Your Hidden Power: Emma Curtis Hopkins Metaphysics for the 21st Century* (Beaverton, OR: Wise Woman Press, 2005), 40.

Hopkins called denial "the omnipotent No."[36] The author has been using and teaching this method for years, witnessing recoveries from supposedly grave conditions, instantaneous remissions, and sudden materialization of financial blessings.

People who have not developed this key often send healing in the form of loving thoughts or energy to others, and seem to find it normal that a significant improvement doesn't follow. Raphael's healing truth won't just make people calmer and more hopeful. If we apply it right, it can literally change circumstances.

A treatment I gave to a baby serves to illustrate Raphael's keys of love and truth in action, and how the details may vary depending on the information that angels bring to light. In April 2015, her parents brought the nine-month-old child to me for healing. Judging from her cheerful demeanor, rosy cheeks, and eagerness to explore my living room, she seemed healthy. The parents, though, didn't look radiant.

As soon as the child was carried into the room, I began looking at her with heartfelt love as I held to the thought that the Higher Power had a solution for her situation. I then listened to the parents' description of her condition. In a tone of soft desperation, her father said, "Since she was born, she hasn't slept more than three and a half hours per night." Neither did the child make up for her lack of rest during the day, when she had only a couple of fifteen-minute naps. Both parents were working full-time, but they had to take turns staying up to watch her. The mother, Ana, is a nurse. She said, "I've had every available test run on her, all of which came back normal. The doctors can't explain her condition and have prescribed tranquilizers." The parents were visibly desperate for a solution and at the same time worried about the side effects medication might have on their baby.

---

36. Miller, *Your Hidden Power*, 43.

After listening to their explanation, I mentally asked Raphael and Mary for guidance. It came to me that she had been labeled as difficult or a problem child. This often happens in family relationships. When someone close to us has anomalous situations or behaviors we often slip into labeling them. It's particularly common in parents toward their children but can also occur with children toward parents, between siblings, or with colleagues, neighbors, or anyone in our personal or public sphere. These labels are false identities whose influence can keep people stuck.

In this case, right after I sensed that she had been labeled, another piece of information surfaced from her mother, who said, "When she does fall asleep, sometimes she cries quietly." It came to me that the child was sensitive and picking up something unpleasant, possibly from another dimension, which made her frightened to go to sleep.

After receiving this information, I began to neutralize it by focusing on the truth that God loved her, and that the only power that could reach her was God's love, so there was no condition or influence to harm her. For about twenty minutes I held to and affirmed this truth, adapting the words to the subtle aspects of the situation that the angels had revealed. I repeated, "This beautiful girl is not a problem child. She's a perfect baby, surrounded by God's love, and God's love is the only power that can touch her. When she's awake and while she sleeps, the only influence there is for her in any dimension is God's love, so there is only good for her, in her, and as her always." I continued to repeat these and similar words, mindfully centering on love as the only influence at work in her life and thoughts. Several days later, a follow-up call revealed that the night after the treatment, their child had slept easily. She has continued to do so since.

In more than two decades, thousands of flight hours with affirmative prayer, and innumerable cases I've been called on to treat, affirmative denials have proven to be one of the quickest ways to intervene. We'll look at why it's so effective and more ways you can apply it. If, after seeing them, you still prefer not to use the word "no," we'll explore alternative methods to achieve notable results quickly.

To dissolve a condition, whether it's physical, emotional, or in any area of life, identify a limiting attitude in your own mind or the mind of the person needing treatment. For instance, if someone tries to convince you their situation is difficult, you can say, "There is no difficulty for Spirit. Spirit knows your condition, how to heal it, and is working to do this, here and now." Remember: when you affirm, you are not trying to convince the other person but rather speaking to your own beliefs.

Wrathful Affirmations

Emotions, finances, and other circumstances can be quickly cleared when we face and neutralize the blocking belief.

Here are more examples. (Feel free to change the word "Spirit" to God, Goddess, Divinity, Infinite Good, Source, or your own preference.)

Dissolving Fear

"In the name of Archangel Raphael, I hold to the truth that my mind receives a constant inflow of divine thoughts, which are helpful, uplifting, and confident, so there can be no low-vibrational thoughts in me."

Counteracting Depression

"I am made in the image and likeness of joy, so I am only open to happy, uplifting vibrations and feelings, now and always."

Improving Circulation

"Divine love pours through my veins in a radiant, powerful stream. No condition or event of the past or present can keep divine love from flowing through me, touching every cell of my body and every vibration of my being, and restoring my wellness now!"

In Case of Tumors or Undesired Growths

"There can be no growth except spiritual growth, because the only power to make things grow is Spirit, who makes only good grow in my mind, body, and emotions, here and now."

Cognitive Wellness

"The Divine Mind cannot be worn down. Nothing can keep the Divine Mind from thinking through me clearly, now and always. My intelligence comes from the Infinite Source, and no condition or event can diminish it or take it from me now or ever." Adapt the idea to affirm for another: *"The Divine Mind cannot be worn down. Nothing can keep the Divine Mind from thinking through (name of person) clearly, now and always. Her intelligence comes from the Infinite Source, and no condition or event can diminish it or take it from her, now or ever."*

Bone Health (Can be adapted for any apparently degenerative process)

"There can be no degenerative process in my bones, because the only true processes are those triggered by Spirit, who only triggers loving processes that free me, strengthen me and lift me up. And Spirit uses any other apparent processes to help me, so only divine processes are taking place and have taken place in my bones, my body and

my world. This awareness allows Spirit to reach into my bones and restore them to radiant wholeness now."

Heart Conditions

"No condition or event of the past or present can keep God from expressing its perfect life through my heart now."

Allergies or Toxicity

"I cannot have any allergic or toxic reactions, because the one substance in my world is divine substance, which helps me, benefits me, and favors me, now and always."

Respiratory Wellness

"Divine love fills the mental and physical atmosphere around me, so only good is touching my mind, emotions, and body. Each time I breathe, this loving, divine atmosphere enters in my sinuses, throat, and lungs, never harming me but lifting me up to wellness, now and always."

High-Risk Conditions

"I cannot be at risk. Love would never put me at risk and love doesn't leave me open to risk. Love lifts me up and holds me in complete wellness whatever the circumstances, now and always."

Contagion or Infection

"We can't catch anything harmful because the only thing there is for us to catch is Infinite Good."

Climate Change

"There can be no harmful substance or effects in Earth's atmosphere. Divine love fills Earth's atmosphere, so only good is touching us through it now."

Accidents and Post-Traumatic Stress Syndrome

"The only true events in my life have been and are divine events that benefit me, free me, and lift me up. Infinite Good uses all events to help me, so no event could have really harmed me. This awareness allows Spirit to erase any seemingly harmful results from my life, mind, and body now."

Finances

"My prosperity cannot be limited. Spirit doesn't limit me or make me depend on people or circumstances for my supply. Spirit supplies me richly through infinite channels, now and always."

You'll find more denials and also affirmations for financial prosperity in chapters 2 and 6.

Put Wrath into Your Words

When you use denials and affirmations to heal, remember Chac Chel and Parnasavari, and apply your power of divine wrath by speaking with authority. Once I was giving an express treatment to a young woman who had come to me for a large, painful lump on her neck. It turned out that since birth, she been besieged by numerous, recurring conditions. Usually, when people hear my healing words, they look enthused and hopeful. In her case I noted a certain despondency. She was so used to hearing her relatives discuss their ailments and to feeling victimized that she doubted the strength of my affirmations. So I began to affirm more forcefully: "God is present right inside your tissues, and right there unleashes its power to free you from any negative appearance! Nothing can limit your wellness!" This affirmation helped me overcome her doubts and the reaction her doubts had caused in me. I continued to repeat this and compatible ideas for another ten minutes, during which the lump stopped hurting and decreased visibly in size.

Enrich Your Wrath by Paying Attention to Your Intuition

The beliefs behind sickness and negativity are like walls of limiting energy, and as you work with the tools in this chapter, you will come to sense when those walls are thicker or harder and you need to affirm in a more commanding tone. You will also sense you have successfully moved through them. An example of this is the treatment I've been giving to a dog named Grissy. When the owner first brought her to me, Grissy had lost the use of her legs. The veterinarian had said that when dogs of her breed reached a certain age, they suffer a sudden, progressive and irreversible atrophy of their muscles. From the beginning of the first fifteen-minute treatment, Grissy began to rouse. On one occasion, I had been using denials and affirmations and suddenly I felt guided to affirm strongly: "I refuse to believe that you can inherit any limiting program. You are infinite being, naturally connected with the wellness that flows from God's mind to you now." As soon as I stated the words, "I refuse to believe ...." Grissy, who had been lying passively in her owner's lap, started moving her head and lifted herself up on her forefeet. Grissy is now able to stand up and her muscles get continually stronger.

Other Wrathful Affirmations

Besides direct denials with "no" and "not," you can use adjectives such as "unlimited" and "infinite" and other words such as "only" and "almighty." The following examples serve for large-scale concerns like epidemics and climate, and you can adapt the idea to whatever your needs and situations.

I was living in Mexico City when the swine virus broke out. Official news outlets predicted the worst, deaths were reported, panic was unleashed. To avoid infection, people were instructed to suspend all group activities, including my classes and workshops. This suspension had been going on for some weeks when I decided to leave town on a personal retreat. Daily, I wrote to Michael, Raphael, and Mary, asking for their assistance. In the letters, I repeatedly wrote the following affirmation, meditating on it as I did: "The Same Mind that knows how to stop this threat is working to do so through infinite channels and with almighty means, here and now." A few days after I had begun this practice, the headlines said that the problem had been contained.

On another occasion, a friend and newspaper director posted on Facebook a photograph of Hurricane Patricia in the stratosphere. I looked at the white spiral in the sky that was supposed to portend great danger for Mexico and the southern United States, a storm predicted to cause the greatest harm of any in history. I thought that something so beautiful couldn't be harmful. I then affirmed, "God's love is in the center of this phenomenon, and only good can come from it. The only things that can storm on this region are divine harmony and good." I later remembered the terrible predictions related to the image and doubted my inner peace, so I began to write the affirmation and also posted on my Facebook page. A few days later, newspaper headlines spoke of a "miracle": Uncharacteristically, American reporters were mentioning the "hand of God" as the only possible explanation for the way in which the hurricane had broken up. Later reports signaled a coastal mountain ridge as the decisive factor in the storm's sudden dispersal. If this was the only explanation, why hadn't meteorologists taken that possibility into account before? One religious organization began publicly praising itself for their prayers, and it's not my intention to do the same. Obviously, people all over were hoping, intending, invoking the angels, and praying for a miraculous outcome. Perhaps a critical mass of people are getting it: that prayer is not about persuading an arbitrary deity to intervene but rather a way of clearing the mind so we can allow divinity to demonstrate true outcomes. What I can vouch for is that when we deny the power of destructive appearances on any scale, sooner or later what we have chosen to believe will appear in our world.

Angelic Mudras: Move Your Hands Wrathfully

Another way to heal with wrath is to move our hands and arms as we affirm and deny. Some years ago I began doing this intuitively to accompany the energy of affirmations and denials with diverse movements to push through beliefs, eliminate blocks, open divine portals, pull out energy knots, cut through negative attachments, and seal the results. My clients gave me positive feedback such as, "My pain didn't go away until you started making those movements," and "When you moved your hands I could see colored lights." So I continued to follow my guidance. I'd been using these movements for more than six years when I discovered that the Tibetan savara healers (mentioned on page 86) also use hand and arm movements in their treatments. In India, certain advanced practitioners of yoga make spontaneous mudras during their meditation. Not only our thoughts and words, but our light bodies serve to channel the energy of healing wrath.

In the exercise section of this chapter and in chapter 6, you will find more on these movements.

Healing with Plant Angels

In Raphael's emerald dimension is a group of beings who heal in their own special way: plant spirits. Since ancient times, their physical properties have played a central role in healing, and plants continue to provide the active ingredients for most medicines today. Through photosynthesis, a process that scientists are still at a loss to explain, they translate sunlight into chlorophyll, generating food directly or indirectly for all the rest of Earth's inhabitants.[37] They also absorb carbon dioxide and convert it to oxygen. Of all the ways plants sustain our world, perhaps the most interesting is the least recognized in industrialized society: as sentient spiritual healers and guides for humanity.

Thousands of years ago, green forests prevailed around the planet: trees were sacred, and the woods were used as living altars. Native peoples considered plants to be sentient beings and would call on their spirits to assist with emotional, energetic, and physical healing.

This viewpoint is not confined to ancestral teachings. A new generation of scientists also consider flora to be sentient, even thoughtful. Plant physiologist Stefano Mancuso goes so far as to affirm that our green brethren are more intelligent than humans. In his book, *Brilliant Green*, Mancuso notes that they have twenty senses as

---

37. "Finally, the Mysterious First Part of Photosynthesis Comes Into View," Futurity website: https://www.futurity.org/photosynthesis-energy -conversion-1711092/.

compared to our five, including the ability to perceive electromagnetic fields and gravity. After ten years of directing the International Institute of Plant Neurobiology that he founded at the University of Florence, the author confirms that plants "talk to each other, recognize their kin and exhibit various character traits."[38] Well aware of relationship, plants think and work as communities. For instance, if a deer begins munching on leaves on one side of the forest, somehow the word spreads and the entire woods emit a toxic or bitter substance to inhibit further predation. Trees promote unity, thriving when they are together, engaging in networks, and sharing resources across species.

The relational aptitude of trees resonates with the feminine approach, and the connection wasn't lost on ancestral cultures, where trees were typically associated with the Goddess. Groves were used as temples, and when cities began to emerge, trees remained a necessary presence at goddess shrines. The Tibetan goddess Parnasavari is closely related to forests. She appears in a skirt of leaves, which is also worn by women healers who venerate her today. In ancient Mexico, a healing goddess called Toci ("Our Grandmother the Nocturnal Physician") was thought to derive her powers from plants and herbs. Among the many ancient trees venerated in Mexico today, the Tree of Infinite Fruit in the northern state of Chihuahua is related to the goddess of fertility and agriculture, Chicomecoatl. For hundreds of years, farmers have visited the tree to pray to the goddess so their crops may prosper.

The universal role of female healers has been suppressed over the centuries, yet flora is still present as a key factor of the pharmaceutical industry and shamanic medicine, and its energy is a numinous, healing presence around the planet. In her book *The Woman*

---

38. Stephano Mancuso, *Brilliant Green: The Surprising History and Intelligence of Plant Intelligence* (Washington, D.C.: Island Press, 2005), 4.

in a Shaman's Body, Barbara Tedlock retrieves myths about female shamans who were destroyed by their envious male counterparts, only to return through foliage. A native Mexican story describes the creator goddess Takutsi Nakawe ("Grandmother Growth"): after fighting the men who wished to steal her powers, she dove underground and from the blood of her heart sprang a Brazil tree."[39]

A similar development has taken place in religious history. Isis instigated and oversaw the resuscitation of Horus. Yet millennia later, Jesus had his resurrection and Buddha his illumination—both without an animus. Or did they? The two Marys were the only companions to stay with Jesus throughout the crucifixion. As for Buddha, his hypnotic eyes, lovely locks, and sensual curves contrast with early representations of a more believable-looking emaciated monk. The changes are the product of the assimilation of the once-honored feminine into Shakyamuni's figure. In the cross and the Bodhi, both Jesus and the Buddha have their tree. Could this be more than a symbol? Could it be that the energy of the plant world helped them complete their spiritual missions?

There's a Hopi teaching about the re-emergence of both plants and the sacred feminine. As author Pam Montgomery puts it, we are entering what is called the Fifth World:

"… [A]n era of "The Great Healing … a time of huge paradigm shift … shaped by the feminine paths of cooperation, non-aggression, inclusiveness, non-competitiveness, service rather than dominance, use of psychic and spiritual gifts, as well technology and living in conscious harmony with nature's ways …. Because of plants' predominance on the planet, their great sensitive intelligence and their ability to heal on all levels, they are … actually instigating this huge evolutionary movement that is spiritual in nature … Plant

---

39. Barbara Tedlock, PhD, *The Woman in the Shaman's Body* (New York: Random House, 2006), 56.

forms from previous worlds are beginning to spring up as seeds. The same kind of seeds are being planted in the sky as stars. The same kind of seeds are being planted in our hearts. All these are the same. This is not a metaphor."[40]

Though the effects of industrial society are in many ways ominous, they also offer an opportunity to share information that crosses cultural and historic barriers. We have access to keys—ancestral and contemporary, scientific and mystical—that we can use wherever we happen to be, and with them manifest wellness.

There are numerous, simple ways you can invoke the healing energies of our leafy friends.

Call on Tree Spirits

Just knowing that they are present and can be invoked enriches our healing. I enjoy calling on them mentally; that way I don't have to pick or cut them.

The first time I did this, I was attending a gentleman in his seventies. He dried his tears as he told me, "The doctors say that my circulation is so bad that they may have to amputate my feet." I felt the need to apply every sort of help. After using other methods shared previously in this chapter, I sat in silence with my eyes closed and attention toward the left, the intuitive side, where it can be easier to connect with invisible helpers. I mentally called on the angels and plant spirits to seal the healing, and saw light presences as well as the spirit of a tall, large tree.

The man and I spoke on a Sunday. The following Tuesday, his wife reported that he had again seen his doctor, who was surprised to note that his circulation was almost normal; he was out of danger.

---

40. Pam Montgomery, *Plant Spirit Healing* (Rochester, VT: Bear & Co., 2008), 111.

Since then, I have frequently invoked tree spirits, or what I call the healing spirits of forests, to support and seal a treatment. Sometimes a tall tree will appear behind the person I'm attending. When this happens, I affirm: "Your healing is supported by a tree spirit, who is behind you, strengthening you and lifting you up to wellness and spiritual growth now."

Discover Your Tree Family

There's a tall, beautiful pine outside my home in Mexico City. I've always loved it and sometimes fought to protect it from neighbors who consider it a nuisance and have tried to hurt it and cut it down despite the fact that it's been declared an ecological monument. This ancient pine is almost within arms' length of the space where I've developed my healing work. As I continued to learn about trees, it came to me that this tree might actually have something to do with the work. One day I noticed an indenture in the bark, a sort of hole where the sap had hardened into the shape of a perfect heart, the size of a large talisman. On another occasion, I came home with some friends at night. They parked next to the tree, shining their headlights on the trunk. We were all surprised to notice a figure that had been formed in the bark. It stood about three feet tall, clearly showing a slightly bent personage clothed in a tunic, wearing a cap and leaning on a tall staff. I often hug this tree, praise its beauty and healing work, and sometimes ask for assistance to persist in my own and to harmonize my emotions and to balance my energy.

Ancient Mexicans saw trees as bridges between the dimensions of matter and spirit, humans and angels. Do you have a special tree near your home or daily activities? It may be a personal guide and healer for you. When we hug them, trees absorb the excess positive ions that we pick up in our urban environments. Hugs are also a great way of sending love to them and receiving their healing intentions for us.

Do Things for Flora

Contact with plant spirits goes both ways. When we assist plants physically and spiritually, we draw closer to their world. Besides hugging and praising them, we can be sensitive and careful when pruning, caring for, or cutting plants. Before entering a park or forest, we can greet and bless the guardian spirits of the place. We can help protect ecosystems by writing letters, sharing petitions, and attending hearings. (Remember: the energy's important and works better if we go about activism in a spirit of love, not of fear.) And we can pray for the trees. For instance, we can affirm: "The forests of the planet are not alone or without protection. The Divine Guardian is with them, watching over them, and working in every way to protect, sustain, and restore them now."

Gather Plant Energies

One of the most effective ways to call on plants' healing energy is by visualizing all the green and growing things around the world, and then connecting them to the part of one's body or emotions that are in need of healing. Once I became sick to my stomach when also experiencing severe menstrual cramps. I sat in the bathtub, focused on the area in pain, and then imagined it became green as it connected to the great sphere of vegetable life around the planet. I felt a lovely vivification and, in less than two minutes, all the pain and symptoms totally disappeared.

Montgomery describes sitting with her back against a tree, just knowing that she's breathing in the oxygen it exudes, and that it's absorbing the carbon dioxide she breathes out. In the city where I live, there aren't too many chances to sit against a tree, but we all do breathe, so I use this image at a distance, affirming, "I breathe in the life of plants, and breathe out love and life to them." While guiding group meditations, I sometimes repeat, "Each breath connects us with the healing life of plants, who produced this oxygen, and who absorb and transmute the carbon dioxide we breathe out."

Exercises with Archangel Raphael

To increase your healing powers, you can apply spiritual technology and activate your light body. Besides Raphael's healing letters and mandala, we will now see original keys like a Healing Truth Candle, angelic tantra to activate your healing heart, and angelic mudras to awaken the healing circuits in your hands.

Angelic Tantra to Activate Your Healing Heart

- In your mind's eye, imagine Raphael and Mary—two great, green archangels—standing before you. Trust your intuition on the details of their appearance; each of us can see angels in a unique, personal way.

- For a minute or so, feel their strong love vibration and behold their radiance, akin to a glowing tree or forest.

- Imagine yourself absorbing their presence into your body until you can feel it glowing.

- Place your attention at the center of your chest and sense that area becoming particularly bright.

- Repeat the following affirmation for six or nine minutes:

  "Raphael and Mary shine in every cell of my body and every vibration of my being. My heart glows with love

> *for the angels, for myself and for others. My healing light*
> *body has awakened, here and now."*

Raphael and Mary Bring the Truth to Light

If some sort of special information is needed to complete the healing of our minds, bodies, and situations, they'll reveal it. This information may include hidden emotional, physical, or energetic factors, as well as the divine truth that will dissolve the condition. Sometimes the information comes in the form of a sign, a book, a health professional, or another outer stimulus that appears spontaneously on our paths. At others, particularly when we're helping people or using affirmations like those shared further on in this chapter, it comes as an inner sensing. The following suggestions facilitate this connection:

1. Close your eyes and see yourself in a place with green growing things that you've visited in the past: a lush garden, a meadow, or a forest.

2. Sense the verdant radiance of Raphael and Mary in your heart, and directing your attention there, ask them if there's something special you need to know for healing.

3. With your attention still on your heart, spend several moments "listening" for the response. It may arise as a phrase, an image, or an inner knowing.

4. If nothing comes to light, repeat this exercise daily, paying attention to outer and inner guidance until it does.

Healing Truth Candle

1. Obtain a light green candle and a black dry-erase marker for writing on non-paper surfaces. (Alternately, you may use a wide strip of white paper to write on with a ballpoint pen and later tape around a white candle or even a lampshade.)

2. On your candle or strip of paper, write "Raphael and Mary," and under them the condition you wish to know more about, for example: "breast health," "self-esteem," "freedom from infection in (name body part)," "joyful and appropriate partnership," "my healthy relationship with money."

3. Light your candle. (Or, if you used the option of the strip of paper described above, tape it around the lamp or candle and turn it on or light it).

4. For a couple of minutes, gaze at and contemplate the words describing your intention.

5. Close your eyes and visualize those words floating against a background of light.

6. For six minutes, repeat the following affirmation:

"The light of Raphael and Mary is now revealing whatever I need to know in order to manifest wellness (happy relationships, prosperity, self-esteem). I am willing to look at those aspects of myself, of my life and world that are coming into view."

Repeat this exercise as often as necessary to reveal the knowledge.

Angelic Healing Mudras

As stated in the section on affirmative denials earlier in this chapter, you can direct healing wrath by using hand movements.

An easy one to start with is this:

With fingers slightly bent, stretch your right arm before you, rotating your hand in a clockwise motion and pushing your palm forward with vigor at the end. Combine this with affirmative denials to push out limiting beliefs. You'll find more examples of angelic mudras in chapter 6.

Raphael's Healing Mandala

Raphael's colors, energies, and symbols will support your manifestation of wellness.

Getting Ready

Before gathering your materials, take a moment to quiet your mind, focus on your intention to heal, and ask the angels, goddesses, and plant spirits to help you manifest it. Hold to your purpose as you put it together.

You will need:

- Bright green (not neon or pale green) paper or poster board and a gold or blue pen, crayons, and/or paints.

- Color images of your healthy self: actual photographs of you running, working out at the gym, dancing, swimming, or doing another activity that requires wellness. Optionally, you can download and print and/or use pictures from magazines, brochures, or the internet of someone who resembles you with a better figure and condition. Remember that you must appear active.

- If you've had or need lab work, you can complement these images with lab studies that you retouch to show normal levels and results.

- Depending on the size of your mandala, 20 to 30 small images of forest-green plants. You can use a picture of your favorite tree or mix different kinds.

- 1 large (1½") and 3 or more small (½") images of Archangel Raphael and his twin flame, Mary. (You can download, cut out, and paste; or if you prefer, draw the images onto the poster board.)

- Your favorite adhesive stick, paste, or glue.

Make Your Healing Mandala

1. Trace a large (10" or more) circle, and line it evenly with the plant images.

2. Draw or paste the image of the angels in the middle, and the smaller images around the inside of the circle to taste.

3. At the top of your mandala, write an affirmation, such as:

"I call on the angels of wellness to activate my healing powers of mind and body, now."

"The divine forces of healing rush to support my wellness. I feel it, I see it, and I receive it now."

"I am made in the image and likeness of divine life, and I enjoy my wellness now."

Center in Your Mandala

Three times a day, spend six minutes looking at your mandala, feeling the energy of plants and angels streaming to you and through you, and imagining yourself enjoying the activities depicted on your mandala.

Keep your mandala secret. Other people's doubts can block manifestation. And pay attention to the signs that appear on your path: a treatment, exercise, or nutrition program or another resource may be a link in the chain of divine healing.

Letters to Raphael for Special Healing Needs

For chronic, critical, or ongoing conditions, there are few techniques as powerful as letters to Raphael and Mary. You can write them in your journal or on a sheet of green paper.

Over the years I've shared many of these letters and received numerous testimonies. I'll share the example of Julie, a single mother with a young son. She recalls that when she came to see me, she had gone to the gynecologist for a routine checkup and tested positive for cervical cancer. She then visited another doctor for a second opinion, who confirmed the initial findings and sent Julie to oncology for a follow-up. When she visited me, Julie's big brown eyes were filled with worry: "I was the sole support for my son, who at the time was seven years old." I gave Julie a letter to the angels of healing with denials and affirmations, which I suggested she write on clean sheets of paper so it would resemble a true missive. As archetypal forms of communication, letters open portals.

Her letter looked like this:

Dear Raphael-Mary,

Please work with my guardian angel to expand my faith, and with the angels of the doctors and all involved to heal the appearance of cervical cancer. I send up my words for your perfect use:

There can be no growth except spiritual growth, because the only power to make things grow is Spirit, who makes only good grow in my mind, body and emotions, here and now. (In each letter, she was to write the affirmation eighteen times.)

Thank you beforehand for your angelic intervention. With love and gratitude, Julie.

After writing the letters daily for two weeks, Julie followed the doctors' orders to visit the oncologist. He ran some tests on her and ended up saying, "There must have been a mistake; your results are normal." She went for a second opinion, which confirmed that she was fine.

As we apply the keys shared in this chapter, we optimize our innate healing powers. Through and beyond these results, we discover a larger meaning of healing. It's a path of reconnection: with ourselves, others, light beings, our magical planet, and with the most amazing of all loves: the Source for whom connection isn't about dependence or submission but about wellness, beauty, and empowerment.

Chapter 4

HOPHIEL AND CONSTANCE: BEAUTY, BRILLIANCE, AND INTUITION

The archangels of intelligence will give you confidence in your gifts and aptitudes, jump-start your creativity, and bring success in cultural, educational, and intuitive pursuits.

Hophiel's wings are made of peacock feathers and his tunic is bright yellow, the color of illumination and the sun, to which he's related. He carries a book and a scroll—symbols of wisdom and knowledge—and a sword with which he cuts through old thought patterns, mental fog, forgetfulness, and unconscious resistance to higher perspectives. Considered an emissary of the sun, he facilitates mental empowerment, supporting intellectual development and new thought patterns. Related to beauty, he also brings prosperity.

His divine complement Constance is a beautiful golden archangel whose penetrating gaze can see beyond our distraction and insecurity, recognizing and rekindling our highest potential. She imparts the dedication, discipline, and strength that supports our persistence to establish new, positive patterns and she grounds our intellectual and subtle gifts.

As angels of awareness, the golden pair have a key role in awakening our Angelic Intelligence. They raise our vibration, facilitate our connection with light beings, and guide us on our light path. They support the growth of our mental, creative, and spiritual skills, and ensure that we assimilate only divine ideas and wavelengths. Like their golden aura, this work strengthens our souls and the radiance of our light body, sealing the latter in the rainbow colors of Uriel's peacock-feather wings.

Hophiel's Chakra Manipura

This chakra is particularly important because it empowers us with confidence and intuition to develop our talents. Yellow in color, it contains intelligence, self-will, and identity. The Hindu goddess related to Manipura is Lakini Shakti. About her, author Cyndi Dale says: "She encourages us to set goals and concentrate on what we need to do—and think—in order to achieve our aspirations...."[41] She calls Manipura "the center of our personal power." Here, "we find the keys for balance and deciding how we are going to achieve our dharma, our life purpose, rather than just live out our karma, our past experiences."[42] In the Inka tradition the solar plexus center is also yellow and, like Athena, related to autonomy, individuation, and fulfillment of one's dreams. The Cherokee version of this chakra is a yellow-orange color. In its light, we can transform negative thoughts and feelings "into higher action."[43]

41. Cyndi Dale, *The Subtle Body* (Boulder, CO: SoundsTrue, 2009), 257.
42. Ibid.
43. Ibid, 295.

Mexican artist Auria Balleza is a practitioner of Auro-Soma, an occult tradition with roots in the Kabbalah that works with colors and the energy body. In a personal interview, Balleza said that according to Aura-Soma, the most important point in our subtle anatomy is at the center of the solar plexus: "It's called the Star of Incarnation, and refers to what you are here to give. It connects to the Earth Star so you can live on the earth plane, and the Star of Soul, which is above the crown chakra. The Star of the solar plexus is the seat of intuition, reason, channeling, and inspiration. It's where we do alchemical transformation and contact the angels." Charles Filmore says that in "its highest phase," the intelligence of the solar plexus works with "the white light of Spirit … in the top of the brain."[44] Mind activity, like that associated with Hophiel, is usually associated with the head. Yet the chakra of the solar-plexus speaks to the importance of confidence and self-direction in developing our mental skills –and these stances radiate from the stomach. In diverse ancient traditions, the stomach was "held to be the seat of the soul."[45] It's interesting to note that doctors have identified a "second brain" in the stomach.[46] It turns out that many thoughts and memories accumulate there, to the extent that this organ has mental impulses of its own. Intuition often appears as a "gut feeling." We need confidence to heed it, just as we need confidence and persistence to "digest" knowledge so that it becomes part of our personal light, and that we may generate our own original work. To trust ourselves and the gut instincts that ground our higher perception is part of Angelic Intelligence.

---

44. Charles Filmore, *The Twelve Powers of Man* (Eastford, CT: Martino Fine Books, 2013 reprint of 1938 edition), 49.

45. Pierre Pallardy, *What Your Gut Instinct is Trying to Tell You* (UK: Rodale International, 2011), 13.

46. Michael D. Gerson, *The Second Brain* (New York: HarperCollins, 1998), 2.

Hophiel and the Goddesses of Wisdom and Accomplishment

It is believed that Hophiel's name was originally Sophiel, due to his connection with Sophia. As one the most ancient of all goddesses, Sophia's name is synonymous with wisdom itself, which was considered a feminine principle. Solomon attributed his knowledge to spiritual encounters with Sophia, in which he "learned it all, hidden or manifest, because I was taught by Her whose skill made all things."[47]

This essence of divine wisdom is expressed through numerous goddesses who resonate with Hophiel, including Athena, Sarasvati, and Lakshmi.

Athena, Goddess of Culture, Confidence, and Accomplishment

Athena is the Greek goddess of culture, wisdom, strategy, and protection. She carries a shield and a lance, and an olive branch of culture and distinction. She rules wisdom, intuition, strategy, weaving, civilization, artisans, discipline, authority, diplomacy, victory, sisterhood, femininity, athletics, self-determination, and success. Athena works with Hophiel and Constance to imbue us with the confidence, discipline, and strength to successfully develop and share our talents. As do many goddesses and archangels, she strengthens our angelic body.

Athena is very important for Angelic Intelligence because of her origins, although they have been buried in past myths, like her birth from Zeus's head. Earlier versions reflect the dignity once accorded to the sacred feminine: Athena was the daughter of Zeus's first wife, Metis. Zeus swallowed Athena so that she wouldn't grow to rival his greatness, but she couldn't be consumed and ended up reemerg-

---

47. Lawrence Durdin-Robertson, *The Year of the Goddess* (Wellingborough, UK: Thorsons Publishing Group, 1999), 26.

ing from his head. Author Brandi Auset calls her "the philosopher, embodying reason," and "the personification of the autonomous female."[48]Athena has her roots in the Libyan goddess Neith or Athenna, a facet of Isis, whose title *Athene* meant "I come from myself." Neith was held in great esteem from predynastic times until the beginning of Roman rule. The Libyan goddess ruled several of Athena's specialties, including weaving. Like Mexican Xochiquetzal, not only did she weave garments for the living but also for the dead, whom she protected with her arrows. These clothes are symbolic of the light body—an essential aspect of Angelic Intelligence that reappears in goddess myths throughout the world.

Neith was the mother of sun god Ra, leading to Athena's golden-yellow color. Although Athena and Neith evolved into goddesses of war, their original victory was enlightenment of the mind and protection of the soul. Like Hophiel, they use their weapons to vanquish negative mental influences, sharing his mission to illuminate, fortify, and protect. Hophiel's scroll and book resonate with Athena's olive branch of wisdom and cultural prowess.

Invocations to Support Your Efforts and Confidence

"Athena and Constance, make your strength rise in me, that I may grow in light and success, now and always."

"Powerful Athena, radiate your discipline through me, so I may bring forth this (book, concert, degree, production) now."

"Hophiel and Athena, please cut away distractions and doubts, and direct me to use my faculties successfully now."

---

48. Brandi Auset, *The Goddess Guide* (Woodbury, MN: Llewellyn, 2016), 13.

*"Assured Athena, bring forth your confidence in me so I may develop
my intuition fully now."*

A bit further on we'll see other tools to receive their support.

Before exploring them, let's consider three other goddesses who
resonate with Hophiel.

Sarasvati, Hindu Goddess of Wisdom, Intellect, and Prosperity

Your beauty [is] equal in splendor to Mount Kailash ...
Perfect skill in oratory, debate and composition ...
Lucid expression thrills every sharp mind, so I beseech you:
Grant me wisdom in writing, debate, and teaching.
—Prayer for Sarasvati by the Second Dalai Lama[49]

Sarasvati shares many of the archangel's gifts. She imparts beauty,
eloquence, scholarly and artistic proficiency, perfect memory, intuition, supreme knowledge, illumination, prosperity, and longevity.
Like Hophiel, she works to awaken our logical, creative, and intuitive abilities.

In her four hands, the goddess carries a sword, a book, a rosary,
and a lute made of lapis lazuli. Like Hophiel, she's connected to
peacocks. Her radiance is associated with the autumn full moon.[50]

---

49. Glen Mullin, translator, *Meditations on the Lower Tantra, From the Collected Works
of the Previous Dalai Lama* (Dharamasala, Tibet: Library of Tibetan Works and
Archives, 1983), 127.

50. Sharron Rose, *The Path of the Priestess* (Rochester, VT: Inner Traditions, 2002),
22.

In resonance with the golden archangel, Sarasvati's sword represents her work as a protector. She frees us from anything that might disturb the harmony needed for creative and intellectual pursuits, including distraction, interruptions, unfavorable planetary influences, and negative mental influences such as nightmares, insecurity, discord, and negative entities.

Her lute of lapis lazuli represents creative, magical, and cultural attainment. Her rosary symbolizes spiritual sciences. Her book signifies intellectual and academic wisdom.

Sarasvati's name means "Lady of the Waters," "Lady of the Lake," or "Flowing One." Sarasvati reflects the Hindu concept which "attributes to women and goddesses the power to give life, but life … is not understood as merely a biological or material phenomenon. Female life-giving power (sakti) nourishes, inspires and empowers on every level…. Sarasvati … pours forth the nectar of knowledge and artistic inspiration, nourishing the mind and spirit."[51]

In her waves of love, divine nectar, and grace flowing from the heavens, we are reminded of Hophiel's subtle processes. His touch isn't physical, but vibrational, as is the substance of Angelic Intelligence.

Like the Hindu goddess of wisdom, the golden archangel supports our mental, spiritual, and creative skills. Aspra says that the eyes on Hophiel's peacock-feather wings represent divine perception and wisdom. In *Invoke the Goddess*, author Kala Trobe says that Sarasvati's peacock plumage represents "the all-seeing divine nature."[52]

---

51. Shaw, *Buddhist Goddesses*, 246.

52. Kala Trobe, *Invoke the Goddess: Visualizations of Hindu, Greek and Egyptian Deities* (St. Paul, MN: Llewellyn, 2000), 6.

Lakshmi, Goddess of Wisdom, Beauty, and Prosperity

Ruler of beauty and abundance, Lakshmi's main color is gold. We'll save a more detailed analysis of her symbols for the chapter on Uriel, archangel of divine supply, with whom she's also connected. However, Lakshmi has important connections with Hophiel. She is known to collaborate with Sarasvati to bring prosperity to those who work to develop knowledge and enlightenment. She is said to have given the god Indra a wisdom beverage called soma.

There's a true story concerning Lakshmi and an illustrious scholar that serves to remind us of how light beings facilitate human access to Infinite Intelligence. In many Indian towns, the golden goddess has been and is deeply venerated. Among her adepts at the end of the nineteenth century was a child math prodigy by the name of Ramanujan. As explained in Robert Kanigel's biography of him, *The Man Who Knew Infinity,* theorems seemed to flow spontaneously through Ramanujan's mind, and he would spend hours a day writing them down. The mathematician said they came from parchments the goddess would show him in visions and dreams.

His importance for the history of math is said to rival that of Newton. Ramanujan's contributions were so advanced that even today, they continue to shed new light on various fields including logic, physics, and humankind's evolving understanding of black holes. He was known to say that an equation meant nothing for him unless it represented a "thought of God."[53]

Like Solomon, who claimed to have been taught by Sophia, goddess of wisdom, Ramanujan's story illustrates the direct, intuitive connection we have with divine intelligence. Although the former

---

53. Robert Kanigel, *The Man Who Knew Infinity: A Life of the Genius Ramanujan* (New York: Simon & Schuster, 1991), 7.

is enveloped in myth and the latter is an extraordinary case, both evoke the unlimited nature of higher mind that can and does flow to us in the form of ideas, inspiration and understanding.

Besides her gifts of wisdom, as goddess of prosperity, Lakshmi works with Sarasvati and Hophiel to benefit those who develop their intellectual, creative, and intuitive faculties.

Hophiel and His Goddess Colleagues Support Intuitive Intelligence

This connection is felt in dreams and visions, and through signs. Most often it seems to come from our own thoughts, which have actually been influenced by angels.

A continual practice of prayer or meditation combined with serving others will naturally lift our vibration, increase intuition, and attract divine guidance, precipitating Angelic Intelligence.

I've experienced this myself. Despite working with spiritual principles since childhood, for many years I couldn't come up with an affirmation of my own. Books were my mentors, and if I didn't have one on hand, I would feel stuck. Eventually, after thousands of flight hours in prayer, some sort of inner shift took place and a stream of original affirmations began flowing. For the last fifteen years, I've been writing daily prayers and angel invocations for Daykeeper Journal and the Mexican newspaper *El Gráfico*, rarely using the exact same phrase more than once. The inspiration flows like a waterfall from a higher source. On the rare occasion when I feel blocked in wording a new thought or beginning a text, I pause and mentally ask the angels for support. The words flow quickly and their quality is superior. I've joked that the angels are one-upping me.

I've also given thousands of individual healings and unblocking treatments, and not one of them is quite like another. As I work with each person, insights about their situations arise, sometimes with messages from their dead loved ones and very specific information that I had no way of knowing previously and that the clients later confirm. While reviewing their needs, I mentally design the affirmations and invocations I'll use in the treatment, yet often end up changing them for ideas that the angels suggest. I'm also guided to move my arms and hands and energy in different ways (some methods of which are shared in this book), as are the healers I have trained and many of those who receive treatments with my methods. Intuition is a natural part of energy healing. When we give our subtle gifts as service to one another, angels gather to work with and through us.

Angels will inspire us for all kinds of mental, occult, and creative activities. It's not that they do our work: we need to put in time, study, and effort. But when we remember to call on them and pause to listen within, the light from above uploads into our minds, accenting our innate talents and vastly improving our results.

Invocation to Receive Knowledge

"Angels of self-improvement, please connect me with the books, the teachers, and the information to develop my understanding and walk my path of dharma."

Invocations to Awaken Intuition

"Hophiel and Laksmi, pour your radiant vibration into my mind and being and fill me with the intuitive understanding of whatever I need to know."

"I see Hophiel's light flowing like golden liquid through my being, awakening my angelic intuition now."

Invocation to Manifest a Space for Your Spiritual Practice

"Angels and goddesses of wisdom, direct and support me in making a space to study (to create, to pray, to visualize, to invoke the angels) and to grow my light."

"Hophiel and Constance, please manifest an inspiring, tranquil physical space where I can study (write, play my music, sing, meditate, journal, and so on)."

Invocation to Focus on Your Light Path

"Hophiel, with your golden sword, please sweep away distractions so I may walk my path of light now."

Invocation to Recognize and Act on Divine Guidance

"Archangel Hophiel and goddess Sarasvati, direct me to recognize and act on divine guidance, now and always."

Invoke Hophiel and Sarasvati at the Full Moon

As noted above, Sarasvati is related to the full moon. When Luna glows bright in the dark sky, she brings light to apparent darkness. It's a perfect portal to call on the angels and goddesses of wisdom.

In the exercise section of this chapter, you'll find a more elaborate full moon invocation.

Dreams: Hophiel's Special Portal

Like Sarasvati, Hophiel is a special guardian of dreams. Through them, he and his goddess colleagues can touch us directly in magical ways.

At some time or another, most of us have received insights and other gifts from dreams. Who wouldn't like to have clearer and more constant access to those gifts? By working closely with Hophiel and his goddess colleagues, you can develop it, protecting your dreams from negative psychic influences and fulfilling your mission even as you sleep.

Dream Interpretation

Everyone dreams. Specialists know this because they can measure the rapid eye movement that takes place when, in dreams, we look at and do things. In his book *The Wisdom of Your Dreams,* Jeremy Taylor says that all dreams are good because they all contain valuable information.[54] Unpleasant dreams can show us things about our need for healing or problems and their solutions. After years of working with my own dreams and those of others, I must say I agree with him, partially. Dreams often bring up what we can't or don't want to see. However, there may be other influences, like fears, worries, imagination, physical processes (such as cold or pain), outer stimuli (fluorescent lighting or a fight or party going on outside your bedroom) and, as discussed in chapter 2, the thoughts of others and entities.

Since pre-patriarchal times, dreams have played a key role in spirituality. Through them you can access guidance, increase intuition, connect with light beings and spirits, heal yourself or another, and

---

54. Jeremy Taylor, *The Wisdom of Your Dreams* (New York: Penguin Books, 2009), 3.

do high spiritual work. When the body sleeps, the mind is free to receive guidance and move through subtle realms.

Some dream messages are simple and obvious. For instance, you might hear a voice that gives you advice. Maybe it tells you to eat a certain food or take a supplement (in which case it's wise to research it and check with a health professional). They also come through symbols, which are an important part of angels' vocabulary. You may see the cover of a book with helpful information, or a folder or the name of a company that reminds you of a deadline you had forgotten or a call you need to make. A dream about a relative or friend may mean they need help or have some good news to share. Dead dear ones can visit us in dreams to ask for prayers or forgiveness, to bring us guidance, or simply to greet us.

There are dreams of warning, as seen in true stories of people who were about to travel but changed their flights after dreaming about accidents that ended up happening. In those cases, the dream saved their lives. When we dream something bad is going to occur— to us, to someone else, or to an entire area or population—it can be a call to action and also prayer. The future is never totally fixed, and not only what we do but how we pray and visualize, can avert and modify certain probabilities. If you do dream of impending disaster, look into it and take whatever measures you can, but remember to use positive affirmations and to ask the angels to intervene. For instance, you can repeat: "Nothing bad is going to happen. Spirit is present and working in this situation, and only good can come from it now." Throughout the chapters of this book you can find many affirmations for transmuting problems of all kinds, and for protection and guidance of others. If you receive a warning dream or vision, a good way to invoke the angels is: "I call on the angels to help in this situation and to direct my actions, prayers, and visualization to allow a divine outcome now."

We can also receive dream guidance of a positive kind. A client of mine who's a nurse dreamt that she was walking through the big, open doors of a certain hospital. The next day she went to see the director, who ended up hiring her for an attractive position.

When you work with Hophiel for dream guidance and protection, you receive clear, constructive messages more frequently. With his golden sword, the bright archangel specializes in removing low-vibrational influences and connecting us with higher wisdom.

Not only do angels guide us in physical actions and solutions, they know our minds are powerful, and they guide us to pray and visualize. The night after attending my class about Hophiel, a businesswoman named Gracy dreamt that two strangers were giving her money. Each of them showed her a wallet full of cash. When they opened the wallets, more and more money flowed, as though it came from a different dimension. She felt it was a sign that good things were coming. I suggested she recall the images from her dreams and use them to visualize herself receiving large amounts of cash. After applying the suggestion, her income grew significantly.

Angels' main project is to support our spiritual evolution. They know our current level and send guidance to move us on our path of light to overcome our attachments, resentments, insecurities, and character defects; and to become braver, more confident, more loving, and more focused on our life mission.

If You're Woken in the Middle of the Night

If a dream or a voice seems to wake you in the middle of the night, try getting up and choosing from the letters in this book to write to the angels. Around 3:30 am is an especially powerful time of day for this angelic activity. When the people in your world are sleeping, the mental airwaves are freed up, and your thoughts meet with little resistance. Often, angels wake people up at this time, or you can wake yourself. In the wee hours, write to the angels, and pray for some special concern you have, for a loved one, or for groups in need like "the animals and trees in the Amazon," "children in situations of apparent abuse or abandonment," and so on. A person or group with special needs may come into your mind intuitively.

Writing to angels is both powerful and calming, and many people fall asleep naturally after making their letters.

Angelic Dream Interpretation

There are universal archetypes or symbols that appear in everyone's dreams. For instance, if we dream about a teacher, it can represent a voice of wisdom within; seeing an automobile can speak to our life direction; a hummingbird can represent a loved one who's passed on, and so on. We don't have space to cover them all here, but at the end of this book you'll find a list of recommended dream dictionaries and encyclopedias.

I'll now share a simple method of dream interpretation that often brings the most important insight you can receive.

1. In the morning on waking, call on Hophiel and/or your guardian angel and spirit guides to help you recall and interpret your dream or dreams.

2. In a notebook or your Angel Dream Journal, write down all you can remember of your dream. Take note of details like people's hairstyle and clothes, types of furniture, features of the place or area, and anything else you remember. Taylor points out that the most surrealistic aspects of a dream often contain the most important symbolism.

3. Read over what you wrote while thinking of each person, thing, and element of a dream as part of yourself. For

instance: your boyfriend can symbolize your masculine self, a store owner could be your role as a businessperson, a doctor represents your healing wisdom, your mother is a facet of yourself that knows how to care for you (or the opposite, depending on your personal history), a stranger who tries to take you somewhere you don't want to go may be a part of yourself that wants to distract you from your true intentions, and so on.

4. Consider all the details as described in step 2, and analyze what their symbolism means to you. For instance, if you dream that you're wearing a pair of pants similar to a pair you had when you were in college, you could be reconnecting with the part of yourself that's preparing for a new life mission.

5. Write down whatever messages you glean from your dream, and then analyze it again for any additional meanings. Often, dreams have various levels of interpretation. A person you know may represent part of yourself, *and* you may also be seeing something about your relationship with that person or being asked to pray for them.

6. If you feel a need for additional clarity, share your dream with a friend or group, and get their feedback. You can ask for additional guidance the next night by sitting up in bed and repeating this phrase ten times before going to sleep: "Angels of wisdom, please show me the meaning of this dream in a clear way that I can easily understand and apply."

7. Do whatever you can to move in the direction indicated by your dreams. Like Ramajudan, the celebrated mathematician who made a discipline of applying the wisdom received from Lakshmi in dreams, our lives can be transformed by actively weaving oneiric guidance into them.

As we act on guidance, our ability to retain and understand it grows, and our web of connections with the magical realm of angels becomes increasingly palpable.

Invocations for the Angels to Take Us to Study, Evolve, and Serve in Our Dreams

Choose from the following and before going to sleep, sit up in bed and repeat it for three to six minutes:

"Hophiel, Constance, and goddesses of wisdom, tonight while I sleep, please take me to learn what I need for my evolution and that of all beings."

"Archangel Hophiel, please work with me to develop my Angelic Intelligence, tonight while I sleep."

"Angels and Guides of Wellness, please teach me to deepen my healing powers, tonight while I sleep."

"Guardian angel, while my body sleeps, please work to free me from whatever separates me from God."

"Angels and goddesses of dreams, please direct me in doing the highest and best spiritual work tonight while I sleep."

"I call on my guardian angel and spirit guides. Please lift me up to best and highest resonance tonight while I sleep."

"Guardian angel, please direct me to serve in the best and highest way, tonight while I sleep."

Exercises with Hophiel, Constance, and Their Goddess Colleagues

The Angel Dream Journal

Integrating the colors and images of Hophiel and Sarasvati, this journal has a high vibration. Seal it with a special blessing.

1. Purchase a yellow notebook or journal, or make one by covering any notebook with bright yellow paper.

2. On a piece of white adhesive paper that's a couple of inches smaller than the notebook, print or draw a picture of Hophiel and Constance.

3. Paste this image on the notebook, with a smaller one of Sarasvati above it.

4. Alternately, paste images of yellow angels and Sarasvati on an existing notebook.

5. Inside the cover, write: "I bless this journal as a portal of the light that angels and goddesses send through my dreams."

6. Place your hands on the journal, as you repeat: "I recognize the omnipresent light that shines through this journal, blessing it as an instrument of angelic wisdom."

7. Each night before going to bed, sit on or kneel next to your bed. Hold your book open to the next blank page and say, "Archangel Hophiel, please write the story of my life on these pages."

8. For a couple of minutes, visualize that Hophiel is bending over your journal and writing in it.

Angelic Dream Incubation

Ancient adepts would devote hours and, in some cases, days invoking divinity and meditating to receive the desired guidance. [55,56] They took ritual baths and fasted or avoided eating heavy foods at night so that digestive processes wouldn't interfere with their oneiric experience.[57]

Full-Day Preparation

1. The morning before you incubate a dream, call on Archangel Hophiel, repeating:

   "Great angel, please guide me with your golden light to prepare for the answer I seek tonight."

2. In a new page of your journal or on a sheet of paper, write: "Please reveal the best solution (decision, course of action) in this situation."

3. Get your mind working on the solution: spend a few minutes thinking of all your options. Make a list of the pros and another of the cons of each option.

4. Take a shower, imagining that the water is a field of golden, liquid light that's pulling away shadows from your aura and touching your mind.

5. Dress in natural-fiber clothing (cotton, silk, linen, wool, hemp).

6. On several yellow post-its or small signs, write the words: "Hophiel guides me in dreams." Paste them in key places: on your bathroom mirror, the refrigerator, your desk, the

55. Scott Cunningham, *Sacred Sleep: Dreaming the Divine* (St. Paul, MN: Llewellyn, 1999), 24.

56. Ibid, 106.

57. Ibid, 160.

edge of your computer screen, and so on, so you can stay mindful throughout the day.

7. If you're spending your day at home, keep a yellow candle lit so you can remember Hophiel, visualize his radiance filling your space, and repeat your request throughout the day.

8. At night before going to bed, go to your bedroom, light a yellow candle, and call on Hophiel by repeating: "Archangel of Wisdom, please come and fill my space with your light."

9. Imagine the great yellow archangel standing behind the candle, and see the rays emanating from him and filling your room.

10. Standing up, repeat three times: "Archangel Hophiel, please pass your sword over my head and solar plexus and cut away any low vibrations that might interfere with my reception of angelic guidance. Seal me in your golden light." As you repeat, visualize Hophiel standing next to you, passing a sword of light up over the back of your head, over the top, and then down over your face, chest, and solar plexus.

11. Sit on the edge of your bed and spend a few minutes reviewing your options in relation to the situation you want guidance for (see step 2).

12. Still seated on the edge of your bed, repeat ten times: "Thank you, angels of wisdom, for revealing what I need to know about this situation (name the situation or bring it to mind), in a clear, positive dream I remember on waking."

13. Blow or pinch out the candle and go to sleep.

14. Keep your Angel Dream Journal (pages 132–133) or a notebook on hand so you can write the dreams or fragments you remember on waking.

Express Dream Incubation

If you don't have time to apply the entire method above, apply the nighttime part, from steps 8 to 14.

Increase the Power of Your Intentions

Besides overseeing nighttime dreams, Hophiel supports our hopes and wishes, and our ability to turn them into effective intentions.

To establish an intention is to open a doorway that only you with your free will can define.

With the support of my mother, who was my first teacher, I have been working with intentions since childhood. Together we would make lists of what we wanted. Over time, I discovered that some of the intentions would manifest but most wouldn't.

To write our wishes can be an act of power. However, we can unwittingly limit it. From the moment we start writing, a little voice whispers, "And just how would this wild dream happen?" "Do you really think simply writing will bring it about?" "Look at your situation, so far from that dream! This is ridiculous!!" These doubts sabotage manifestation.

Some years ago I came up with a method that shortcuts around self-sabotage, facilitating the sensation that our dreams have already come true. Since then I've shared it with thousands of people in my prosperity courses, in many cases personally helping them to perfect their application, and being witness to their outstanding results.

Missive of Manifestation: The Letter to a Confidant

Write this imaginary letter in your Angel Dream Journal or on a sheet of yellow paper.

1. Call on Hophiel, repeating: "Angel of Light, please inspire my intentions in resonance with the angelic book of my life."

2. Letting your intuition guide you, make a list of the most important things you would like to see happen over the next several years. Cover different areas that together express your dream life. You can include subtle goals such as achieving illumination or inner peace, developing discipline or deep faith, working with the angels, awakening your intuition or healing gifts, or remaining centered in love for yourself and others. Write wishes for physical or emotional wellness, romantic happiness, professional or creative success, and financial independence. Include intentions for others: the health of a dear one, your child's happiness and spiritual direction, the balancing of Earth's climate. Don't make your list so extensive that it becomes scattered, but do cover several key areas.

3. Choose a confidant to write your imaginary letter to. This is an inner exercise for your own mind. Although you won't actually be sending the letter, vibrationally speaking it's important to choose a real person you would share great news with, someone that you're sure will be sincerely happy for you. It could be a sibling, a best friend, a teacher, a coach, or a parent. If your confidant lives in another city, it will be easier to imagine you're writing to them.

4. From the moment you begin to write, imagine that this is a rough draft of a real letter you're preparing to send in

which you're sharing the good news of your dreams come true. Be as detailed as possible.

For instance, you might start by saying, *"Dear Karen, I'm writing to share my joy about all the good things that have been happening in my life…".*

Imagining that you're sharing real news and in your own words, describe all the blessings from your list of intentions as though they have completely consolidated. Adapt and enrich the following examples:

I'm living in the house of my dreams. It has a big, beautiful library, next to a lovely forest that I can see through the living room, kitchen and bedroom windows… There's an inspiring meditation room where I love doing my daily inner work and contacting the angels. My prayer life is rich and fulfilling… I'm strong and completely healthy. I go on walks, swim, go the gym, and dance. My yoga practice has grown significantly and so has my social media presence—with over a million followers. My classes are full. Hundreds of people come from all over, experience great results, and are happy to pay good money for my services and recommend me. Through this and other channels, my income is about four times more than it was five years ago. I finished my book and it has been published by a major firm.
I continue with altruistic activities, giving a free weekly class at the local community center and volunteering at an animal shelter where I have met some very positive human friends.
My mom is doing better than ever. She enjoys her morning walks, traveling, and the many blessings life has given her. I told her I was going to write you and she sends her love, too.

*We really have so much to be grateful for. There's a guest room
for you whenever you decide to visit and enjoy the trees and
peace of this setting that I know you'll love.*

Hugs in light,

[Your name]

Additional Tips for Effective Manifestation

Remember to focus on the final result. For instance, if you want to
travel, don't write: *"Our bags are packed for a trip to sacred sites around
the world."* Rather, write: *"Our trip to the sacred sites in eight countries
was awesome. We interacted with a variety of native teachers and made
lovely friends who seem like spiritual family. We learned a lot and soaked
up spectacular beauty and great vibrations. We ended up having more than
enough money for extras and our income continued to flow while we were
traveling, so we were even able to get gifts for friends and family."*

Be concrete. Don't just say, *"Prosperity is flowing for us"*—spec-
ify your monthly income or the types of expenses it allows you to
cover: *"We've had more than enough to live well, travel frequently, and
help some worthy causes."* You may use the option shared in the letter to Karen above, saying, *"My income has almost tripled in five years"*
or a similar comparison. Apply this to healing, harmony, or other
intentions. Describe things tangibly and visually to open a quantum
space for manifestation.

When manifesting, you want the universe to handle the how. For
instance, don't write: "I went on a cruise where I met a new man."
Instead, write: *"I have a new love who's kind, intelligent, spiritually
aware, successful, and we are passionately attracted to one another."*

If you have a partner and want a happier relationship, don't
mention the person's name. Just say, *"I'm living (or going out with) my
dream woman. She's the kindest, most positive person. She gets along with
my kids from my first wife, loves nature and music like me, and there's a*

strong, mutual attraction. We're growing together spiritually and financially." If your current partner can respond to the intent, your relationship will improve. Otherwise, they will move out of your life and someone new will appear.

Avoid discussing your letter or showing it to others. Doubts or envy can block manifestation.

You can rewrite your letter on a frequent, even daily, basis. Each time you do, live the experience as though you were really communicating your news.

Besides a letter for long-term goals, write letters for short- and medium-term goals.

After writing, remember to be mindful of your intuition, signs, changes, and opportunities, including to act on them. You are a key agent of your new good.

Setting your intentions is particularly effective at the new moon portal.

Ritual to Establish New Mental Patterns

Hophiel and Constance support new mental patterns. People who practice meditation and positive prayer often find themselves slipping back into negative thinking. This key will help you remain in a higher wavelength.

1. After a session of positive prayer or meditation, light a yellow candle.

2. Gaze at the candle; register the bright, golden color in your mind and then close your eyes, holding the golden glow in your mind and watching it grow into two bright angels. They may appear as tall, winged beings or simply fields of yellow light. You may perceive one with a sword—that's Hophiel—and the other, Constance, as more feminine.

3. Visualize Hophiel passing his knife above and around your head, then down over your face and solar plexus, and repeat: "Archangel Hophiel, with your sword of light, dissolve lower thought patterns from my mind and body."

4. See Constance come close, feel her touching the top of your head with one wing, and your solar plexus with the other, and repeat: "Angelic Constance, please imbue me with your strength and hold me in divine thought patterns, now and always."

Full Moon Invocation of Archangel Hophiel and Goddess Sarasvati

1. Before gathering your materials, repeat: "Hophiel, Constance, and Sarasvati, make of this lunation a window of angelic light that awakens me and the world to our full brilliance."

2. Take a moment to imagine yourself surrounded by many yellow light beings who are putting a brightly shining, golden tunic on you.

3. Hold to the sense of being dressed in golden light as you acquire or gather: a yellow candle, a stick of sandalwood or jasmine incense, a goblet or glass of water, and some daffodils or other yellow flowers.

4. Repeat: "Hophiel, Constance, and Sarasvati, please shine your light through this lunation, cutting through any low vibrations and radiating deeply into my life and the world."

5. Look at your candle and imagine you can see an angel standing inside it.

6. Light the candle, seeing how the angel's aura grows through it, expanding into your space as many small, winged beings flow out on its rays.

7. Light the incense, saying: "This is an offering for the angels, the goddesses, and my ancestors and guides whose wisdom has nourished mine." If you know the names of your guides, say them. You can also mention special ancestors, like "My grandmother, the scientist," or "my mother, who gave me books and taught me to be kind."

8. With your left hand, pick up the goblet and dip the fingers of your right hand into the water, sprinkling it around your aura as you repeat three times: "Angelic grace purifies my energy, pouring love and light through my mind, heart, and body, into my world."

9. Sit in a comfortable position and continue to repeat this affirmation for six minutes.

The full moon is an especially apt time for beginning any of the activities in this chapter. Whenever you happen to look at the full moon, you can imagine you see Sarasvati, Hophiel-Constance, or one of their swords inside Luna's bright circle.

Protect and Bless Your Birth Chart

From my years of experience as an astrologer, I can vouch that a natal chart is a treasure trove of information. Among other things, it shows our psychological tendencies, talents, aptitudes, past lives, vocational direction, and types of business, work, and occult application that can bring prosperity. For many centuries, certain influences have been considered beneficent and others malefic. Besides the stars themselves, there are beliefs around those influences that have accumulated from the collective mindset of diverse historic periods. Sometimes that mindset was manipulated by kings and ruling priests who promoted mass hysteria by labeling certain alignments as terrifying portents. Fortunately in our time, astrology has become increasingly constructive. However, present and past labels on certain configurations and aspects can intensify their challenging influence.

When reading someone's chart, I bless it to transmute the apparent challenges. I'll now share how you can this yourself.

1. On a white sheet of poster board, paste or draw your natal chart wheel.

2. Using paint, pastels, or a felt-tip pen, draw bright yellow rays around the circle, as though it were a sun. If you like, you can add some orange, red, and/or gold along with the yellow rays.

3. Paste or draw a color picture of Hophiel or Sarasvati in the center of the chart wheel.

4. Place your hands on the chart and repeat slowly and with intention: "Spirit (God, Goddess) loves me and hasn't made me to be subject to negative influences. Omnipotent good touches me through all conditions, including these configurations. I bless my moment and chart of birth, knowing that only good can come to me, is coming to me, and will come to me through them, now and always."

To bless another, repeat the above steps using their chart wheel and adapt the blessing to the second person ("Spirit loves you"… etc.).

Invite the Angels to Organize and Renew Your Library or Bookshelves

One of the greatest blessings of the twenty-first century is our access to books. Hophiel supports us in building, organizing, and renewing our personal library so that we have the best titles for each phase of our development and reading pleasure.

The following exercise will help keep your books in order and keep the right titles flowing as you give away those that no longer serve you and invoke angelic support for new ones.

1. Stand before your bookshelves. Put your hands together in a sign of reverence and repeat: "Hophiel, Constance, and Sarasvati, please help me organize and renew my library." Imagine numerous yellow angels and dakinis (female light beings) come near the bookshelves, surrounding them with golden light.

2. For a moment, close your eyes and see them touching your books and moving them around, taking some out and filling the spaces with new ones.

3. Open your eyes and go over your books. See which ones you won't be likely to use or read again. Take them out and put them in a box or bag for later donation to a library or friends who would appreciate them.

Note that depending on the condition and size of your present collection, the following steps can take up to several hours or more. You may prefer to schedule a little time each day, say, ten or fifteen minutes, to apply them.

1. If you don't have already have your books in order, choose a shelf or space for each type, a space for books on healing, another for angels, goddesses, prayer, dreams, travel, architecture, cooking, organic gardening, or your own pet topics.

2. Begin to rearrange them, visualizing yellow angels and dakinis working at your side and feeling the excitement as you "watch" them bring in new books and add them to your collection.

3. When you're done reorganizing your bookshelf or shelves, once again stand before them, hands pressed together, and repeat: "Thank you, angels, for your support. Please

> connect me with the highest and best titles for my current phase of growth and reading pleasure."

Make sure you get the obsolete titles you set aside (step 3) out of your space quickly. Give them away to friends and relatives who will enjoy them, to a seniors' center, or to a local library. You could even sell them to a used bookstore, but don't let ambition keep you from clearing them out. The universe responds to a vacuum, and the angels need space to bring you new titles.

The angels will send you books as gifts through humans and they'll also put them on your path at a bookstore, online, or at the local library. Pay attention and act on angelic guidance to acquire or borrow them.

Hophiel's Flowers

For Academic, Artistic, and Intellectual Achievement, Invoke Carnation

The botanical name for this flower is *Dianthus caryophyllus*, evoking the goddess Diana. As a warrior goddess, she resonates with Hophiel's protective facet, bringing strength to set the necessary limits with ourselves and our environment and to follow through on our projects. The spirit of carnation helps channel our energy in successful works.

Connecting with Carnation

Even today, Oxford students wear and give one another carnations as a sign of luck and support for exams.[58] Besides using them on mandalas for academic, intellectual, or creative success, you can:

---

58. Alexandra Jane, "Four Weird Oxford University Exam Traditions You Won't Have Heard Of," Topuniversities.com, May 2017. https://www.topuniversities.com/blog/four-weird-oxford-university-exam-traditions-you-wont-have-heard.

- carry this energy with you by pinning a carnation to your blouse or jacket

- keep a carnation or bouquet on hand while writing, studying, or working on something creative

- paint or draw or picture of a carnation on the workbook for your academic or creative project, or on top of a pile of books, papers, or other materials you are using for it

- use a picture of carnations as a screensaver for your tablet or computer

- take a carnation bath

- send someone carnations as a success blessing

- invoke the spirit of carnations to bless a project (see below).

Carnation Bath for Confidence and Success

This is a great way to cleanse your aura of the shadows of insecurity and connect with the energies of Athena and of carnations.

1. In two to three quarts of water, boil a half-dozen carnation flowers for five minutes.

2. Take them off the stove and let them steep for another ten minutes.

3. Strain the water and let it cool to lukewarm.

4. Take a shower or bath. After you finish, ask Athena to wash away insecurities and anoint you with confidence and success for a creative or intellectual undertaking.

5. Visualize the goddess standing next to you, a great light shining from her head, heart, and solar plexus.

6. Hold the container with the carnation infusion above your head and imagine that Athena is also holding it with her hands.

Pour the infusion over your head and imagine that Athena is washing away insecurities and anointing you with confidence and success.

Invoke the Angels and Goddess of Carnations

Bring together in one place whatever materials you have for a cultural, creative, or intellectual project. Depending on the endeavor, these may include your computer, books, papers, paints, brushes, canvas, a musical instrument and partitures, and so on. Putting your hands on these materials, call on the spirits of these flowers:

> *"Carnations of the planet, please me bless with constancy so that I may work until my talents flower in tangible results."*

> *"I invoke the goddess who brought forth this lovely, lasting flower to inspire me with beautiful, lasting results."*

> *"Spirit of carnation, please strengthen me to set effective limits and complete this (book, project, symphony, degree, etc.) with success and beauty now."*

Use Carnations to Bless Others

People give flowers for diverse events such as birthdays, weddings, funerals, and of course on romantic or sentimental occasions. They are given to artists, speakers, and winners of accolades, sometimes thrown on stage. Angels bring us flowers all the time, as do loved ones who've passed on. Knowing about their magical energy, we can apply a new paradigm and send flowers to support a friend or dear one who's working to finish an intellectual, academic, or creative project. Carnations have the perfect energy for this. Along with the bouquet you might include a card with a small picture of an angel or wings along with the words, "Angels inspire you in your work (studies, art, etc.)." The bouquet can be physical or intentional.

Just close your eyes and mentally "send" them carnations, imagining that a bright yellow angel or the goddess Athena is delivering them. You can also visualize the person on stage receiving a prize, degree, or recognition of some kind before a large audience that applauds and throws the person carnations.

To Awaken Your Intuition and Protect Your Confidence, Invoke Mugwort

A wild shrub, mugwort's flowers resemble delicate lavender-colored brushes. Her botanical name, *Artemisa vulgaris*, derives from the goddess Artemis, the Greek equivalent of Roman Diana, who supports self-reliance and confidence. Mugwort flowers awaken intuitive wisdom and free us from the intentions of others who have blocked our success and weakened our confidence.

Exercise to Retrieve Your Confidence and Trust Your Intuition

1. Light a bit of mugwort smudge or lavender incense, repeating as you do: "This is an offering for Hophiel-Constance and for the spirit of mugwort, whom I ask to clear my energy of any influences that block my confidence and ability to trust my intuition."

2. Light a yellow candle, visualizing that a tiny, bright angel comes into your space through the flame and grows to be taller than you.

3. Repeat: "Hophiel-Constance, please work with the spirit of mugwort to clear my energy of thoughts from others projected on me, and restore my confidence and trust in my intuition."

4. Visualize Hophiel holding a small, light purple flower in his hand, and "see" him passing it all around you with sweeping movements that clear out your energy.

5. See him put the flower into your solar plexus, where it is absorbed.

6. Thank the angels and mugwort spirit.

Mugwort to Support Your Dream Wisdom

Put mugwort leaves or a picture of mugwort flowers inside your pillowcase.

Before going to sleep at night, sit on the edge of your bed and repeat three times: "Spirit of mugwort, please fill my dreams so I may grow in wisdom, consciousness, and healing power."

Mugwort for Insight in Meditation and Journaling

Before meditating, put the palms of your hands together and repeat three times, "Spirit of mugwort, please accompany me in this meditation, so that my wisdom may grow and my spirit evolve with angelic direction."

Use a yellow notebook for journaling and paste or draw a mugwort flower on it. Each time you are going to write in your journal, touch it with both hands and repeat: "Spirit of mugwort, please accompany my journaling so that I may retrieve wisdom and clarity and heal my memories and perceptions now."

Hophiel's Mandalas

Choose from the intentions related to Hophiel: intellectual and creative achievement, beautifying your space and appearance, or following your light path. Considering the variety of Hophiel's areas, you may enjoy making more than one mandala.

Mandala for Academic, Political, or Intellectual Achievement

Before gathering your materials, take a moment to quiet your mind and focus on your intention for success as an author, musician, artist, craftsperson, public servant, or academic. Ask Hophiel-Constance and Athena to direct your talents and efforts to the goal. Hold to your purpose as you put it together.

You will need bright yellow paper or poster board and a red or gold pen, crayons, and/or paints. (Because of the variety of images on this mandala, your paper or poster board should be large enough to draw a 12 to 14" circle on it.)

Color images of your maximum desired result. For example, if you want to finish a degree, go online and download an existing degree from that same institution, or if you can't find one, put it together yourself, integrating the logo of your preferred university or institution, adding your name, the date you wish to graduate, and the words "Honor Student" or any other personal accolade. If you aspire to being a well-known artist or musician, Photoshop a magazine, adding your own picture as though you are on its cover. If you would like to become a senator, put your picture behind a podium, with a plaque and your title. Whatever your aspiration, think big and focus on the consolidated result. If you're an aspiring painter and make a mandala with a picture of a painting, it only ensures you'll make a piece of art or perhaps see someone else's. Be sure you include images of large-scale success.

Pictures of money: again, think big. When visualizing money, people often make the mistake of using relatively ineffective pictures like these: cartoons of trees with dollar bills, money floating in the air, low-denominational bills, small amounts, or messy piles of money. Instead, use orderly, opulent pictures such as a briefcase full of cash, a check for a large amount made out to your name, or orderly piles of $50 or $100 bills that you can easily imagine having on your desk or table. In chapter 6, you will find more details on visualizing prosperity, but it's also a great way to complement your intellectual and creative achievements.

- Depending on the size of your mandala, include 30 to 40 small images of carnations.
- 1 large (1½") image of Archangel Hophiel and his twin flame Constance. (You can download, cut out, and paste; or if you prefer, draw the images onto the poster board).
- 3–6 smaller images of goddesses Athena (for achievement) and Lakshmi (for prosperity).
- Your favorite adhesive stick, paste, or glue.

Make Your Mandala for Intellectual, Political, or Creative Achievement

1. Trace a large (12" or more) circle, and then line it evenly with the carnation images.
2. Draw or paste the image of the angels in the middle, and the smaller images around the inside of the circle to taste.
3. Paste the pictures of your achievement and money evenly around the mandala. Don't crowd the circle; each image should have room to be surrounded by the background color.
4. At the top of your mandala, write an affirmation like one of those that follow:

   "Angels and goddesses of achievement, fill me with confidence, discipline, and focus. Bless me with success in this (book, concert, degree, production, political achievement), now."

> *"Angels and goddesses of success, cut me free of feelings of unworthiness, so I allow my light to shine, now and always."*

Center in Your Mandala

Spend six minutes three times a day looking at your mandala.

Imagine the carnations of the world encircling you and sending their support for your achievement. Repeat the affirmation, feeling the angels and goddesses directing and supporting you in your project. Finally, spend two minutes imagining that you're enjoying the achievements depicted on your mandala, and knowing that you're worthy of them.

Keep your mandala secret. Other people's doubts can block manifestation. And pay attention to angelicities (signs, synchronicities, and opportunities) that appear on your path: a tutor, a class, a contact, books, new ideas. Follow your intuition and act on it, as well as doing the normal work required for your achievement.

Mandala to Beautify Your Space and Appearance

Far from being materialistic, beauty nurtures our soul. When called upon, Lakshmi and Hophiel-Constance literally bestow this gift upon us. The following mandala opens a space for beauty in your self-image and life.

Before gathering your materials, take a moment to quiet your mind and focus on your desire to increase beauty in your space and appearance. Say: "Hophiel-Constance and Lakshmi, please direct my efforts and connect me with my divine right to experience and radiate beauty."

Use the same materials as described in the previous mandala with these changes: Instead of carnations and pictures of Athena, use small white lotuses and pictures of Lakshmi. Exchange the images of success and money for:

- small, color pictures of yourself at your most attractive (alternately, pictures of someone who resembles you at your most attractive. They may be well-coiffed and dressed, working out at the gym, or in a bathing suit with a great figure.)

- pictures of a beautiful wardrobe or shoes and items of clothing

- small, color pictures of beautiful surroundings you'd like to enjoy (for instance, a garden, or a lovely home, room, or furnishings)

- As with the previous mandala, trace a large (12" or more) circle, lining it evenly with the lotus images and drawing or pasting of the angels in the middle, and the smaller images around the inside of the circle to taste.

- At the top of this mandala, write:
  "Angels and goddesses of beauty, with your grace please beautify my image and space."

Center in Your Beautification Mandala

Spend six minutes three times a day looking at your mandala.

Imagine the lotus flowers of the world gathering to bring forth beauty in your world. Feel the angels and goddesses touching your surroundings and appearance. Finally, spend two minutes imagining that you're enjoying the conditions depicted in your mandala.

Keep your mandala secret. Other people's doubts can block manifestation. And pay attention to angelicities (signs, synchronicities, and opportunities) that appear on your path: an exercise class, plants you can purchase, a piece of furniture or an item of clothing an inspiration to cut your hair, polish the floor, wash the carpets, varnish the doors, or otherwise beautify your space. As you act in whatever way you can to manifest beauty, it will open a path for more beauty to enter your world.

Mandala to Walk Your Light Path

After clarifying the intention of this mandala, affirm: "Angels and goddesses of illumination, please direct the creation of this mandala so that I may walk my light path, here and now."

- Use the same materials as described in the previous mandala, with these changes: Rather than lotus, use mugwort flowers. Instead of Lakshmi, use pictures of Sarasvati. Omit the images of beautification.

- Trace a large (10" or more) circle, and then line it evenly with the images of mugwort flowers.

- Draw or paste the image of the angels in the middle, and the smaller images around the inside of the circle to taste.

- From the bottom line of the circle, draw a double line leading to the center, like a path that goes to the angel or goddess whose image is there.

- Above or to the side of your mandala, write: "Flowers of dreamtime, please hold me in your soft embrace and protect me as I walk my light path now."

- Under your mandala, write this affirmation:
  "This circle is a window that opens onto the luminous realm of Spirit, which flows into me and into the world."
  After the affirmation, write this invocation: "Hophiel and Sarasvati, please take my hand and lead me on my path of light."

Center in Your Mandala

Spend six minutes twice a day applying these steps:

1. Repeat the flower invocation three times, feeling their embrace as though these delicate blooms were surrounding you and pressing softly against your skin.

2. Repeat the affirmation for three minutes, feeling the light of Spirit shine through the circle like a sunny window, shining around you and into your being.

3. Repeat the invocation, observing the path and feeling that you are moving on it directly to the angels (or the goddess if you chose to put her there).

Through Constance, we have seen the importance of persistence. Break through the inertia that might distract you from using this mandala daily. You can meditate with it for periods of twenty-eight days. Take breaks and use a different mandala, write your letters, and use other techniques from this chapter and from this book. Pay attention to the angelicities that appear on your path: a course, a dream, a book or books, a teacher, a journey. Follow your intuition and act on the opportunities Hophiel and Sarasvati will send in response to your intent.

Letters to Hophiel

Write to Hophiel, Constance, and their goddess colleagues for success in creative, academic, and intellectual pursuits, to improve memory, retention, and mental clarity, or to develop your intuition.

Write the letter on bright yellow paper, or use gold ink on white paper. Use or adapt the following examples:

Letter for Success in Creative, Academic, and Intellectual Pursuits

Dear Hophiel-Constance,

With your sword of light, please cut away insecurity and distraction; and strengthen my confidence, discipline, and focus so that I manifest success in this project (my master's degree, book, painting career, or another related goal). I send up my words for your perfect use:

> *"No condition or situation can keep Infinite Intelligence from expressing itself successfully through this project now."* (Write this affirmation six or twelve times.)

I bless you for your light and love. With gratitude, [your name].

Letter to Improve Mental Clarity

Dear Hophiel-Constance,

Please pour your golden light through my mental circuits, clearing my mind so that my thinking is bright and quick.
I send up my words for your perfect use:

> *"The all-knowing mind of Spirit (or the Goddess, or God), thinks with perfect clarity through me, now and always."* (Write this affirmation six or twelve times.)

Thank you beforehand for your angelic intervention. With love and gratitude, (your name).

Letter for Improving Memory and Retention

Dear Hophiel-Constance,

Please touch my mind with your empowering light and strengthen my powers of retention, so that I remember true information (for this exam or presentation, or to master this language or field of study, etc.) clearly and well.

I send up my words for your perfect use:

> *"Infinite Intelligence knows all and remembers all true information easily, in and through me, now and always."*

Alternate affirmation:

> *"My memory is a divine gift that cannot be limited or taken from me. I give thanks for my perfect memory now."*

(Choose one affirmation; write it twelve or eighteen times.)

> *"Bless you for working to optimize my faculties. With love and gratitude, (your name)."*

Letter to Awaken Your Angelic Intuition

Write to the angels and ask them to increase your intuition in general or some specific gift such as clairvoyance (intuition through images and pictures), clairaudience (hearing information and messages from angels and spirit guides), or clairsentience (the ability to intuitively feel or sense things).

Write this affirmation eighteen times in the letter:

> *"Angels guide me, and I am naturally receptive to their messages, now and always."*

Conclusion

Every time we have a realization, learn something, or achieve a new level of creative, intellectual, or spiritual mastery, our light grows, and ,with it, our link to Hophiel's golden network. By consciously invoking and engaging with this network, our light is multiplied.

Along the way, Hophiel, Constance, and their goddess colleagues support our confidence, discipline, prosperity, talent, and personal magic. They touch us on all levels, in all undertakings of the mind and spirit. Directly or indirectly, they all connect with Hophiel's true mission, which resonates with this fragment of a Sanskrit prayer to Sarasvati:

> *"Take my hand.*
>
> *Lead me on the sacred path to enlightenment.*
>
> *For the sake of all beings, open my heart.*
>
> *Lift these veils of ignorance.*
>
> *Wake me and the world from slumber."*[59]

Believe in your intuition, cultivate your talents, apply your magic. Call on the angels and goddesses of illumination and include all sentient beings in your intention. Walk your path of light.

---

59. Sharron Rose, *The Path of the Priestess* (Rochester, VT: Inner Traditions, 2002), 22.

Chapter 5

CHAMUEL AND CHARITY: LOVE, HAPPINESS, AND SELF-ESTEEM

Love is not just a sweet feeling; it's a power that's present in the very fabric of reality, constantly working to lift us into the realm of divine good. Chamuel and his divine complement Charity work to precipitate our connection to this power, to awaken its spark in our hearts and its activity in our minds, relationships, and world.

These are the pink archangels who bring happiness in relationships with others and with ourselves, fuel empathy, dissolve harsh attitudes, rekindle passion, harmonize our connections, heal our lives and self-esteem, and lift our vibration so we can more readily connect with angels, who abide on the wavelength of love.

Pink is the color of Chamuel's tunic and Charity's dress or robes. Chamuel's symbols include a heart, a rose, and a cupid with a bow and arrow. Charity is often depicted with golden hair streaked with pink, and a pink dress with golden belts and accessories. As her name suggests, she promotes kindness and helps us shift from hard attitudes into gentler ways of perceiving ourselves and others to heal divisiveness in personal and political scenarios. When we work to cultivate and share these vibrations, angels can more easily reach through to our dimension, touching us and guiding us.

In prayer, meditation, and other altered states, people often see these angels as a field of pink light, sometimes with gold rays or sparkles. Chamuel and Charity are connected to Anahata, the heart chakra, the center of love in our energy body that the pink pair help develop. Just as the physical heart pumps blood throughout the body, the pink archangels work incessantly to pour love through our spiritual heart and into our beings, relationships, and world.

Chamuel and the Goddesses of Love

Since ancient times, love has been associated the sacred feminine, so we find more goddesses related to Chamuel than other archangels. From cosmic, omnipresent Isis to sensual Xochiquetzal and gentle Kuan Yin, different deities specialize in different kinds of love. To explore them brings Chamuel and Charity's rich gifts into relief.

We will see magical keys to open your life to love. At times you will be guided to work with pink. The effects of this color are always positive. Pink inspires generosity and love. It harmonizes our thoughts, emotions, and surroundings. If someone sends us negative intentions, we can surround them with pink light and send them kind thoughts. This neutralizes the harm, touching their highest self, and precipitating divine outcomes. Bright pink communicates intense love; soft pink, impersonal or friendly love. The harmonizing effect of this color is so tangible is that it has been used to calm prisoners.[60]

Besides special exercises, this chapter includes numerous invocations, and affirmations to increase our love quotient, harmonize our

---

60. Jacob Liberman, OD, PhD, *Light: Medicine of the Future* (Rochester, VT: Bear & Company, 1991), 48.

emotions, and manifest happiness. As you apply them, remember to hold your attention on your heart chakra at the center of your chest and visualize that it radiates pink. To kindle passion, red is effective.

Isis, Resurrecting Your Good

Egyptian Isis was known as a loving, omnipresent mother, who supported people in all situations, from the mundane to the transcendent. A guardian of women, she oversaw marriage and family, fueling devotion and respect between parents and children and the obedience of husbands—yes, you heard right—to their wives. Whoever invoked her could count on her loving assistance, independent of their religion or social status.

When Osiris was murdered, Isis searched high and low to retrieve his body and bring it back to life. This shows how divine love accompanies us in the most dire experiences, lifting us up in victory and new life.

With the advent of patriarchal religions, the image of an all-loving Mother gave way to divinities that inspired guilt and fear. Today, Chamuel and Charity work alongside Isis to heal these beliefs and restore our conscious access to omnipresent love.

Invocations and Affirmations to Reconnect with Omnipresent Love

"Angels of love, please heal my soul from the programs of the world and reignite my connection to loving Source now."

"The true substance of reality is love, and the angels guide me to perceive it, now and always."

"Omnipresent love works through all circumstances and situations, producing only good for me (for us), here and now."

"Chamuel, Charity, and Isis, please direct me to perceive the love that's present in me, in others, and in the world, now and always."

Invoke the Resurrecting Power of Love

Chamuel frees us from the idea that we are alone in a difficult or hostile world. He reconnects us with Omnipresent Spirit who, like Isis, is always listening to our words of faith and uses them as doors to act in our relationships and, for that matter, every aspect of our lives.

Nancy's story shows the magic of this reconnection. Having been adopted at an early age, she visited me with issues of abandonment. Her adoptive mother loved her but had several children of her own who resented Nancy's presence. When she was a teen, one of her siblings decided to inform her that she was adopted. The news upset Nancy deeply. She felt alone and was overcome with the urge to know the identity of her biological parents. Nancy's adoptive mother would only tell her that the couple had been very young and weren't in a position to raise a child.

By the time Nancy came to see me, her adoptive mother had passed on, taking the secret of her parents' identity with her. The angels sent me an image of the deep river of Spirit's love pouring through her life. I began to affirm:

"Spirit's love pours like a deep river through your life path, touching you through all situations. You have never been alone, you have never been abandoned, you've never experienced absence because Spirit's love has always been with you, filling your life and finding a way to touch you. When a human channel has disappeared, Spirit has found other ways to touch you, always opening the highest and best channels .... Knowing this, we forgive any person that for whatever reason couldn't remain in your life. As we watch it flow, the deep river of God's love washes away any difficult memories or impressions. Nothing could have really hurt you because Spirit has been using all situations to touch you with its kind power that only generates good for you. And you will never be alone because the deep river of Spirit's love continues to flow and touch you, appearing through the best and highest human channels, now and always."

I loved the image of the river of Spirit's love, flowing and powerful, whose archetype runs deep in the collective unconscious. Around the world we find river goddesses who bring healing and abundance, including Irish Airmed, Egyptian Anuket, Celtic Coventina, Hindu Danu, Finnish Vellamo, and Hawaiian Haumea, to name just a few.

As for Nancy, she visited me the following month to thank me. Her adoptive mother, now deceased, had appeared in a dream and given her the names of her birth parents.

I decided to share this treatment in a live Facebook transmission (now in Spanish on my YouTube channel). People responded enthusiastically and many posted comments. To those who mentioned healing needs, I suggested they adapt the words and repeat:

"Spirit's love pours like a deep river through my world, touching me through all conditions. As I watch it flow, the deep river of God's love washes away any challenging or painful appearance. Nothing could have really hurt me because Spirit (Goddess, God, Divinity) has been using all situations to touch me with its infinite power that only generates good for me. By observing this loving activity that touches me through all conditions, I allow it to heal all things. Nothing has truly hurt me because the only thing that comes into my world is God's good."

Numerous testimonies began to flow. One woman said she had suffered from degenerative arthritis and for some time hadn't been able to walk without intense pain. After repeating the above affirmations persistently, the pain subsided, her leg healed, and she was walking normally in a matter of days. Another woman commented that after pronouncing the affirmations hundreds of times, some large moles disappeared. Others reported healing of personal and family relationships.

A bit further on, you'll find adaptions of this treatment, enriched with angel invocations to heal our childhood and love histories.

Religious styles come and go, but the omnipresent love exemplified by Isis remains with us. It awaits our attention to lift our spirits, harmonize our hearts and relationships, and literally transmute our circumstances.

Venus, Roman Goddess of Love and Happiness

The Roman version of Greek Aphrodite, Venus, is the goddess of romance, partnership, love, and beauty. Like Egyptian Isis and her Mexican counterpart Xochiquetzal, Venus is associated with doves.

Like Chamuel, her color is pink. The archangel appears with Cupid, Venus's son.

Auset says that Venus "dispels troubles and turmoil, gifting devotees with happiness and joy."[61] Besides love, she rules fortune and victory. She works with Chamuel to harmonize relationships, awaken our charm, bring happiness in partnership, and, perhaps most important of all, restore our capacity to value and care for ourselves.

---

61. Auset, *Goddess Guide*, 77.

Through the archetype of Venus, we're reminded that successful relationships don't depend on our ability to manipulate others or use the "right" words to induce attraction or cooperation. When we tune in to the vibration of love, we naturally attract the highest and best connections and open the way for right outcomes in our existing associations.

Affirmations and Invocations to Attract True Relationships and Heal Your Self-Esteem

"Archangel Chamuel, awaken the love-power within me, so that I attract the best and highest partner for the current phase of my life now."

"In the name of Archangel Chamuel, I declare myself free from karmic attachments and open to the true and joyful relationships that resonate with my consciousness now."

"Chamuel and Charity, please free me from concern about the approval of others and direct me to value and care for myself, now and always."

"Chamuel-Charity and Venus, pour your pink radiance into my world, and lift my relationships to the wavelength of divine love now."

"Chamuel and Venus, direct my affection toward myself so I may receive the wonderful love experiences that Spirit sends me now."

"Angels and goddesses are working to ignite the love-flame in my heart. I see it, I feel it, and I radiate it now."

"I don't resonate with a low-frequency network. I'm a loving, conscious being and attract only positive, kind, angelic contacts now."

Xochiquetzal, Aztec Goddess of Sacred Sex and Alchemical Partnership

The Aztec goddess of love, marriage, and women is surprisingly like Venus. She rules the love-magic of flowers, especially marigolds, and is connected to the dove—in resonance with both Venus and Isis. Like them, Xochiquetzal embodies transformation, reminding us that relationships provide one of the most important areas of spiritual growth. Like Aphrodite—Venus's Greek predecessor—she's sometimes depicted in rich, golden clothes, gold being one of Chamuel's colors. Both her rainbow radiation and her golden persona allude to the light body that she helps awaken through sacred marriage.

There's been a lot of misinformation around Xochiquetzal. When the Spaniards arrived in Mexico in the sixteenth century, the monks attributed "sex sins" to both her and her companion goddess, Tlazolteotl, an attribution that has no basis in the Mexican concept of these goddesses. Xochiquetzal evokes Chamuel's work to heal us from toxic beliefs around the physical act of love, like guilt, shame, and objectification. They transform physical intimacy by restoring it to a vibration of sacred love and joy.

> *"Archangel Chamuel, please bring into my life an appropriate, true partner with whom I may share divine love and physical intimacy, now."*

> *"In the name of Archangel Chamuel, I declare myself free from guilt and shame related to sex, my enjoyment of sex, or sexual encounters of the past."*

> *"Angels of love, please bless my bed and awaken the fire of joy in my love life, here and now."*

"Xochiquetzal and Chamuel, please direct me in happy, positive growth in my relationships now."

"Angels and goddesses of love, please bless my sex life with sacred love that fuels my partner's and my lover's evolution and awakens our light bodies, now."

"Zadkiel and Chamuel, please pour your pink and purple light into this relationship (family, connection, and so on), aligning us in harmony and forgiveness now."

Red Tara, Tibetan Goddess of Healthful Romance and Spiritual Ecstasy

Worshiped in certain Buddhist and Hindu traditions since antiquity, the gifts of the goddess of blissful relationships are timeless. She presides over romance and sexual happiness of an appropriate, uncontaminated kind. She overcomes low-vibrational lust and strengthens our discernment in choosing positive relationships. Most important of all, she works to enlighten and awaken the spiritual ecstasy in our hearts.

Her symbols include a red lotus and a fully drawn bow with an arrow made of tiny lotus blossoms,[62] evoking Chamuel's bow and arrow. Red Tara is traditionally invoked at dawn or dusk, when the sky is red. Isn't it interesting that these are also the best hours to observe love-planet Venus?

Like Venus and Xochiquetzal, Red Tara favors sexual and romantic fulfillment. She also works with Chamuel to heal the shadow side of our love nature. These two beings can free us from false attachments, help us distinguish love from lust, purge humanity of rape

---

62. Shaw, *Buddhist Goddesses*, 340.

and toxic sex, and connect us with a joy that can't come from people but instead from the infinite Source whose temple is in our hearts.

Invocations and Affirmations to Awaken Your Innate Capacity for Joy, Release Toxic Relationship Patterns, and Manifest Positive Partnership

(Repeat them especially at dawn or dusk, when the sky is red.)

"I'm not stuck with negative relationship patterns. The angels of love are with me, working in every way to free me and guide me to true happiness now."

"Archangel Chamuel, please connect me with a partner who supports my joy and evolution as I support his/her joy and evolution now."

"Red Tara and Chamuel, please awaken my heart in divine ecstasy, now and always."

"Chamuel and Red Tara, please apply your magic and free me of possessiveness and negative attachments now.

"I put this relationship in the hands of the angels, and I am free to enjoy the present moment now."

"Red Tara and Chamuel, please transmute humanity's toxic desires and awaken our divine affections now."

"Goddess of healthy love, please free the children and any other victims of toxic desire now."

"Red Tara, please transmute any false attachments so I may manifest a truly happy partnership now."

"Chamuel and Red Tara, please help me release my relationships so that I can be fully available to Spirit's love now."

"Chamuel and Red Tara, free me from the tendency to project my happiness onto a romantic (sexual, marriage) relationship, now and always.

"Angels of love, please guide me to discern the truth about this relationship and to make divine choices in my love life now."

Before looking at more ways to transmute attachments and manifest bliss, let's see another of Chamuel's goddess connections, a very important one.

Kuan Yin, Asian Goddess of Compassion

Like Chamuel, the goddess of mercy has her temple in our heart chakra. Venerated in China, Japan, and Korea, she carries a jug of magic healing water and is known for the infinite compassion that flows from her orchid-flower heart. She loves all people regardless of their social position and is ready to heal and assist them in this life or beyond. In her we find similarities to Isis. You may recall that Isis was known as "the listener," as is one of Kuan Yin's two divine assistants. However, Kuan Yin doesn't focus on partnership or pleasure but, rather, on universal embrace.

Besides attending our requests, Kuan Yin fuels our compassion quotient. Angels are currently very busy working on this aspect of humanity's evolution. As a species, we have slipped into apparent indifference about what happens to others, to animals, and to the earth in what has become the "me civilization." People drive around in their luxury cars, which in and of itself is fine, but they often seem to care more about having the latest model than about what they can do to help others. There are many ways to express caring: through a smile or encouraging word, by writing a letter to Congress in defense of a vulnerable population or cause, rescuing an abandoned pet, reviewing the impact of our daily habits on animals and nature, or simply holding to compassionate, nonjudgmental thoughts anytime we encounter people.

In times of apparent chaos, the angels work overtime to pull us out of this vibrational sludge, igniting our heart power in healthy ways that benefit us and others and lift the planetary frequency. The angels are delighted to respond when we invoke them.

Kuan Yin illustrates this faculty of Angelic Intelligence. She resonates with Charity, whose name speaks to divine generosity, the freedom to truly care, and to see beyond the harsh labels of the collective mindset, viewing others and ourselves with a divine and merciful gaze.

Affirmations and Invocations to Strengthen Compassion

"I invite Kuan Yin and Charity to shine through my heart, clearing my perception so that I see myself and others with lovingkindness, now and always. Archangels of love, touch my mind and renew my natural joy and kindness now."

"Chamuel and Charity, please pour your bright pink essence through my heart, and free it so I may radiate love for myself and others now."

"Divine love is present in all political exchanges, acting to support harmonious, fair agreements now."

"Charity and Kuan Yin, open the door of my heart so I may channel divine love into the world now."

"Angels of compassion, pour your pink light through these streets (this situation) and awaken the love in these people's minds and hearts now."

"Archangel Chamuel, attune my heart to your pink light of kindness, which I radiate to all, here and now."

"Charity and Chamuel, guide me to develop my love nature while sustaining healthy boundaries now."

"Charity and Kuan Yin, please take my heart into your hands, cleanse it of harsh attitudes, and fuse it with the merciful heart of Spirit now."

Blessing Others Appropriately

Kindness may be simple, but it's not always easy. Have you ever wanted to help someone but feel like you just can't do enough? Do you find yourself concerned about getting pulled into another's victim trips or being taken advantage of?

An aspect of Kuan Yin's work sheds light on these situations. Consider this fragment of a poem on the compassionate goddess:

Though beings oppressed by karmic woes

Endure innumerable sorrows,

Kuan Yin's miraculous perception

Enables her to purge them all. [63]

---

63. John Blofeld, *Bodhisattva of Compassion: The Mystical Tradition of Kuan Yin* (Boulder, CO: Shambala, 1978), 108.

The goddess's greatest magic is her perception! By beholding others in the light of spiritual truth, she doesn't take on the weight of their circumstances, but rather transmutes them with this divine power, a power you and I can also use.

When someone inspires your compassion, don't get stuck in their appearance. Change your thoughts and open the way for the Divine Helper to appear.

Affirmations and Invocations to Help Others

"You are in the company of innumerable angels, and they are guiding and supporting you now."

"You are not alone or without assistance, the Divine Helper is with you, attending and sustaining you in every way now."

"You are not alone or overwhelmed; Infinite Good awaits you, filling your path, inundating your world, and facilitating all situations now."

"Angels love you; angels are guiding you; angels are showing you the way."

"All that can be coming to you or through you is Infinite Good."

"Angels of love, please awaken my divine perception to bless this person now."

"Angels of love, please awaken my perception so I can see the divine truth for myself and others now."

Repeat these phrases or adapt and use affirmations from other chapters depending on the person's need—for guidance, healing, urgency, and so on.

If we come across someone with a special need, we can gift them with our consciousness. One night I was walking down a city street and there was a woman lying on the ground, apparently unconscious. Another bystander had called an ambulance, but it was Friday night and the vehicle seemed to be stuck in traffic. I stood there in the dark and began to affirm: "You are not alone or without effective attention; the Divine Doctor is with you, attending you and caring for you now." After about three minutes, the ambulance appeared. A paramedic got out and approached the woman, who was stretched out on the cement with her eyes closed. I continued to affirm for her, and before the paramedic could touch her, she stood up and was able to walk.

If we see someone asking for money, we can apply our Angelic Intelligence and take a moment to step away from judgment, instead applying thoughts like the following to shift our perspective out of lack: "The Divine Provider accompanies and supports you now." If we give the person a handout, we can avoid thinking their need is great or our contribution small and instead imagine we're giving an opulent gift to a millionaire.

When we want to help someone, we often think they're in a weaker position than we are. Invocations and decrees such as the ones above can precipitate divine connection, as can the simple act of visualizing them surrounded by angels or in the wings of their angel. We don't have to wait for special occasions to apply our Angelic Intelligence, which also helps us avoid the subtle trap of spiritual arrogance, a trap I'm acquainted with.

The other day I was at the bank, sitting across from the manager while he looked at his screen to ascertain my eligibility for a new credit card. Like most bank consultations, this one seemed to drag on, and I began to get impatient. I decided to transmute this feeling by mentally affirming, "There is only Infinite Good in this situation for me." It occurred to me to affirm for him, too. The inspiration made me catch myself in a moment of pride. Somehow I had assumed that this man in a suit who had obviously studied business administration or another "materialistic" degree and was (according to my estimates) "only" a banker, was therefore not a special, spiritually conscious being (like me), and was somehow further away from the Divine. As I mentally repeated the words, they helped me correct my distorted perception: "You are entirely surrounded by Infinite Good and it's the only thing you will find in all your situations." The labels dissolved, and I had a moment of silent unity with this man who was and is as worthy and special as me and also of unity with the divine love that was equally blessing both of us.

Blessing Unpleasant People

There are times when it seems impossible to be harmonious. If someone abuses or tries to get the best of us, it's only natural to get on the defensive. We might want to bless them but can't let our guard down—and it may be that we *shouldn't* let it down. Turning on your heart doesn't mean turning off your common sense. If your integrity is threatened, the angels will wave red flags. Pay attention, follow your intuition, and take care of yourself and your dear ones. Standing with angels is a place of strength, not fluff.

However, the most common situations aren't a matter of physical security but rather irritating interactions made more stressful because we have to deal with the person or people on a regular basis, such as a family member, in-law, a boss, or collaborators. We have a right to choose whose energies we allow in our intimate circle, but there are situations where we can't exercise that choice directly.

Like Kuan Yin with her miraculous perception, we can transmute this feeling. Repeat: "Only God's good is reaching me through you, now and always." Affirm it verbally, and if necessary, write it many times. In my experience either the person's behavior will change or something in the situation will shift and you won't have to deal with them.

Invocations to Transmute Challenging Relationships

"Kuan Yin, help me stay in compassion and transmute my perception of this person's influence now."

"Chamuel and Kuan Yin, touch my heart and spirit so I may anchor my attention in the divine love that touches me through this person, now and always."

"Kuan Yin, please help me discern how to deal with this person and this situation now."

The Angels Help Heal Your Inner Child

Our angels want us to be harmonious, but true angelic harmony is a vibration from within, not a stiff smile that glosses over our wounds. Chamuel and his goddess colleagues can help us to realize true self-love.

As explained in chapter 1, much of our inner discord is fueled by resentments and will harmonize magically when we practice forgiveness. We recommend reviewing that chapter and using Zadkiel's tools frequently. We can also be affected by wounds or lacks from our childhood that keep us from loving ourselves and connecting to positive situations. Negative entities use such patterns to hold us down.

In the exercise section of this chapter, you'll find a very powerful method for going within, re-constellating your family patterns, and healing your self-esteem with the help of the angels.

Affirmations and Invocations to Set Effective Limits

"Angels of self-esteem, please guide me and strengthen me to set effective limits now."

"Chamuel and Charity, please shield me from manipulation and strengthen me to act in my own best interests now."

"I am not alone or without support to set effective limits. My angels are with me, guiding me, motivating me, and strengthening me to stand up for what I need to, now and always. Thank you, angels."

Exercises with Chamuel, Charity, and Their Goddess Companions

Angel Constellations

To one degree or another, most people carry wounds from childhood. Scars of abandonment and abuse can lie in our subconscious like dark secrets, fueling an inner dialogue that subtly sabotages our harmony and self-worth.

If you feel as though this is something that could be affecting you, you'll be surprised at the results of this simple exercise that helps change your inner dialogue, face the shadows, and transmute them with angelic love. The angels crown the process by freeing and blessing your entire family tree.

This exercise is designed to take about ten minutes daily.

1. Purchase a pink notebook, or make one by covering any notebook with pink or red paper. Alternately, use the angelic diary described in the previous chapter.

2. Each day in the morning, open your notebook to a new page and affirm: "The angels guide my inner journey to embrace, accept, and love myself."

3. Then write: "Today, I remember this shadow from my childhood."

4. Write a single difficult experience or memory that comes to your mind; something that has affected your self-esteem. On the next pages, you will find some real-life examples taken from my groups.

5. Turning your attention to your parent or whomever perpetrated your suffering (someone different may come up each day or you may find yourself turning to the same person repeatedly), tell them in writing how the experience made you feel. Stand up for yourself as you would have liked to at the time if you had known how.

6. Repeat: "Archangels Chamuel and Zadkiel, please reveal what made this person act that way." Take a moment to listen within, ponder their history that could have contributed to their behavior, and follow your intuition to imagine what caused it.

7. Write: "I understand what led you to do this (explain any understanding that has arisen). I know that according to your consciousness at the time, it was all you could do. I forgive you. However, I'm not going to accept the hurt this caused me. I declare myself free of the idea that I deserved that kind of treatment. I release you and I also release myself, because I deserve to be happy and love myself."

8. Repeat the following words slowly and mindfully, imagining that you can see the angels of your family tree as winged beings, a field of light that coalesces nearby, or in whatever form they appear to you: "Angels of my family tree, please come here and use my awareness, forgiveness, and empowerment to open a door of healing. The love of Spirit flows through my family tree, freeing and blessing all. Only good has come through my ancestors and through this experience."

Example of Steps 3 through 7 (from the journal of a mother and businesswoman)

"Today, I remember this shadow from my childhood: I was four years old when my mother would stand by and mutely observe as my father yelled at and whipped my sister and I. This made me feel totally belittled, particularly since she was a loving, intelligent woman whom I admired. Her passive acceptance of the situation made me feel labeled as though I deserved to be humiliated and beat. This is a dark secret. None of my friends' fathers would do this. It created an atmosphere of fear and denigration. I sometimes denigrate myself when I don't attend to my needs, stick to my own limits, or fight for my interests.

"Mother, I understand that Dad convinced you to maintain a united front, and I believe you when you say you fought with him about his abuse of us behind closed doors. I know it was all you could do with your level of consciousness at the time. I don't judge you; I love you, forgive you, and set you free. But I'm not going to keep the secret anymore. I'm not going to stand passively by. This treatment was not right. Your complicity, though unwitting, was not right. I deserve to be stood up for, and I'm going to start doing this for myself: voicing my needs, taking action on my own behalf, and releasing people and situations that seem to put me down or relegate me. I'm going after what I want and assuring myself that I am worthy of good treatment and support."

Follow Up on Angel Constellations

Do the above exercise each morning for at least twenty-eight days or until it becomes a habit to talk to yourself in a new way. Each time, allow new memories or details to arise. When we invoke the angels, they work directly in our beings and lives. They also attract complimentary tools, people, and situations to us. In the case of Angel Constellations, these may include a therapist or support group, guidance in dreams, opportunities to talk with family members, additional books, new friends, or work situations that support self-value. Be mindful of opportunities and act on them.

It's important to complement your new inner dialogue with an active commitment to gain self-respect. Similar but not quite the same as self-esteem, self-respect is something we acquire when we behave in ways we find admirable. These include: making our best effort, being congruous with our professed ideals, being honest, treating others with the same consideration we want for ourselves. These behaviors send a message to our inner self that we are more interested in our own approval than the approval of others.

Invocations and Affirmations to Support Your Inner Child and Build Self-Respect

"Archangel Chamuel, throughout this day, please direct me to treat myself with love."

"Chamuel and Charity, please heal my inner child so that I am open to the highest and the best (partnership, friendships, marriage, family dynamics, company, collaborators, or goal)."

"Angels and goddesses of love, please support and enrich my inner work (therapy, 12-step process, journaling, and so on), so that I may heal my self-esteem and build my self-respect, quickly and in peace."

"I opt out of any plan that weakens me or brings down my vibration."

"Archangel Chamuel and goddess Venus, radiate your pink light into my mind so that I see myself and others with love."

"Archangels Chamuel and Michael, please shield me from negative relationships and surround me with sincere and positive people now."

Reworking Relationships

The tone of our relationships is important to our quality of life. Besides the angel prayers, letters, and other mystical methods in this chapter, here are some practical tips to complement your inner healing:

- Cultivate connections with those who treat you well.

- If someone is abusive or disrespectful, stand up for yourself.

- In long-standing relationships, creating new dynamics can take time. Be persistent so others know you mean business.

- Be open to listen to the needs and feelings of others; they're worthy too.

- The goal is not to go around arguing or picking fights, but rather to send a message to your inner child that you mean business about your limits. Remember, you've vowed not to be an accomplice of your childhood abuse or abandonment.

- If abuse recurs or arises, calmly and directly tell the person involved that you don't deserve this treatment and you're not going to take it. If they refuse to change their ways, set an ultimatum. If they continue the abuse after that, follow through on your limits. This congruence is decisive in building your self-respect.

- There are some relationships we can't choose, such as with a boss or work colleague. However, there are times when we can exercise our freedom and leave.

- There are times when we just don't know what to do. We might be stuck in a mutually antagonistic dynamic. We may want to be harmonious but feel scared of being used. Maybe we feel too financially, physically, or emotionally entwined to make a break. Or we could just be confused.

The following steps are designed for such situations:

1. Ask Chamuel and Charity for help. Repeat: "Angels of love, in a clear way please reveal the solution for this relationship, and strengthen me to act on your guidance now."

2. For nine minutes a day, use affirmations to work on your perception. For instance, you may repeat:

"Only Infinite Good is touching me through this person and this situation,"

Or: *"I am not alone or exposed to toxic or limiting influences. The Divine Companion is with me, filling my home and my world with his (with her/its) presence. My Divine Companion is always kind, truthful, harmonious, uplifting, successful, motivating, fair, and positive,"*

Or: *"The substance of this relationship is divine. It's a dynamic, loving substance that works to help us now."*

1. Choose from the tools for forgiveness in chapter 1 and spend ten minutes daily applying them.

2. Often, the situation will improve spontaneously. If it doesn't, stay mindful of the first opportunity to get out, and use it. Or make the opportunity.

Rose Quartz Heart Tuning

Quartz is a natural conductor of electromagnetism, and so is your heart. Rose quartz has a special mission to purify and lift humanity's love vibration. It can remove accumulated hard feelings (some of which may cause breast lumps) and, according to Hazel Raven in her book *The Angel Bible*, "quickly dissolves self-condemnation, low self-esteem, self-deprecation and selfishness."[64] It also softens the tension behind aggressive behaviors.

As an emissary of the magnetic earth, quartz can draw out vibrations that are not aligned with love.

1. With a piece of rose quartz in your right hand, lie down.

2. Ask the angels of the rose quartz to participate in this heart tuning.

3. Take a moment to feel luminous, pink beings gathering around you.

4. Place the quartz on the center of your chest.

5. Repeat: "Angels of the rose quartz, please draw the shadows of sadness, self-deprecation, fears, or imbalances in my love nature (name emotions you wish to release) from me."

6. Pause to feel a pulling sensation as the dense energy is pulled up by the quartz and released into the ethers.

---

64. Hazel Raven, *The Angel Bible* (London: Octopus Publishing, 2006), 317.

7. Repeat: "Attune my heart to your transparent love-light now."

8. Repeat steps 5 through 7 for another six minutes.

An especially effective time to start this exercise is at the new moon. Continue during the first fourteen days of the lunar cycle or until the next full moon.

Love-Energy Tip

Besides applying the affirmations, invocations, and practices shared in this chapter, we can fuel our harmony by wearing pink clothing or accessories and keeping pink quartz flowers on hand.

Chamuel's Magical Flowers

Of the pink archangel's many flowers, we'll explore Venus's rose, Xochiquetzal's marigold, and Red Tara's red lotus.

The Rose

Roses have long been connected to the Goddess, and in ancient times the flowers themselves were venerated as divine beings. Considered the flower of Aphrodite and Venus, in Pagan Europe the rose was known to awaken the spark of romance and passion. Montgomery says that the spirit of rose is helpful for healing a heart that's been deeply hurt.

Many authors speak of rose's gifts of beauty, gentleness, and love. What's notably absent from wisdom literature is the power of her thorns. Considered an undesirable feature, they're actually an essential part of the planet's defense system. In energy work, pointed objects represent protection and are connected to Archangel Michael's sword. The failure to note this aspect of rose's symbolism reflects humanity's collective resistance to recognize the importance of self-defense on the path of love. Just as the rose plant's thorns serve to protect its delicate flowers, so the angel of the rose protects our hearts from undesirable energies that we may bring forth along with the subtle yet glorious beauty of our love nature.

Invoke the Rose Tree to Heal and Protect Your Heart

Have on hand rose oil and rose incense.

1. While you light a stick of rose incense, repeat: "This is an offering for the angels of roses, whose presence I request to heal my heart and protect my energy so that my love nature can blossom like a fair rose."

2. Sit in a comfortable position, imagining you're relaxing on a large, comfortable loveseat covered with pink rose petals. Imagine that you can feel the silky petals with your fingers.

3. Begin to breathe deeply in the following way: imagine that you're taking the air directly into your heart, hold your breath for three seconds, and breathe out through your mouth, imagining that your exhalation clears your heart.

4. After a minute or so of breathing this way, begin to visualize a rose tree standing tall before you: strong, green, and filled with pink blossoms.

5. Repeat: "Rose Tree Angel, please encircle me with your green branches and shield me with your thorns that repel any influence, being, or person that would interrupt the flowering of my heart."

6. Visualize the tree's branches extending around you in a circle. Imagine the diameter is about ten feet and you are in the center, safe and comfortable.

7. Repeat: "Rose Tree Angel, thank you for protecting me so that my heart energy can heal and flower."

8. Take a bit of rose essence oil and rub it lightly on the center of your chest.

9. Visualize a pink rosebud at that same point and spend a couple of minutes sensing that it opens and grows, until it becomes full and radiant...

10. Repeat the following words for six to nine minutes: "Divine love fills my heart and I am reconnected to my true nature of love that I radiate to myself, to Spirit, to the angels, and to all beings now."

11. Repeat: "Thank you, Rose Tree Angel, for protecting my heart. Relax your branches (watch as the circle goes back into the tree), but if unkind intentions come near, make your thorny shield appear, and in a ray of pink light, send them back to their source."

Red Lotus

This flower radiates a strong energetic fire capable of burning through false attractions, enlivening the spark between lovers, of love for life, and of longing for union with the Divine.

Red Tara uses her flowers to free your heart of false attractions and unleash your love and bliss.

1. Light a bright red candle.

2. Breathe deeply and slowly: inhale through your nose but imagine that the air enters through your heart; pause for three seconds after each inhalation, and exhale completely through your mouth.

3. As you continue to breathe slowly and deeply, gaze at the candle and imagine that you can see a heart a shining inside of it. With each inhalation, watch the glowing red heart expand until it spreads out around the candle into your space, eventually enveloping you completely.

4. Repeat: "Red Tara, please shower me with your flowers and cleanse me of any false attractions, attachments, or romantic fixations now."

5. In your mind's eye, see a canopy of tiny red lotus blossoms streaming down around you. Hold to this vision for three minutes as you feel the flowers pouring over you and cutting away any attachments both from you to others and from others to you. If somebody in particular comes to mind, focus a little more on the dissolution of that attachment.

6. Imagine that gold dust begins to mingle with the tiny red lotuses as you repeat three times: "Archangel Chamuel, lift the vibration of my love nature to its highest, freest, and most joyous expression now."

7. Visualize a red lotus in the center of your heart and affirm six times or more: "My heart is free to enjoy the moment and to love others, myself, and Spirit in healthy ways, now and evermore."

Before going to bed at night, take a few moments to stand at the edge of your bed and mentally greet Tara and Chamuel. Visualize a canopy of red lotuses and gold dust flowing over your bed.

Marigold

"Marigold" means "Golden Mary" or "Golden Lady from the Sea." Like the other bright flowers from Xochiquetzal's magical tree, marigolds evoke the connection between love and the light body.

Marigold Love Blessings

If you're touching your partner either in intimacy or simply by taking their hand, you can imagine you're sending golden flowers from your heart that go directly to the other person's light body.

You can also mentally send golden flowers to a loved one who is no longer on the earth plane, directing them into their light body.

Chamuel's Mandalas

Mandala to Heal and Love Yourself

Before gathering your materials, take a moment to quiet your mind, focus on your intention to heal your inner child, and come to respect and love yourself. Ask Chamuel-Charity and Venus to direct your mind and process. Hold to your purpose as you put it together.

- Bright pink or fuchsia-colored board and a red or gold pen, crayons, and/or paints.

- A photograph (preferably color) of yourself as a child in addition to a recent one where you look happy and well-dressed and groomed. If you like, take advantage and Photoshop your figure, hair, and so on. This is not as superficial as it may sound. We attract what we visualize, and your looks are apt to evolve in the direction of the photo.

- Depending on the size of your mandala, twenty to thirty small images of pink roses or mixed pink with white.

- A large (1½") image of Chamuel and his twin flame, Charity. (You can download, cut out, and paste; or if you prefer, draw the images onto the poster board.)

- 3 to 6 smaller images of the goddess Venus.

- Your favorite adhesive stick, paste, or glue.

Make Your Mandala for Self-Love and Healing

1. Trace a 10" circle and line it evenly with the rose images.

2. Draw or paste the larger image of the angels in the middle.

3. Paste the picture of yourself as a child above this angel image, slightly to the left, and the picture of yourself as an

adult at the same level but slightly to the right, so that they balance one another.

4. Paste the smaller images of angels and Venus around the inside of the circle to taste.

5. At the top of your mandala, write an affirmation like one of the following:

"My first priority throughout this day is to treat myself with love."

"I am not alone or without support to heal my inner child. My angels and spirit guides are with me, working in every way to free my heart and restore my self-esteem now."

"I am a radiant expression of divine love, and I embrace myself in this certainty, here and now."

Below your mandala, write, "Roses of the world, please encircle me with your love, and restore my heart chakra now."

Center in Your Mandala

Work with this mandala for nine minutes each morning.

1. Spend about three minutes repeating the invocation to the roses of the planet and feeling how their energy flows into your heart chakra, heals it, and makes it strong and bright.

2. Devote about three minutes to look at your childhood picture, talking to that child with words of tenderness and love as you radiate pink heart energy to her or him.

3. Spend another three minutes looking at your adult self, sending pink light to her/him from your heart, and repeating the affirmation you wrote above your mandala.

If you like, use the above mandala before applying your Angel Constellations (pages 176–178) or another exercise from this chapter.

Mandala to Manifest a Happy, Passionate, Healthy Love Partnership

Before gathering your materials, take a moment to quiet your mind, focusing on your desire to manifest a happy, healthy love partnership. Ask Chamuel-Charity and Red Tara to direct the efforts of this mandala and align you with a happy, healthy, and passionate partnership.

1. Follow the instructions for the previous mandala, using red paper or poster board, 30 to 40 red lotuses instead of roses, and pictures of Red Tara instead of Venus. Substitute the pictures of yourself for color pictures of happy partnership. Choose pictures of couples whose faces aren't visible, so you are open to the angel's choice of a partner for you. Depending on your desired results, these may include: a pair of interlaced hands on top of a sheet or quilt, a couple walking on the beach holding hands, sitting at a nice restaurant, or hugging in bed; a groom's hand putting a ring on a bride's finger, a marriage certificate with your and your spouse's names, "My true love," and so on. If you already have a love object and the person is available, Photoshop the pictures using his or her face and your own, and his or her name alongside yours on the marriage certificate.

2. Make sure your mandala is not choked or crammed with too many pictures. They can be sparse and relatively small so there's a margin of red around each one. Also, don't paste them in a crooked position; keep them straight.

3. At the top of this mandala, write:

> *"Chamuel and Red Tara, please fill my life with divine love and manifest a healthy, passionate partnership (marriage, boyfriend, etc.) that resonates with our paths of divine bliss."*

4. Under your mandala, write:

> *"Spirits of Love-Flowers, please gather around and attract my true love to me in resonance with my highest and best good."*

5. Inside the mandala, write:

> *"The angels know how to manifest a healthy, happy, passionate relationship and they work to do this. I see it, I believe it, and I receive it now."*

Center in Your Mandala

Spend six minutes three times a day sitting with your mandala, as you:

1. Repeat the invocation to the spirits of love flowers, sensing how they gather and attract your true partner to you.
2. Repeat the request to Chamuel and Red Tara.
3. Enjoy the pictures of happy partnership, as you repeat the affirmation inside the mandala.

Keep your mandala secret. Other people's doubts can block manifestation. And pay attention to angelicities (signs, synchronicities, and opportunities) that appear on your path. If you want to meet someone, you may receive an invitation to a new place or group; a stranger or an old acquaintance may appear unexpectedly on your path; you might feel the urge to make a trip, visit a spiritual center, or attend a class; you could receive an offer to improve your figure by going to the gym. You want something different, and it's important to demonstrate your willingness by showing an openness to try things.

Mandala to Expand Your Social or Professional Circle

After clarifying the intention of this mandala, affirm: "Angels and goddesses of love, please direct this creation so that I may connect with the friends (colleagues, clients, business associates, etc.) corresponding correspond to my true, angelic network now."

Follow the instructions for the previous mandala, using medium-bright pink paper or poster board, pink orchids, and salmon roses for the flowers, omitting the goddess images. Substitute the pictures of couples for color pictures of groups of people. If you're looking for friends, use a small to regular-sized group or individual photos of ten to twenty faces, depending on the number of new people you wish to attract. If you're interested in a much larger network for work or a cultural, political, or spiritual project, obtain pictures of dozens, hundreds, or thousands of people. Choose photos of people you haven't seen before who look happy and positive and as though they resonate with you. Patricia Betancourt, National Sales Director of an international company, cut out a hundred small faces of women for the mandala for her team and it soon grew significantly. If you're using faces, they should be small enough to fit without crowding your mandala.

Above your mandala, write: "Angels of love, please bring into my life the best people for the current phase of my happiness, success, and spiritual growth."

Under your mandala, write this: "Roses and orchids of the planet, please make new, happy connections appear and blossom for me now."

Inside your mandala, write one of these affirmations:

"The guardian angel of each person knows who's part of my divine network and guides them into my life. I see it, I believe it, and I receive it now."

"My inner light attracts to me the perfect people to relate in joy, peace and love now."

"I'm surrounded by angels, and only good vibrations and influences can reach me, now and always."

Center in Your Mandala

Spend six minutes twice a day applying these steps:

1. Repeat the flower invocation three times, feeling the energy of roses and orchids encircling you and shining on you.

2. Repeat the angel invocation.

3. Gaze at the picture, enjoying the idea that these are your friends (collaborators, group, and so on). As you do, repeat the affirmation inside your mandala.

Written Requests to Chamuel

Write to the Archangel of Love when:

- you sense that past attachments don't let you find true love
- a certain relationship seems impossible to heal
- you've tried other methods and haven't been able to manifest true love
- you're addicted to the approval of others
- you need special help to broaden your social or business network

- you wish to break through blocks to awakening your divine heart of love
- you've done all you can to heal a relationship and you still feel stuck.

Write these letters in a pink notebook or on sheets of pink paper. When requesting freedom from old patterns and attachments, direct your missive to both Chamuel and Michael. If the letter is about a long-standing relationship problem, write to Chamuel and Zadkiel. Check the following examples.

Letter to Attract Your True Love

Carla was an attractive executive who had friends and suitors but no real love prospect. She was concerned that she may never find happiness. I suggested she use the following letter, combining it with the letter to the confidant from chapter 4 and the mandala for a happy marriage shared in this chapter. A few months later, through a series of unexpected circumstances, she met a man who looked and acted like the angelic husband she had wished for. They're now happily married and have two beautiful children.

To Archangels Chamuel and Charity

Dear Archangels,

I praise your radiant mission to bring happiness and love to all beings. Please work with my guardian angel and the guardian angel of my true love—whoever he or she may be—so that we meet soon and share true, divine companionship, growing together spiritually and materially ... (add other characteristics you desire in the relationship).

I send up these words for your perfect use:

The angels know who the best person is for me, and they work
to attract and connect us to one another now.

(Write the above affirmation nine or twelve times.)

Thank you, my dear, pink archangels, for working to bring me
fulfillment in partnership.
Blessings,
(sign your name)

Letter to Dissolve Past Ties and Find True Happiness

Write to Chamuel and Michael, asking that they "work with the
guardian angels of all involved to dissolve any karma and any attachments from me to others or from others to me, from this incarnation or any past life, that might delay my manifestation of true love."

Write the following affirmation nine or eighteen times in the
letter:

"I release all the people I've ever been involved with to their true hap-
piness now (if someone in particular comes to mind, pause
and say, "I release you.") Archangel Michael works through the
guardian angels of all involved to cut any obsolete ties from me
toward others or from others toward me. I give thanks for the path
of true love that opens before me now."

Letter to Broaden Your Social or Professional Network

Using the above guidelines, write to Chamuel and ask that he please
renew and expand your social network with "sincere, stimulating,
spiritually aware people" or your professional network with "positive, kind, productive, mutually supportive people."

Write the following affirmation six times or more in your letter:

"The angels know the best and highest people for my (social network, professional network, spiritual group, or client base), and they are guiding them to me now."

Letter to Release the Fixation on Others' Approval, Heal Your Inner Child, and Manifest a True Partnership

Write to Archangels Chamuel and Raphael, asking that they work with your guardian angel to heal your inner child, release attachment to the approval of others, and manifest true partnership.

Include the following affirmation six, nine, or eighteen times:

"I am not alone in my desire for healing and happiness. My angels and spirit guides are with me, working in every way to free me from negative patterns or attractions, and supporting my emotional wellness, self-love, and easy connection to a true, positive partner (husband, girlfriend, lover, etc.)."

Your Fire-Flower Heart

The following connects with what has been the most important experience in my life. When I was a child, my parents told me God didn't exist. I didn't quite believe them, sensing that there was something there but also that it wasn't quite like what our churchgoing neighbors thought. One day when I was having an emotional crisis, I was gifted with a glimpse. I had said, "God, if you exist, please take over my life." At that moment, a dark space around me opened and suddenly a presence reached through and touched me. It didn't have a hand with fingers or a head of white curls. It was an indescribably beautiful, intensely powerful light whose touch filled me with Infinite Love and total bliss.

The experience only lasted for a moment, but from then on I knew that for me, Spirit existed and that it was love, light, power, and freedom. For some time afterward, I couldn't find this experience described in religious texts. They all seemed to speak of punishment, sin, or karma in addition to a sort of bipolar divinity: half-kind and half-ogre. The closest I found was St. Theresa's ecstasy, where an angel pierces her heart, causes an ecstatic love-union. However, this encounter also caused her intense pain; what touched me contained no suffering. Eventually, I came across descriptions of individual experiences very similar to mine in non-dogmatic texts, although the people who had them (including Richard Bach in his book *One*), didn't always identify the source of their bliss as a supreme being.

After that joyous encounter, I knew that this presence accompanies us all, constantly inviting us to reconnect (an understanding confirmed by my later metaphysical studies). For the time being, we seem stuck in a world of shadow where our greatest joys and pleasures are meager reflections of our true destiny. But Infinite Love is right there with us. It's the most glorious and kind companion, father, mother, and lover we could dream of. The angels are guiding us all to retrieve this original, sublime connection. In the meantime, as we walk the path home, we can develop love not only for people, nature, and ourselves but for the source of all good: Spirit, Goddess, God (Infinite Love doesn't care what we call it).

The following treatment is a way of giving something back to the One who gives all. It's also a powerful way of fueling a sublime kind of passion.

Repeat the following prayer nine or eighteen times, imagining as you do that you're sending bright, flaming flowers from your heart:

"Dear Mother-Father (Goddess, God, Sublime One, Love), I love you with all my heart and all my soul and all my being and I send you flowers from my fire-flower heart."

After using this key, two things happened: a few days later, a lovely woman who attended my classes brought me an enormous, beautiful bouquet that looked just like the large orange and red flowers I imagined in the prayer.

And a few years later, I learned of a Slavonic myth about the "fireflower," a name I thought I'd invented but perhaps received from the angels or picked up from the collective unconscious. This mythical bloom grows on the fern plant once a year at midnight on Summer Solstice. It's protected by forest devas, and he or she who succeeds in getting past them to seize the flower will "understand the oracular language of trees ever afterwards."[65] The most beautiful aspect of the myth is the symbolism of the fire-flower itself. It represents the "essential gift of the Goddess's love."[66]

What does her love bring us? We tend to think of divine kindness as a gentle energy that's up there somewhere, distant from our lives with their longings and challenges. To look at love-goddesses around the planet brings new light on this vibration and its gifts. There's omnipresent Isis, guardian of women with powers of resurrection; Venus, who brings joy, charm, romance, and also self-esteem and roses that sweeten our hearts and shield them; Xochiquetzal, who lifts our intimacy to a higher vibration and awakens our light body; Red Tara, who knows all about toxic attraction and applies her magic to transmute it; and Kuan Yin, who opens our heart of compassion, teaching us to heal in ways that don't weaken us but actually fuel our faith.

The love of these goddesses may radiate in sweet shades of red, gold, and pink, but it's a strong, savvy, empowering force that

---

65. Walker, *Woman's Dictonary*, 426.
66. Ibid.

the angels now bring us. As we persist in working with Chamuel, Charity, and their flower companions, our heart radiation will grow, eliciting the kindest possible response from life and from sentient beings. Infinite Love will manifest not as a distant ideal but as an active presence that pours through our shadows, healing and transmuting them and manifesting tangible, happy experiences in relationship to ourselves, others, and the Divine. It won't leave us smiling submissively on the sidelines like good little sufferers bent from the weight of our karma and that of others. It will dissolve our load, restore our joy, and put us on our feet so that we stand straight and tall, like a god or goddess in the sun.

Chapter 6

URIEL AND GRACE: CODES FOR ANGELIC ABUNDANCE

Uriel and his divine complement Grace specialize in divine providence. Glowing through the ruby ribbon in the angelic rainbow, they dust us with the gold of spiritual and material riches. They may appear in red tunics, or as a glowing ruby field sparkling with gold flecks. Uriel has several symbols:

- a parchment, representing divine vision and wisdom.
- a book, symbol of the mental work required for peace and abundance
- a sword, to cut through limiting programing and low-vibrational thought fields
- a hand with flames, symbolizing the divine desire, love, and power that expresses in everything we give and receive

Uriel connects with the root chakra, Mudladhara, related to survival and sustenance in the physical realm. Known as the angel of the presence, Uriel represents the tangible manifestation of divine good as abundance in our worlds.

His twin flame, Grace, is sometimes depicted as a strong woman with thick, dark tresses. She supports our reconnection with the infinite Source whose loving power pours into our material situations, filling them with joy and plenty. She awakens us to our divine birthright of prosperity and fuels the inner fires of gratitude that increase our peace, happiness, and supply.

As the events of 2020 have brought home, economic systems can and do change. But Source is unchanging and responds whenever we turn to it in consciousness, making Uriel's work particularly important in our times. When applied, Uriel's codes lead to material mastery. Besides prosperity, the ruby-gold archangels promote success, work, ecology, peace, devotion, divine desire, vigor, resilience, creative will, and the physical and magical use of our hands.

Uriel and the Goddesses of Earth, Opulence and Productivity

In their goddess companions we find codes to connect with the blessings of the ruby archangels. Uriel's name relates to the Sanskrit, *artha*. This is also the root of the names Urth, Urda, Ertha, and other goddesses of nature and abundance. In India, *artha* refers to both Mother Earth and material prosperity. It is also the Roma word for money, and our English word "earth" derives from this same root. In ancient times, our planet was not seen as an object to be exploited but as a sentient being who gave lovingly of her bounty.

Of the many goddesses related to Uriel, we'll focus on the Hindu Lakshmi and Celtic Brigit. A deity of both cosmos and earth, Lakshmi unleashes supply from the infinite dimension of Spirit, while Brigit—whose persona evokes an active, talented woman—supports personal productivity.

Lakshmi: Reconnect to the Source

The Hindu goddess of success, beauty, and abundance, Lakshmi's appearance is laden with symbolism. Like Uriel, her main colors are red and gold. Evoking the archangel's flame, the Vedas say she's "lustrous like fire." She's richly bedecked in garlands, jewels, and amulets.

The most popular of all Hindu deities, Lakshmi is closely related to the lotus. Born from this sacred flower, she carries one in her right hand, with it bestowing spiritual and material riches. Her jewels are made of gold and silver, the precious metals of alchemy. Her amulets offer protection from fear, envy, and low-vibrational forces that would block success, beauty, and abundance.

Often accompanied by elephants, Lakshmi's blessings enter our lives with earth-shaking force, chasing off the appearance of limitation. The elephants pour waters on her head, representing the goddess's rich mind powers. Her blessings are the result of the ongoing, ever-present action of divine intelligence and grace that flow for all sentient beings.

Lakshmi has a special resonance with Grace, Uriel's divine complement whose name, as we have seen, evokes the loving activity of Spirit that flows unceasingly to cover our situations. The goddess's mind powers resonate with Uriel's book, symbol of the mental work required to manifest abundance. As Lakshmi's elephants stamp out limitation, Uriel's sword cuts away limiting beliefs, such as scarcity and lack of personal worth.

Before exploring their keys, let's consider two other blessings that Lakshmi bestows and that speak especially to our times. Through her connection with royalty, she brings success to illuminated rulers and aligns the minds of corrupt ones so they exercise their power for the collective good. Once restored to an ethical mindset, she brings success to the latter as well. Also, Lakshmi works to protect Mother Earth. As we learn to precipitate our abundance, we can enrich our magic for these angelic missions.

Unblocking Your Abundance

If our supply comes from Infinite Grace, why do so many have to struggle for it? The common mindset is filled with low-vibrational thoughts and images, enforcing a quantum field of limitation. As discussed in chapter 3, our perception exerts an organizing force on situations. Until we lift our minds to a higher frequency, our life is invaded by this limiting field.

Lakshmi's bright, rich image contrasts with the dark ideas about money that prevail in the West. Her archetype challenges the myth that spirituality is somehow at odds with wealth. In resonance with Lakshmi, Uriel's red color evokes the connection to Earth that forms part of the angelic rainbow and part of our experience as incarnated beings. He and Grace direct us to accept this connection and release any unconscious resistance we may have to money. To collaborate with them, we can open our minds to visualize abundance and erase the beliefs and attitudes that tend to block it.

The following keys are adapted from experience with thousands of people in my courses and personal sessions over the last twenty years.

Establish Your Intentions for Abundance

This may sound simple, but it's an important first step that has more to it than you might think, as you will see in the following method that focuses on material prosperity, worldly success, and spiritual progress.

1. Light a stick of cinnamon incense, repeating: "This is an offering for Archangels Uriel and Grace, whom I now ask

to touch my mind and facilitate effective intentions for worldly and spiritual success."

2. On a sheet of red paper or in your angel diary (described in chapter 4), describe in writing what you want to manifest. It's important to be concrete. Don't just say, "I want prosperity," or "I wish to be successful," or "I would like to live abundantly." Instead use sentences that trigger your imagination and generate a tangible picture, like the following examples:

"I hear my phone ring and feel its smooth, cool surface as I answer it and my business partner says, 'Good news! The deposits have gone through.'"

"I see myself giving my spouse (child, partner, parent, spiritual guide, charity) a check (or a pile of cash) and I experience the joy of sharing."

"I open my safe (briefcase, drawer, secret door, or your favorite place to keep cash) and see that it's filled with neatly arranged stacks of fifty- and hundred-dollar bills. I take a few bills out and am happy to see that there's so much left."

"I'm boarding a plane with my kids, greeting the flight attendants who kindly guide us to our seats in first class."

"I hear a new message going into my phone. I look at it, open it, and see that a large deposit has been made to my account.

"I look up my bank balance and see that there is $250,000 in my account."

"I'm sitting across the desk from my bank manager (stockbroker, etc.), who looks at me with a smile and tells me my credit's been approved (or my yield is very high, or another piece of good news)."

> *"I open my wallet and see that it's packed with a large wad of high-denomination bills."*

A note about financial intentions: Over the years of I've often heard people say they're waiting for a certain deal or situation to materialize so that they can have funds. What they don't realize is that they're mentally conditioning their supply to come through a single channel. When we hold on tightly to a certain client, sponsor, company, deal, or situation, we don't allow our good to flow.

What does this have to do with visualization? When you work with the above keys, include at least one image of funds without stipulating the giver or channel. That will keep the door open for money to manifest in Spirit's perfect ways.

1. Clarify your intention for spiritual progress. Because of the subtle nature of these goals, an excellent way to precipitate results is to visualize that you're talking about them with someone. Consider these examples:

   > *"I imagine myself sitting before my spiritual teacher. They look into my eyes and I hear them say, 'You've achieved illumination.'"*

   > *"My students (colleagues, siblings, relatives) are telling me that the angel messages I channel are completely accurate."*

   > *"I'm talking on the phone with my mom (daughter, friend), saying, 'I feel so fulfilled with my spiritual life and results.'"*

   > *"I'm sitting with my best friend on her living room couch and telling her that I've entirely forgiven myself and others and am continually centered in love."*

2. Complement your financial and spiritual intentions with goals for success in work or another meaningful activity. Use or adapt the following examples:

   "I imagine myself picking up my phone and hearing my friend Julie's voice as she congratulates me on the success of my YouTube channel."

   "I'm on a boat at sea, standing next to the captain. He says to me, 'We've been able to save more whales this year and you're part of this team.'"

   "I visualize myself on stage at a company event, holding the trophy for first place in sales and listening to the warm applause."

   "I imagine that I'm looking at my business page on Facebook and it has 1,000,000 followers."

   "I'm on a video call with my agent, who tells me, 'We've closed the deal and it's attractive.'"

   "I imagine that one of my colleagues is with me. She smiles and remarks, 'We've healed hundreds from all kinds of conditions, and you're an important part of this.'"

   "I see myself in a beautiful auditorium, finishing a conference before a large crowd, hearing the enthusiastic applause."

3. You can use similar scenes to clarify intentions for others, imagining that your daughter, son, sibling, or friend is sharing the news of their spiritual and worldly advancement.

4. When you're done writing, you'll have at least three intentions: one each for financial prosperity, spiritual progress, and success.

5. Placing your hands over your list, repeat: "Uriel and Grace, please direct me to visualize calmly, clearly and frequently, opening a quantum space for Spirit to consolidate this or something better, for the greatest good of all concerned."

The simple act of writing your intentions opens a door of free will, allowing a flow of grace. You can keep that door wide open by following up and using the list as a guide for daily visualization.

Do it like this:

- Three times a day, devote six to nine minutes to reviewing your intentions.

- Begin each session by repeating, "Uriel and Grace (or angels and goddesses of abundance), please direct my attention so I can open a space for prosperity, success, and spiritual evolution now."

- After reading each intention, pause to close your eyes and for two to three minutes, evoke the scene, experiencing it tangibly in your mind. When visualizing money, touch the check or bills. Hear the characteristic timbre of the voice of the other person or people in your scenes; get into the contentment your achievements inspire.

- You don't have to spend a long time reviewing your intentions, but frequency is important. Try to visualize at least three times daily.

- After each ten-minute session, say: "I leave the results in the hands of the angels." Take it in a spirit of fun as though it were a game and don't let it turn into a source of stress.

This last step is important and encloses a secret that can vastly improve your manifestation. Often people don't experience the results they want because they visualize with a sense of anxiety, as though they had to work hard on it. When the need seems great, the time short, or the desire intense, it's not easy to stay calm. Also, we are used to thinking that success comes from pushing ourselves. When it comes to visualization, this approach is counterproductive. Perhaps like many people, you have had the occasional experience of visualizing in a nonchalant, almost indifferent way, and receiving surprisingly good results. Without you knowing it, your lack of intensity let the outcome flow unimpeded. Be persistent, live what you're imagining as though it were already so, but try giving your goal a light touch. Hold to the truth that you really don't have to work hard. In an absolute sense, you aren't generating anything new. Spirit has already manifested your good. You're just opening a quantum space so the finished results can download, so to speak, in the world of appearances.

Invocations and Affirmations to Concentrate on Abundance

"Archangel Uriel, please direct my attention to the abundant good that is here for me now."

"I give thanks that I am divinely guided to apply my inner powers of abundance, now and always."

"Uriel and Grace, with your sword of fire, please burn through distractions so that I can visualize my abundance clearly now."

"The angels of abundance inspire my vision of the rich good that Grace is manifesting, here and now."

Visualization offers a powerful tool to break through the limiting images that cloud the collective mentality. It opens a quantum space that allows your results to precipitate tangibly. Further on in this same chapter you'll find an abundance mandala that reaffirms this opening.

Dissolving Mental and Emotional Blocks

We'll now see some examples of the most recurrent attitudes and beliefs I have come across in my work, along with affirmations you can use to transmute them. Read through them; choose the decrees that resonate for you, and repeat them for nine, eighteen, or twenty-four minutes daily.

Ritual to Empower Your Abundance Affirmations

Do this when you're beginning a new cycle of inner work for abundance, or, if you prefer, each time you use the affirmations and tools in this chapter.

1. Light a stick of cinnamon incense, repeating, "This is an offering for Uriel and Grace, whom I ask to free me from any unconscious blocks to abundance and strengthen my conscious connection with the Source."

2. Light a red or gold candle, and imagine the above-mentioned presences emerging from the candle one by one as they float into your space.

3. See these radiant beings reach out their hands or wings, and feel them as they touch your mind.

Effective Solutions for Common Blocks

Release self-pity and resentment. All of us go through stuff; at times, life can seem like a cross to bear. It's important to recognize our feelings, but we can easily slip into a self-image of victim that becomes reinforced when we complain about our situation to others. The self-applied victim label works like an unconscious pact that tends to attract unfair circumstances and block the flow of divine supply.

Besides reviewing and using some of the tools shared in chapter 1, you can apply the following key: Mentally turn to Uriel's divine complement, and say: "Archangel Grace, please help me send intentions of prosperity to those who have blocked, envied, or been unkind to me or my loved ones." Then repeat for ten minutes: "In the name of Archangel Grace, I now send rich blessings to whoever seems to have offended me. I see them successful, prosperous and happy, and my own good flows to me freely now." Do this each night before your last visualization session. Your intentions will be elevated to the frequency of alchemical love, where no conditions can block them.

Self-pity is closely related to resentment, and it tends to dissolve when we center in forgiveness. But it's worth reviewing our inmost feelings; if we discover this shadow, we should erase it.

Some people really seem to have the deck stacked against them. Just today, a woman named Mayra came for an unblocking treatment. She works as a manager in an insurance company, yet most housecleaners make than she does. As a child, both of her parents had abused her, after which her mother left her with relatives who had continued to abuse her emotionally and sexually. As an adult, she was stuck emotionally and financially. Fruit of an unhappy marriage, she had a daughter. Since she couldn't pay rent, the two of them ended up living with Mayra's dad, who would continually hit her up for money and treated her like a wife rather than a daughter. She was in physical pain and chronically dizzy. I explained to Mayra that for whatever reason she had incarnated in such a challenging situation, as long as she continued lamenting her bad luck or karma, she would continue repeating similar patterns. It was up to her to begin applying her mind powers to visualize, connect with, and believe in the Infinite Good that was working to heal her and open a new path.

After treating her with the help of angels, the pain and dizziness disappeared, as did her sadness. With a personal history like that, her follow-up will be important.

Prayers to Dissolve the Effects of Past Problems, Challenges, and Other Apparent Disadvantages

"By Uriel's divine sword, I declare myself free of any unconscious pact I may have had with limitation."

"I have not been marked by disadvantage. The only power to mark me is Spirit (God, Goddess, or your own favorite name), who has marked me with divine facilities in all things. I am marked as a beloved child of Spirit and attract support, opportunities, and prosperity from the entire universe now. The angels use my awareness to erase any other apparent marks or labels that I've put on myself or received from others, and they weave the divine mark of good into my aura, awareness and life now."

"Archangel Uriel, with your sword of fire, please dissolve any unconscious attachments to ideas of victimhood or injustice and cut away entities who have lodged in me through these experiences. Uriel has freed me and Grace guides and blesses all involved, now. Thank you, angels, thank you, Mother-Father."

"I release any unconscious attachment to victimhood, and my life is a divine victory, now and always."

If You're Experiencing Lack

We're used to thinking of reality as what we can see, touch, smell, taste, and hear with our physical senses. From this perspective, there can be lack and limitation. From the divine standpoint, lack cannot exist. Omnipresent Spirit fills all creation, and there is no lack in Spirit.

A young couple named Will and Denise came to consult me. They had a great idea for a restaurant but didn't have the funds to start it. I affirmed for them, "There can be no lack of funds or support for you, because Spirit fills your world and there is no lack in Spirit. Spirit is always full of good, so you have plenty of funds and plenty of support now ..." After repeating these and compatible words for some time, I closed with an affirmation to bring in the angels: "The angels have used my faith to open the channels of good that overflows into your situation now." They later told me that a few days after this treatment, an aunt came to visit from out of town. In casual conversation, she mentioned that she had received some profit from a business deal and was wondering how to invest. Denise told her about her plan and the aunt decided to support their venture for a share of the profits. They eventually bought her out and now have three restaurants.

Adapt this affirmation if you seem to lack time, opportunities, contacts, or love: "There can be no lack of time or opportunities for me because Spirit fills my world and there is no lack in Spirit. Spirit is always full of good, so I have more than enough time, opportunities, contacts, and love now."

If You Feel It's Too Late for You

Renea was an executive manager in her late fifties. She had a good job in the public sector, but her department was due to be phased out. Neither she nor her children seemed to have much to build on. She came to me for an unblocking treatment and set her intentions for financial success and happiness. The following affirmation came to me: "You are not an age or a situation—you are infinite being, unblockable, unstoppable, uncontainable, and always in contact with all the good the flows from the divine mind to you now." A few days later, Renea's husband, who had left her some years before and was living abroad, called her son and said that he had a large house and wanted the family to join him. He even said, "If your mother wants a room to herself, there's one for her here."

If You're Going through Hormonal Changes or Another Challenging Cycle

Monica is a psychologist and dance therapist who came for healing. She was worried because hormonal changes were making her mind cloudy and she couldn't concentrate like she used to. It immediately came to me to affirm: "Your wellness cannot be cyclical, it comes from God, who sustains your wellness and lucidity, not sometimes but always." She came to see me five weeks later, saying that her mind had become very clear and her teaching practice was once again satisfying. If your business or work seem to be affected by seasons, affirm: "My success can't be seasonal; it comes from God, who makes all seasons and all cycles successful for me, now and always."

If You Think Your Good is in Another Place or Time

A woman named Sylvia had relocated to a town that turned out to be a nightmare. The people were nasty and there were no job or business opportunities. She had spent all her money just surviving in her first months there. I gave her the following affirmation: "My good isn't somewhere else. My good can't be in another place or another time. My good is always where I am. It comes from Spirit who makes it appear as true opportunities and financial supply, here and now." I began to affirm for her, also adapting the affirmation and repeating it for myself. I never heard from Sylvia again, so I honestly didn't find out what happened with her, but the experience produced some interesting results. After some months of affirming this way, things I needed began to precipitate spontaneously. Friends and relatives showed up at my house with strangers who ended up supporting my work and several people sent me unexpected, generous donations. When my son and I were on vacation in a big city and had trouble getting cabs, I would stop and affirm for a couple of minutes: "Our good can't be somewhere else. Our good is always where we are. It comes from Spirit who makes it appear as a taxi for us now." Taxis would suddenly appear, and my son got used to my peculiar way of calling them.

The good that's yours can't be left behind or separated from you. It's always where you are. Whatever it is you need—opportunities, information, financial supply, or sincere friendship—adapt the above affirmation, erase the appearance, and allow it to precipitate.

If Your Inheritance Has Been Withheld

A man named Edward consulted me a year after his father passed on. After going through a grieving process, he had to deal with the fact that his sister, who was named executrix of the will, had been very unclear about the accounts. Despite the fact that their father had stipulated his holdings be divided equally among all his children, she seized them and fought to exclude Edward. I affirmed for him, "Nobody can withhold your divine inheritance what Spirit has stipulated for you appears through perfect channels now." Edward wrote down the affirmation and used it in a letter to Archangel Uriel, writing and repeating it eighteen times daily. Some months transpired and his sister still didn't release the holdings. However, suddenly

Chapter 6

and unexpectedly, Edward received a hefty share of a trust fund his grandmother had established some years before. The amount was greater than the amount his sister had withheld.

If Someone Blocks Your Progress

When she first visited me, Joanne felt frustrated. A sales director of an international company, she was committed to her work and her productivity showed it. However, instead of being pleased with her progress, Joanne's boss seemed to feel threatened and had made a veritable campaign of convincing management that Joanne's successes were based on unethical practices. My client kept working, but she felt that the company heeded her boss's gossip and, as a result, didn't give her the recognition she deserved. Among other affirmations, I suggested she repeat: "My progress cannot be limited, my progress cannot be sabotaged. God doesn't hold me back or make me depend on people for my progress. God lifts me up and moves me forward to my best and highest place with its almighty means now." She had been coming to treatments with me and using this decree and other methods in this chapter for about three months when she received an unexpected call from the company. Of hundreds of directors, she was among only four selected to participate in the prestigious national committee, where she now enjoys solid recognition.

If You Feel Alone or Helpless

Karina is a young mother and businesswoman who's married to David, a professional soccer goalkeeper. David had signed with a major team that told him he would begin as substitute, with a chance to eventually become the principle goalkeeper. However, that eventuality never seemed to come. Time went by and they continued to hold him as a substitute for the principle, who was a well-known star. David saw few minutes on the field, which limited his visibility and the possibility of other teams noticing him. For several years, he tried to renegotiate his contract so he could either sign with another team or be a principle player. The team manager wouldn't support him for either option. Karina wrote to Archangel Michael, asking that he intervene with the guardian angels of those involved (as described in chapter 2), and also used this affirmation daily: "My husband is not alone or without effective representation. The Divine Agent is with him, going before him in all negotiations, representing his interests, touching the understanding of those involved, and moving in this situation in every way to assure a successful outcome and a true contract for him now." She had been doing this for several weeks when the principle goalkeeper stopped showing up for games and her husband had more chances to shine, which he did, winning a cup and attaining a more public profile. Soon after that, he was called by another team to play as regular goalkeeper with an attractive contract, and the original team finally let him go.

Depending on your situation, you can adapt the above affirmation, replacing the words "Divine Agent" for "Divine Publicist," "Divine Sponsor," "Divine Partner," and so on. At one time, I was very frustrated about not having an effective, dedicated assistant. I began to affirm, "I'm not alone or without effective support. The Divine Assistant is with me, working with love, order, and efficacy to help me in every way." A young woman who was working for me at the time suddenly became much more harmonious, dedicated, and effective, making a major difference in my work.

If You Feel Unworthy

Many people tell me that they feel unworthy of prosperity. However, unworthiness has no basis in divine substance, and the following affirmation can sweep such thoughts away: "I hold no thoughts or feelings of unworthiness, because the only true thoughts and feelings are divine, and divine thoughts never sabotage or limit me: they help me, elevate me and connect me with divine good. By Uriel's sword, I wipe away any vestiges of self-limitation, and I am free to receive the success and prosperity that flow to me, here and now."

If You're Faced with Numerous Challenges

Fatima is an eCommerce specialist in her thirties who was working for a major supermarket chain when she was fired in a rather rude and belittling manner. She began taking unblocking treatments with me, following up with visualization, angel invocations, and similar suggestions. A few months later, an international company contacted her from out of the blue. They ended up hiring her as country manager with significantly higher pay and a much more meaningful activity (in online education) than her previous job. A few weeks after she started, the situation became challenging. One Sunday in her unblocking session, she told me that some of her suppliers weren't responding and her personnel, hired by the previous manager, were creating conflicts. Fatima was feeling overwhelmed. I affirmed for her, "The only thing for you in this situation is Infinite Good. You're not alone, Infinite Good fills your workplace and activities, supporting you in every way. From the field of Infinite Good, all the help you could need now appears." As I repeated these words, I saw a luminous field filling her workplace and situation, and from it all kinds of help was coming. The following Thursday Fatima came to my weekly empowerment session and told me that everything had changed for the better things were again flowing in her favor.

May these examples inspire you to face your fears, speak them down, and watch the blocks dissolve as the flow of grace is restored, and with it, your good. After your prayer sessions, ask Uriel to use his sword and cut away limiting thought patterns so you may remain in conscious connection with the Source. As you work with affirmations and invocations like those shared here, your understanding will expand and you'll find yourself inspired to create your own.

"Archangel Uriel, please direct me to choose, understand, and work with the best affirmations to allow my good to flow, now and always."

Uriel and Grace Fuel Gratitude

We're used to thinking of gratitude as a social courtesy, but it's so much more. The act of giving thanks triggers positive emotions, lifting our vibration. This optimizes the multiplying effects of paying attention to the good. My healers and I have had thousands of opportunities to experience this power. When someone comes to us in pain, we ask the person if the pain's subsiding after several minutes of treatment. When they confirm their initial relief, we often repeat words such as: "I give thanks for the amazing, tangible action of Spirit that's working in you and will continue to do so until you're completely well." Such affirmations fuel the healing process and in most cases the pain completely disappears. Gratitude will multiply all good things, including supply.

"Uriel and Grace, please touch my mind with your divine fire and fuel my awareness of gratitude, now and always."

"Angels and goddesses of gratitude, direct me to appreciate my blessings and lift my gaze to the infinite, loving Source, now and always."

Affirmation: "I'm not moved by appearances. I contemplate my past and present blessings and give thanks to the Loving Source that generated

> *them. I have faith in the divine supply that continues to pour into my*
> *life, here and now."*

We don't have to wait for occasions of need. If we cultivate gratitude as a habit, we become active collaborators with the flow of good, keeping our vibration high and our channels open. To stay in the flow:

Keep an image of Uriel and Grace in view from your bed so that even before rising, you remember to give thanks: for wellness, for the new day, for life, for Spirit's love, for a few important blessings you can think of.

Before sitting down to eat, give thanks for your supply. (In chapter 7 are blessings for the table.)

When you receive money, opportunities, or blessings of any kind, mentally thank the angels and the Infinite Source of your good fortune.

When you're feeling rushed or blocked by people or situations, look for something you can mentally give thanks for.

At every opportunity, express your gratitude to people. Thank a family member for sharing a meal or taking a message, thank a client who pays you, thank a waiter who attends you well, or the person who sweeps the streets for keeping them clean.

Write thank-you cards and letters to people who have made a positive difference in your life: a parent, a teacher, a friend, a coach, a sibling, and so on, and make an effort to act on your gratitude by giving something back to them.

Prepare red index cards with Uriel's image or name on them, along with the words, "Thank you." Place these cards in strategic places: by a mirror, on your laptop, in your wallet, and so on to remember to give thanks.

Gratitude Envelopes

The Chinese celebrate their new year by giving money in red and gold envelopes (Uriel's colors) to children and single adults as a sign of luck. A wealthy developer hired me for several services: giving courses to his personnel, helping him visualize his company's expansion, and blessing his developments so they would sell more quickly. Besides paying for these services, he would give me cash gifts in red and gold Chinese New Year envelopes, which seemed to go with his opulent aura and results.

The following envelopes are designed to save for a vacation, business investment, or some other special goal.

1. Obtain or make a large, bright red envelope for each goal.

2. Paste or draw an image of Uriel and Grace in the middle of each envelope.

3. Below the image, write: "Thank you, angels, for supporting this manifestation of (write the goal, amount you need, and date)." Alternately, instead of writing the goal, paste a colored picture of it.

4. Determine a percentage of your income (2 percent, 5 percent, etc.) you'll set aside to meet your goal. It's usually more effective to set aside a small amount regularly than to wait until you have a large "extra" sum.

5. Each time you add money to the envelope, take a moment to give thanks and visualize it overflowing. You can also fill it with play money to facilitate visualization. If it does overflow before you reach your goal, you can make more envelopes, or put part of it in a special account or safe.

It's interesting to note that the word "grateful" comes from the Latin *gratus*, the same root as the word "grace." Etymologically, it means "more in grace." Since our good flows from grace, gratitude also puts us more in abundance. A bit further on, you'll find another special key to connect with Uriel and deepen your capacity for gratitude.

Bless the Earth with Divine Substance

Human perception tends to be trapped in the appearance of the senses, leading us to think that the earth, and anything else that's tangible, as merely matter. From a metaphysical perspective, the substance behind all appearances and all matter is divine. As an expression of Spirit, it's not inert or limited to time or space. It's a loving, intelligent, dynamic substance that, like Lakshmi's magical lotus, actively works to produce good. The same holds true for Earth herself, her climate, and her atmosphere.

In connection with the Angel of Trees, the following meditation is designed to bless our planet, its climate and atmosphere, in the awareness of divine substance.

1. Imagine that you are sitting in a forest against a tall, strong tree. It may be an oak, a pine, a redwood, or whatever species comes to your mind.

2. Say, "Angel of Trees, please use the energy of this meditation to heal the forests and the planet now."

3. Begin to breathe slowly and deeply.

4. Inhale in through your nose and imagine you can smell the scent of the tree. Exhale through your mouth, emptying your lungs each time you do.

5. As you continue to breathe this way, feel that you, like the tree behind you, are sending roots that sprout from the bottom of your feet and reach into the earth below. With each exhalation, the roots go deeper into the ground.

6. Imagine that you have branches reaching up into the sky, growing higher with each inhalation.

7. When you feel that your roots have gone several feet into the earth, and your branches have reached several meters into the sky, repeat for six minutes:

    "The true substance of the earth is divine; it's a loving, beneficent substance that works to generate positive results for the planet and its inhabitants now."

    "The true atmosphere of the planet is a divine atmosphere, charged with love, which can only generate good for the entire planet now."

8. After each repetition, send the awareness of divine substance through your "roots" into the earth, and up through your "branches" into the atmosphere.

9. Imagine your roots recede back into your feet, your branches come back into your arms, and give thanks to the Angel of the Trees.

Brigit, Goddess of Comebacks and Personal Productivity

Like Uriel, Brigit's colors include red and gold. Evoking Uriel's flame, Brigit rules the sacred fires of creativity and transmutation. A triple goddess, she embodies three sisters, each specializing in a kind of transmutation. As goddess of poetry and creativity, she turns ideas into tangible works. As a healer, she transmutes illness to health and esoteric secrets into applied wisdom. As the spirit of smithcraft, she changes rock into metalworks. A major goddess throughout the British Isles, her footprints were known to leave a trail of eternal spring and bounty.

Brigit's fire is the flame of Imbolc, the Pagan celebration of February 2 that honors the sun when it reaches its midpoint between

Winter Solstice and Spring Equinox. In keeping with European traditions, the Mexican goddess Coatlicue symbolically brings forth the newborn sun at Winter Solstice. February 2, celebrated as Candlemas Day, coincides with Coatlicue's emergence from her forty-day postpartum reclusion.

In some parts of rural Mexico, the ancient tradition of postpartum respite is still in use. Relatives do the housework and cooking and attend the new mother, who spends her time resting, taking herb baths to firm up her tissues, and eating tasty, nutritious food. These days are considered vital for her recovery from the birth process and her production of quality milk for the baby. When they're done, women return to their normal, productive activities.

In ancient Europe, where this tradition was also kept, Brigit was known to oversee women's return to activity. Today, the reclusion of the goddess is also a symbol of those times in our lives when for some reason or another we retreat from normal activity and focus our energy inward. We may do this to heal from a challenging situation or to deepen our spiritual consciousness. Besides its relation to postpartum recovery, the forty days—like the Israelites' forty years in the desert—are symbolic of a complete cycle. After such a period we can re-enter the world renewed, move forward with our productive activities, and like the sun at Imbolc, let our light shine.

It's no coincidence that Brigit is an active, radiant archetype. She supports people who wish to make a comeback of some kind, as well as those who are shining their light in ways both magical and productive. She blesses environmental and women's causes and helps us successfully manifest our life's work and purpose. At once a healer, a priestess, an artist, a warrior, and a bride (a word deriving from Brigit), she's a mirror for today's woman and sensitive man who cover diverse fronts at home and beyond.

In ancient Ireland, people would celebrate Imbolc by lighting fires and walking around, blessing crops. If you are making or intending to make a comeback of some kind, you can evoke this archetypal energy of encouragement with the following ritual.

1. Light several tea candles and walk around your home or workspace as you place them in different spots and affirm: "I bless the angelic light that shines in my space, my life, my prayers, and my work, lifting me up, now and always!"

2. As you continue to walk around affirming this way, visualize angels floating around with burning lights.

Like the Brigit's many facets, Uriel's varied symbols represent the spectrum of intellectual, esoteric, and productive activities that contribute to our holistic progress. Uriel's sword cuts away distraction and self-doubt, and his light directs our talents and energies in focused, productive ways.

An experience of my friend and follower, Mexican actress Yekaterina Kiev, exemplifies this combination. A single mother, she had been taking courses, reading books, and applying her mind powers in visualization and affirmation. Her young adult son was going through an emotional crisis that put extra demands on Yeka's time and attention. Right when his crisis came to a head and she was feeling overwhelmed, she got a call for casting. It was programmed for the next day and she was to parody a Mexican politician. She asked for some lines to study and they told her that there weren't any; she would have to come up with something on her own. It occurred to her to look for videos of the politician, and she came across a television interview on YouTube that she could parody. She worked on her voice and gestures to get the character down and even wrote a monologue with several original jokes.

The next day at the casting, the producers loved her performance. She was the only actress who had actually worked on the personification. Yekaterina recalls another actress explaining to the producer that she had just returned from a trip and didn't have time to prepare. She got the part, and they even used some of her jokes in the first episode. She immediately went from having an irregular income—common for actors—to earning an attractive salary. The program, called *La Parodia,* was a huge success on television and social media. It went on to have another season and made several live tours around the country, for which she also got paid. They're now preparing a third season.

Her experience displays the goddess's dual powers of prosperity. She applied inward tools: studying, affirming, and visualizing, and made the extra effort to seize the moment and focus all her abilities to ground her good fortune when opportunity called, despite the challenges at home.

Invocations:

"Archangel Uriel, please awaken my motivation and direct me to begin anew and shine my light now."

"Uriel and Grace, please move me on my best path for the current phase of my success, prosperity, and happiness now."

"Uriel and Grace, help me care for myself and prepare for my new good now."

"Archangel Uriel, please direct me to use my opportunities with focus and courage now."

Uriel's Flowers

Iris and Company

The lovely iris brings together three flower symbols that connect with Uriel and are related to one another:

Iris: flower of faith and hope; fleur-de-lis: symbol of wisdom, bravery, and meaningful, prosperous labor; gladiola: flower of strength, persistence, and victory. You can call on one or all of these flower spirits: Iris to strengthen your faith so you can manifest more easily, fleur-de-lis to apply your talents successfully, and gladiola so you may persist productively and vanquish blocks to victory.

Cut through Self-Sabotage with Gladiola

Have on hand a cylindrical, ruby-red candle, your journal or angelic diary, a pen, and a red gladiola or a picture of the flower.

1. Light the candle.

2. Ask your personal angels and spirit guides to help you identify ways in which you might be sabotaging your own success.

3. Write: "I would be fully on course with my life purpose or success if it weren't for my tendency to ..." (complete the sentence in your own words with all the answers that come to mind). Some examples include:

   "... if it weren't for my tendency to fear not getting it right, which makes me unconsciously seek distraction."

   "... if it weren't for my tendency to feel I just don't have enough time, so what's the point of trying anyway."

   "... if it weren't for my tendency to think that if my relatives see my work, they'll criticize me even more than they already do."

"...if it weren't for my tendency to waste time on social media."

"...if it weren't for my tendency to feel that I'm not worthy."

"...if it weren't for my tendency to start things and then give up before I finish ..."

"...if it weren't for my tendency to postpone dealing with challenges."

The goal is to detect the emotional patterns and habits that keep you from making your best effort in your work or chosen purpose.

1. Look at the gladiola for a minute, letting its image saturate your mind.

2. For a few moments, look at the candle, observing its red glow and imagining that within it you see a gladiola flower.

3. Close your eyes and imagine the candles rays extending throughout the room, sending as they do luminous, red gladiolas.

4. Bring to mind the habit or habits you detected in the inner dialogue you wrote in step 3.

5. Repeat: "Angel of Red Gladiolas, please cut through these patterns and any other energies that may block my progress."

6. For about 6 minutes, imagine the red gladiolas flowing right through you, dissolving your fears and any shadow patterns that have held you back.

7. Open your eyes, press your palms together, and make a gesture of prayerful gratitude toward the candle as you say, "Thank you, beautiful gladiola, thank you, angels and spirit guides."

Lakshmi's Lotus

The lotus is an essential flower and symbol to Egyptian, Hindu, and many different Asian mythologies; it's usually related to the mother-goddess, purity, illumination, and spiritual wisdom. In order to bloom, the lotus blossom must rise through the mud. This is taken as a metaphor for spiritual growth and self-improvement, which require that we move through the challenges of the world in order to flower in all our splendor.

Lakshmi is known as Lotus Goddess or Lotus Lady. The lotus she carries in her right hand is a living magical wand she uses to communicate grace, impart healing and prosperity, and consolidate our positive manifestations.

Lakshmi's Lotus Blessing

Have on hand a red candle and a picture of Lakshmi (easy to find on internet).

1. Light the candle.
2. For three to four minutes, observe the candle, imagining you can see the goddess glowing within the candle.
3. Close your eyes and imagine that you are watching Lakshmi's image grow until it surrounds the candle and becomes a life-sized image of the goddess, seated on a lotus and glowing in red and gold. Place special attention on the lotus flower she holds in her right hand.
4. Visualize that she touches you with her magical flower as you repeat three times: "Beautiful Lakshmi, please touch me with your magical lotus, connect me with the flow of grace, and consolidate my divine manifestations now."

Goddess Invocation

"Glorious Golden Goddess, touch this situation (project, purse, bank account) with your magical lotus and precipitate divine results in it now."

Uriel's Mandalas for Material Abundance and Success in Your Life Mission

The Best Images for Financial Prosperity

Before enumerating the materials you will need for this mandala, I'll share a brief guide of images, adapted from my years of teaching, that will improve your results.

Avoid pictures that just imply abundance. A cartoon of a briefcase with a dollar symbol or an illustration of a tree with dollar bills falling from it may be cute and creative, but they won't provide the realism that allows your imagination to produce something concrete. Look for color photographs of large quantities of cash, ingots, gold bars, and other monetary instruments.

Make sure the money looks neat. Divine good tends to flow in orderly ways. If we use a picture of a large but messy pile of bills, it won't flow as well, and the money may come with a messy situation of some kind. If the bills are floating in the air, it will be hard to imagine you have them in front of you, ready to use.

Choose from and combine images such as:

- orderly piles of large-denomination bills ($50, $500, $100)
- a wallet packed with money
- a hand or hands holding, giving, and/or receiving large amounts of cash
- an open briefcase or safe filled with cash
- numerous ingots, gold bars, or similar

- your bank statement, edited to show much higher deposits and transfers to your account
- checks for large amounts made out to your name.

You can find premade checks for visualization online, but they're not the best. Thousands of people have been looking at and visualizing those images, so you would be working in a more crowded mental space. It's better to download or make real-looking checks. You can scan one you received, erase or change the account holder's name, erase the quantity to write in a higher one, and change the date. You can add the name of someone you wish to do business with, as if that person or company had paid you. If you want to receive a scholarship, edit the check as though the account holder was the school or fund who will pay you. You can download an image of a lottery check and Photoshop it, adding your name as the winner. You can even use your own checks, making them out to yourself. Just be sure to white out or edit the account holder so it doesn't look like you're the one paying.

Carla, a businesswoman and participant in my courses, put tall piles of play money on her desk. On top of each pile she put a smaller pile of real cash so it would look authentic. Her husband took pictures of her sitting at her desk behind these piles, holding more cash in her hands. She followed the recommended instructions and, of course, worked on her business, which grew about 1,000 percent in five years.

Getting Ready

Before gathering your materials, take a moment to quiet your mind; focus on your intention to manifest prosperity; and ask the angels, goddesses, and flower spirits to collaborate. Hold to your purpose as you put it together. You will need:

- Bright red paper or poster board and a gold or blue pen

- Color images of monetary instruments (use above guide)

- Depending on the size of your mandala, 30 to 40 small images of white and pink lotuses, 1 large (1½") and 3 or more small (½") images of Archangel Uriel and his twin flame Grace. (You can download, cut out, and paste; or draw the images onto the poster board, if you prefer.)

- 1 to 3 small images of goddess Lakshmi and/or the so-called Hand of Fatima or a 1½" image of Lakshmi in the middle of your mandala

- Your favorite adhesive stick, paste, or glue.

Make Your Mandala for Material Abundance

1. Trace a large (12" or more) circle, and then line it evenly with the flower images.

2. Draw or paste the image of the angels or the goddess in the middle, and the smaller angels and goddesses around the inside of the circle to taste.

3. Add images of financial abundance (described above), distributing them in a symmetrical fashion. Leave a margin of the colored background around each one. Don't turn them at an angle—crooked images can attract crooked people and results.

4. At the top of your mandala, write an affirmation, such as:

"Angels support my financial abundance, and I'm worthy of receiving it now."

"I give thanks that the angels help me visualize and manifest rich prosperity now!"

"*Large amounts of money flow to me from the hand of the goddess. I see it, I believe it, and I receive it now.*"

"*I give thanks for the financial supply that the goddess pours into my life in a rich, golden stream, now and always.*"

"*My finances are protected by angels and my wealth is divinely insured, now and always.*"

Tapping Your Abundance

Spend at least six minutes three times a day enjoying your mandala in the following ways:

1. As you begin each session, call on the spirit of the flowers, repeating something like, "Magical Spirit of Lotus, please activate my intuitive connection with prosperity so I may allow it to flow to me now."

2. Choose and repeat one of the following requests to Uriel and Grace:

   "*Uriel, Grace, and Lakshmi, please direct me to use my inner and outer gifts successfully now.*"

   "*Angels and goddesses of prosperity, please help me enjoy my present good and manifest greater good now.*"

   "*Lakshmi and Uriel, please put me in resonance with divine prosperity so that I may receive and share it now.*"

   "*Angels and goddesses of abundance, support me in visualizing and manifesting financial independence now.*"

3. Spend a couple of minutes calmly repeating the affirmation on your mandala, as you imagine that the resources shown are your own.

4. For another couple of minutes, close your eyes and bring the images to mind again (visualizing with one's eyes closed optimizes the effect). Imagine you are touching the money, taking some in your hands, and experiencing the joy of knowing there's much more.

5. Open your eyes and thank the angels, the goddess, and the flower spirits for their assistance.

Complement this mandala with the review of your intentions as described in this chapter and with monetary instruments you can hold, such as checks, real and play money, a bank statement that has been retouched to show large deposits and a higher average balance, and similar papers. When you visualize with the mandala (steps 3 and 4), look at these instruments too. The combined energy of your hands, eyes, and imagination enriches the results.

Remember to keep this practice secret. Other people's doubts can block manifestation. Also, stay mindful of changes—even subtle ones. You're resonating in a new way, opening to greater good, and this opens new doors. Pay attention and be ready to walk through them.

As I sometimes remark to my groups, tongue-in-cheek: Since nothing is impossible for divinity, maybe one day you'll hear a knock at the door and when you answer it, you'll find Lakshmi floating on a giant lotus, attired in red and gold silk and flanked with elephants on either side. Maybe she'll be carrying a silver platter with a check in your name for $200,000,000. Miracles do happen, and we can't limit divinity. But it's safe to say that the results of your intention are apt to slip into your life in less dramatic ways. Pay attention to and act on the signs: a new job or business offer, a coach who appears on your path, an opportunity to improve your credentials or professional skills through study, a chance to refinance a loan or property, or an idea for a new line of work or to promote your product or services. You may be intuitively guided to get up earlier to research, develop your options, or spend more time using the tools in this book.

Affirmation: *"Angels of abundance, please guide me to recognize my true opportunities and act on them wisely, now and always."*

Mandala for Success in Your Life Mission

Before gathering your materials, take a moment to quiet your mind, focus on your intention to manifest success in your life mission and ask the angels, goddesses, and flower spirits to collaborate. Hold to your purpose throughout the process.

Follow the instructions for the previous mandala, changing the lotuses for fleur-de-lis or iris, Lakshmi for Brigit, and using only two images of money.

According to your profession, integrate pictures of your success. For example:

- If you're a painter: Create a picture of a large, attractive studio filled with your paintings and people looking at them. Put a sign with the word "Sold" on most of the pictures.

- If you're in sales: Make a picture of yourself standing on a stage with the president of the company, receiving the keys to a car you won or another important prize.

- If you're a healer: Make a picture of yourself standing on stage before a large audience, alongside a best-selling author on the subject such as Bruce Lipton or Larry Dossey. Alternately, use a picture of yourself before a large group of people, surrounded by images of the archangels and a screen behind you with the words, "Renowned Healer, (your name)."

- If you're an ecologist: Redesign the cover of a science or environmental magazine, integrating a picture of yourself, your name, and a caption such as, "Reforesting the Earth," "Cleaning the Seas," or the particular cause that attracts you.
- If you're a scientist: Create a document of a science prize you would like to win with your name and the date of your goal.

Choose from the following affirmations to write on your mandala:

"Spirit knows my true mission and supports me to succeed in it."

"Thank you, angels, for directing and promoting my success."

"I am worthy of shining in my chosen field. I believe it, I see it, and I receive it now."

"I thank the angels for supporting my joyous achievements, now and always."

Connecting with Success

Spend at least three minutes three times a day, enjoying your mandala in the following ways:

1. As you begin each session, call on the spirit of the flowers, repeating: "Please direct me in my true mission and move me to use the opportunities that angels are bringing me now."
2. Repeat: "Archangel Uriel, please align my imagination, thoughts and actions with my best and highest success now."
3. Spend a couple of minutes repeating the affirmation on your mandala and compatible thoughts that come to your

mind, as you imagine that you have already obtained the results in the pictures.

4. For another couple of minutes, close your eyes and bring the images to mind again (visualizing with one's eyes closed optimizes the effect). Imagine you can touch the prize, hear the applause, or enjoy the presence of the angels.

5. Open your eyes and thank the angels, the goddess, and the flower spirits for their assistance.

Don't discuss your goals or the results that begin to manifest as you work with your mandala. Other people's doubts or envy can block manifestation. Also, in resonance with the example of the actress described earlier who rushed to prepare for a sudden call to casting: take the actions that common sense, intuition, and angelicities suggest so you can be ready to use the opportunities that will flow in response to this tool.

Manifestation Gratitude Ritual

People sometimes ask me what they can do with mandalas and related tools once they have manifested the results.

1. In your fireplace, barbecue, or a large, fire-proof container, start a fire.

2. Put your mandala or mandalas in the fire (if necessary, cut into pieces first).

3. Repeat: "In a fire of gratitude, I celebrate these manifestations and give thanks for the divine and angelic support that facilitated them."

4. As you watch the fire, repeat, "Thank you, angels. Thank you, Mother-Father." Feel the flame of gratitude in your heart that rises upward to the realm of Spirit, elevating your being.

Uriel's Magical Hand

Uriel holds a flame in one hand. This is a sign of divine desire, loving deeds, prosperous work, and magical manifestation.

The word "human" contains the Latin root, *manus*, "hand," in acknowledgment that our hands are part of what make us human. In palmistry, the thumb indicates will, and the human thumb really has been an instrument to develop and express our will. The relatively large size of our thumbs gave us an evolutionary advantage over other primates. Increased dexterity in turn triggered changes in the human brain. The combination has enabled our species to make more things and exert greater influence on our environment, molding our world in accordance with our will and intelligence.

We can jump-start another phase of evolution by learning to use our hands in conscious connection with our spiritual will. One way to do this is to send love through our hands as we go about our daily activities and work. Whether touching a keyboard, taking a shower, wiping the counter, or opening the door for someone to enter the room before us, we can consciously use the moment to send love to the object of our action, or to the higher power who made this action possible. Whether or not we're actually touching someone, sending love through our hands awakens the energy currents that naturally tend to flow through them.

Our hands are an important part of Angelic Intelligence. In Asia, practitioners of ancestral traditions send chi (vital energy) and make mudras (signs and gestures used in dance and to favor certain psychic and spiritual states). Reiki is one Eastern healing modality involving hands.

However, most practitioners of affirmations and positive prayer have yet to consciously apply the sacred energy currents that are subtly triggered when we apply our mind powers. Our decrees are instruments of free will, as are our hands. In fact, the word "manifest" comes from the Latin *manifestus*, meaning "to discover, reveal, or catch by hand." By combining certain hand movements with your prayers, you can literally wipe away undesirable appearances, mold divine substance, and give form to what you are speaking.

Angelic Mudras

These movements began to emerge spontaneously in my healing work, and I've discovered they make a big difference in the results experienced by my clients and the healers I've trained. For the first time in print, we'll see some examples of these movements that you can easily integrate into your own spiritual and healing practice. As you apply them for yourself and others, you'll begin to get in touch with the subtle currents in your body that become activated in prayer. Continue to heed these sensations and the angels will guide you to generate additional movements that enrich the results of your words.

1. Choose something you wish to unblock or heal.

2. Say, "I call on the angels of sacred energies to direct me in using my hands to support my prayers, unblock low vibrations, and manifest divine victory, here and now."

3. Choose an affirmation that suits your situation (from pages 179 and 180 in this chapter, or pages 95–98 of chapter 3) and repeat it. As you do, focus on the energy within and around you. Try to detect a resistance. It may come as a doubt in your mind, or you may feel it as a thick sort of energy around or before you. When you're able to capture the resistance, continue to affirm, this time in a firmer tone of voice, with authority, and integrate one or more of the hand motions shared below. Continue to practice until the movements become fluid and you experience greater power in your prayers.

Push through Blocked Energy

1. Stretch your right arm before you with your fingers in a natural position, slightly opened.

2. Move your hand three times in a gentle, clockwise motion.

3. Quickly pull your arm back, bending the elbow slightly.

4. Bend your fingers slightly in a kind of hook position and quickly straighten your arm, pushing your hand forward firmly, as though you were pushing something away with your palm.

5. Make the above movement from 1 to 6 times until you feel the block subside.

6. Throughout this process, remember to continue affirming.

Whirl Out Negativity

1. Put your right hand near your body, or if you're treating another, near their body.

2. For three seconds, rotate your hand rapidly in a spinning motion with your fingers slightly open. The effect is almost like a rake that's whirling invisible dead leaves.

3. Stop the whirling, and close your fingers as though you were grabbing the dead leaves or energy that your movements stirred up.

4. Quickly open your fingers and with a pushing movement, throw the energy away.

Sweep Out Entities

1. To apply when treating another: Sit in front of the person.

2. Turn your hands around and bring them together in front of you, at the level of the person's head, so that the backs of your fingers touch lightly in the middle.

3. As though you were opening a pair of curtains, separate your hands about 2 ½ to 3 feet apart.

4. Going down from the head, in front of the face, then the chest and stomach, repeat the above movement, bringing your hands together and separating them, as you sense the energy moving aside like curtains.

Bring In the Angels

After a prayer session, walk around your space, visualizing the angels filling it. As you do, repeat: "Angels fill this space tangibly." Form a sort of cup with your right hand (your left if you're left-handed), and lift it up and down as you walk as though you were planting an angel each time you put your hand down.

The Hand of the Goddess

The so-called hand of Fatima and similar archaic depictions are powerful symbols of protection and divine providence. You can visualize that one of these hands touches your mind, your purse, or a part of your body as you ask Lakshmi to bring prosperity, light, healing, or another request.

Uriel and Grace are Earth's special guardians. Imagine the ruby couple touching the minds of politicians with their luminous hands.

Affirmation: *"The angels touch the minds of world leaders, inspiring them with divine desire and divine action now."*

We've seen ways of using our hands to receive, to bless, and to unblock. As we develop this aspect of Angelic Intelligence, it's important to remember that our hands are also instruments of giving. To enjoy their full benefits, we can remember to act as divine channels for others and for the world. We can share of our bounty with those in need, give offerings and gifts, donate our time, knowledge, or work for another or for a cause. Such actions bring joy to the heart and also

Chapter 6

trigger the divine circulation that flows to us from the hand of God, of Goddess.

Invocations

"Uriel and Grace, please use me as an instrument of grace for others and for my world."

"The angels of circulation direct me to give in generous, appropriate ways that benefit all involved, now and always."

"I invite the hand of the goddess to touch the world through me, now and always."

"Angels and goddesses of prosperity, please help me enjoy my present good and manifest greater good now."

According to Sufism, all desire is sacred because it's fueled by the one true desire—union with the Beloved. When you finish a session of visualizing, using affirmations, or working with angels, you can bless your intentions. Imagine that Uriel touches your heart with his flaming hand and lighting it. Then repeat, "Uriel-Grace, please use the energy of my desires to fuel the one true flame that burns in my heart: the desire that all sentient beings be joyously open to Grace."

Letters to Uriel: Deepen Your Gratitude and the Power of Your Abundance Affirmations

To deepen your gratitude, write to Uriel.

The benefits of gratitude are increasingly recognized. To experience them more deeply, each night before you go to sleep, write a daily gratitude inventory. Review your life and day to recall and write down your blessings. Don't only express *what* you're grateful for; use the chance to reaffirm your inner powers of gratitude, as in the sample that follows. Include this inventory in a letter to the ruby archangels, whose mission it is to align us with gratitude. Write your letters on bright red paper, in blue or gold ink. Do them at night before going to sleep for twenty-eight days or an entire lunar cycle.

To Archangels Uriel and Grace

Dear Archangels,

I praise your radiant work to restore humanity's vibration of gratitude. Please collaborate with my guardian angel so that I can develop and sustain this consciousness.

I send up this inventory of gratitude for your perfect use:

I'm deeply grateful for the chance to be alive.

I'm fully appreciative of all the love I receive.

I'm grateful that my daughter is healthy, kind, and independent.

I'm happy and grateful for this morning's beautiful walk.

I'm full of gratitude for the strength and health I have.

I'm grateful for my energy and enthusiasm.

I'm so grateful for the market there is for my work.

I'm deeply appreciative of all the beautiful people in my life.

I'm grateful for my grandchild's laughter and hugs.

I'm full of gratitude for the sales I had today.

I'm so grateful for my wonderful mother.

I'm happy and grateful for having work that I love and that helps others tangibly.

I'm deeply grateful for the Divine Presence that's with me always.

Thank you, my dear, ruby archangels, for working to raise my mentality and vibration.

Blessings,

(sign your name)

The following missive lifts your abundance affirmations to their highest frequency.

Letter to Achieve Lasting Prosperity

Ask the archangels to direct you in the highest and best inner and outer efforts. You can add, *"Wield your divine sword to free me from any unconscious blocks to affluence that I may have inherited, formed or received from entities or from the collective mind."*

Write the following affirmation 12 or 18 times in the letter:

"The angels direct me to manifest abundance. I see it, I believe it, and I receive it now."

Alternately, write an affirmation. It's important that you resonate with the words. Once you decide on an affirmation, it's good to stick to the same one for at least twenty-eight days or a complete lunar cycle, so its effect can saturate your deep mind.

The archangels of abundance are not making us wait for some far-off day to support our spiritual and worldly progress. They know about abundance and facilitate the whole spectrum. They lift our gaze upward. They support our visualization of holistic good for ourselves and others. They collaborate to unblock apparent limitations. They direct us to enjoy the moment as we develop gratitude, generosity, and meaningful work. In connecting with their love, guidance, and power, we discover that prosperity is not so materialistic after all. It's part of our rich angelic pathway.

Chapter 7

GABRIEL AND HOPE: BIRTH, BLESSING, SPIRITUAL REBIRTH

White light contains all the other colors, and Archangel Gabriel and his divine complement Hope shine through the last, white ribbon of the angelic rainbow. These are the angels of rebirth, blessing, cleansing, newly incarnate souls, divine messages, water, good news, emotions, flowers, and the moon.

Their symbols include a lily, representing pure, new life, and a trumpet, to awaken our inner angelic essence. They're connected to Svadhisthana, the sacral chakra of the womb and the forces that are capable of birthing offspring, artistic and creative works, and one's own divine identity. They're also related to Sahasrara, the crown chakra of purity that links our personal energy to the higher realms. It's interesting to note that these two centers are related in the Hindu chakra system: the goddess of the sacral chakra, Rakini Shakti, is said to drink the nectar of the crown chakra.[67]

Gabriel is the archangel of "I am" who works to support us in recognizing, affirming, and enlivening our higher self. Each of

---

67. Dale, *The Subtle Body*, 256.

us has a divine identity and mission, and before we incarnate on the earth plane, the angels announce them to our co-creative self. During our lives, they continue to connect us with this message, fueling our Angelic Intelligence, and activating our glorious light body and divine DNA.

Gabriel's divine complement, Hope, keeps alive our positive expectancy. Even in the midst of life's trials, she stokes the flames of hope that keep our vibration high and our minds open to positive outcomes. She motivates us to persist in our spiritual practice and angel connections, preparing us to emerge from each challenge on a higher, more luminous level. She and Gabriel can appear dressed in white tunics, with majestic wings of white and beige feathers, or as fields of white light with gold rays or specks.

Gabriel and the Goddesses of Purity and Renewal

The messenger archangel is connected to all things pure, including the apparitions of virgin goddesses or white-light ladies who have been reported around the world.

During a Toltec ceremony near Guadalupe's shrine in northern Mexico City, I had a personal encounter with the Virgin. Our Venerable Mother Tonantzin, as the natives called her, was hovering over those present and shielding our space with her wide and golden rays. My amazement was greater since until that moment I had relegated the Virgin to the realm of legend. When she appeared, I immediately knew who she was because along with her visage, which was made entirely of gold light, she emitted a very palpable radiation that can only be described as chastity. She preceded to "show" me her magnificent church, built in recent times near her ancient shrine on Mount Tepeyac. Telepathically, she communicated that its striking architecture has a divine energy purpose.

Since ancient times, millions of Mexican pilgrims have flooded the city each year in early December to visit this site. Often they travel on foot, sometimes taking up to three months to reach the shrine, called *La Villa de Guadalupe*. In the sixteenth century, after the Spaniards arrived, Tonantzin was fused with La Virgen de Guadalupe. Mexicans began to use the latter name, alternately calling her Tonantzin-Guadalupe. In testimony to her enduring place in the national heart, she's been named patron saint of all Mexico (1737), Queen of Mexico (1895), and Empress of the Americas (1945).

My encounter with Guadalupe-Tonantzin shed light on the mystery of virgins who are said to appear in various locations around Latin America and Europe. After that experience, I understood why people who've seen her know, like I did, who she is. All my life I'd been reading about the virgin archetype as interchangeable with "the maiden." I now understand her from a different perspective, one I've never read or heard about. I propose this as a new contribution to the study of goddesses that deserves more research: The Virgin's chastity isn't a physical characteristic; it's part of her essence as a light being. It doesn't come from the world of matter; it's a radiation, an ontological condition, a force unto itself.

We get a glimpse of the original meaning in various deities. Take, for example, Juno, the Roman goddess of women and marriage who would renew her chastity on a yearly basis. Juno was called by several epithets that were later bequeathed to Mary, including Rose, Lily, Star of the Sea, and Queen of Heaven. When conceiving her son Mars, one of many hero gods born to virgins, she rejected her husband, preferring to impregnate herself with a lily, the same flower carried by Gabriel when he told Mary she would conceive by the Holy Spirit. Egyptian Isis was all at once a virgin, a lover-wife, and a mother. In the Mexican pantheon, Tonantzin is a facet of Coatlicue, a goddess described in chapter 1. The reader may recall that the latter is a mature woman who, while sweeping her temple, experienced a chaste conception of sorts: being impregnated by a ball of colored feathers. We noted that her sweeping symbolized inner cleansing and the feathers an angelic connection. Through these goddesses, we can see that chastity is not principally a reference to a biological condition and much less a moralistic label, but a purifying, divine power that we can invoke to renew our beings.

With light, cleansing, guidance, optimism, blessings, and magical flowers, Gabriel and Hope help us recover this gift of renewal. *Gabriel* means "God's strength," reminding us that renewal is an inner choice that requires fortitude, a quality Gabriel imparts when we request it. As for Hope, her name expresses a positive expectancy that, like true purity, isn't based on outer events. Through working with these archangels, I've learned that in Angelic Intelligence, the vibration of hope doesn't refer to wishful thinking or attachment to a specific outcome.

We can invoke Gabriel and Hope or their angelic colleagues together or separately, depending on our needs and situation, as in the following examples.

Invocations and Affirmations

"Gabriel and Hope, please cleanse me of low vibrations and restore my pure, radiant essence now."

"The angels help me release the past and move into my new good now."

"Archangel Hope, please restore my trust in the Infinite Good that awaits me and awaits all beings now."

"Archangel Gabriel, please wash away the shadows of the world, so I may be restored to my original purity and joy now."

"The angels of life direct me on my soul-path and strengthen me to walk it now."

"Pristine Mother, fill me with your chaste essence and free me from attachments and addictive tendencies now."

"Gabriel, please bring me messages that reconnect me to me true self now."

Tantra with Tonantzin

This exercise lifts your vibration, purifies your energy, and fuels the gold-white radiance in your light body. It also dissolves the energy imprint of sexual or emotional abuse and toxic intimacy, without affecting positive attraction. Start it on the new moon and continue for thirty days.

1. In a place where you won't be interrupted, get in a comfortable position.

2. Repeat: "Please come before me, Tonantzin-Guadalupe."

3. Imagine you can see the Virgin or a luminous lady standing or floating before you, made entirely of translucent, golden light.

4. "Venerable Mother, please fuse with me and imbue me with your precious purity."

5. Repeat to yourself, "My body is not made of flesh, it's made of light so that it easily receives Tonantzin's light now."

6. Feel the Virgin's light fusing with yours.

7. For three minutes, hold to the feeling of her vibration in you as you affirm: "Tonantzin is here, purifying, renewing, and lifting my vibration now." As you affirm, feel the

energies of purification and of renewal radiating through your body.

You can start with three minutes and, if you feel guided, work up to six, nine, or twelve minutes or more.

Alternately, use the same method to fuse with Gabriel and Hope.

Angel Water Magic

Since ancient times, water, Gabriel's element, has been related to the sacred feminine[68]. The Aztec goddess of water, Chalchiuhtlicue, shares many of Gabriel's attributes. She presides over newborns and "blesses them in their first bath."[69] Her clothes are decorated with water lilies, in resonance with Gabriel's flower. Chalchiuhtlicue's symbols underscore the connection between water, blessing, and birth. Astrologically, Gabriel is connected to Cancer, a water sign that relates to mothers and is considered the door through which the soul incarnates. These metaphors confirm that Gabriel uses blessings and water to support our births and rebirths.

The historic apparitions of luminous ladies, seen by Joan of Arc and Bernadette Souberous of Lourdes and called virgins—both took place near healing springs[70]. As for Fatima, Portugal, the area was considered arid at the time of the apparitions. However, a short time later the so-called, miraculous springs of Fatima were discovered there.[71] Like Gabriel, water also relates to cleansing and is a great transmitter of information. When we infuse the liquid with

---

68. Rianne Eisler, *The Chalice and the Blade* (San Franscisco: HarperSanFrancisco, 1988), 21.

69. Auset, *Goddess Guide*, 23.

70. John Hancock, *Supernatural: Meetings with the Ancient Teachers of Mankind* (New York: The Disinformation Co., 2007), 317–318.

71. https://www.tfp.org/miraculous-springs-fatima/.

a high vibration, it transmits this energy wherever it's sprinkled or applied. This is the wisdom behind holy water.

Angelic Intelligence includes the understanding that matter is susceptible to transmutation and that our perception can lift it to a higher frequency.

Experiments confirm water can carry and transmit energy, information and emotions. In the 1990s, renowned French biologist Jacques Benveniste proved that it serves as a vehicle for electromagnetic information. Among other experiments, he recorded the sound-signatures of certain chemicals. When the signals were played to water, its molecules reacted as though they had been affected by the chemicals themselves[72].

Also in the 1990s, Japanese author Masaru Emoto became famous for his experiments with water. He froze samples with different words written on the containers, and then photographed the ice crystals. Harsh words like "you fool" produced unpleasant, chaotic crystals, while words like "love" and "gratitude" produced beautiful ones.[73] He also experimented with water from different locations. The crystals generated in samples from Lourdes spring in France were similar to those produced by samples labeled with the word "angel."[74] On one occasion, Emoto took samples from a polluted dam in Japan. Its molecules looked dark and shapeless. A Shinto priest then spent an hour praying over the dam. New samples showed that after the prayers, the molecules formed bright white crystals.[75] Emoto shared these and hundreds of related images in his books.

---

72. "Jacques Benveniste and the Memory of Water," Q-mag.org, https://q-mag .org/jacques-benveniste-and-the-memory-of-water.html.

73. Masaru Emoto, *The Hidden Messages of Water* (New York: Simon & Schuster, 2011), 13.

74. Ibid, 128.

75. "Dr. Masaru Emoto and Water Consciousness," The Wellness Enterprise website, https://thewellnessenterprise.com/emoto/.

In a less-known but equally fascinating experiment, photographer Rose-Lynn Fisher took pictures of the molecules of dried tears. The samples varied dramatically depending on the emotion behind them. For instance, tears of laughter produced pleasant images, while tears of grief generated a pattern resembling long, sharp knives. Tears from cutting onions produced molecules with a striking resemblance to foliage.[76] In the book *Spiritual Ecology*, shaman Sandra Ingerman shares an experiment she did, polluting containers of pure water to make it more acidic. With this liquid on hand, Ingerman's groups would do ceremonies to focus on their own divinity and, in the shaman's words, "feeling ourselves as the power of the universe, the divine source of light and universal love."[77] The water would become more alkaline. Their visualization and results are another example of Angelic Intelligence through Gabriel's magical phrase, "I am."

Angelic Blessed Water

You can invoke Gabriel to make you own angelic water magic.

By connecting our attention with divine truth, affirmations open a powerful door that literally transmutes the substance we behold. One of the keys of Angelic Intelligence is to combine not only requests but affirmations with visualizations with invocations of angels, producing a superlative wavelength that optimizes our magic.

To make angelic blessed water, hold a non-plastic container of water in your hands. Imagine that Gabriel and Hope are right there with you, touching the liquid, as you repeat three times mindfully:

---

76. Joseph Stromberg, "The Microscopic Structure of Human Tears" *Smithsonian* magazine website, November 19, 2013, https://www.smithsonianmag.com/science-nature/the-microscopic-structures-of-dried-human-tears-180947766/.

77. Sandra Ingerman, contributor, *Spiritual Ecology: The Cry of the Earth* (Pt. Reyes, CA: The Golden Sufi Center, 2013), 211.

"I recognize the Infinite Good that fills this water, communicating the energy of love wherever it's dispersed." Store this water in a non-plastic jar or bottle. You can keep a glass, bottle, or your own favorite vessel with angelic holy water on your altar and use it to cleanse and bless your space and person as described in this chapter.

Invocations and Affirmations to Heal Our Emotions, Earth, and Oceans

"Gabriel and Hope, please surround the earth with your legions of light, and pour the waters of hope over the planet now."

"The river of Spirit's love flows through me and through all the earth, washing away any accumulated toxins or karma, and reviving us with its high vibration now."

"The oceans are filled with Infinite Good and this force prevails over any appearance, so only good is coming to them and from them now."

"The love of angels flows through my heart, dissolving any acid thoughts and restoring divine purity now."

"I am a living manifestation of divine harmony, hope, and strength."

"The love of angels touches the planet, dissolving acid thoughts from all receptive minds and acid conditions from the oceans, now."

Gabriel and Hope Cleanse Your Space

Do this ritual at the full moon, and repeat if:

- you move into a new place
- you sense dense energy
- you've been feeling despondent

- you've had a draining visitor
- there's been an argument or low-vibrational conversation in your space.

Have on hand a white candle and a stick of jasmine incense.

1. Light the incense and repeat, "This is an offering for Gabriel and Hope, whom I ask to join me in cleansing and purifying this house (room, space) now."

2. Take a cup with angelic holy water (see above) and walk about your home or the place you're blessing, sprinkling it on the walls and floors, in the corners and covers, even flinging some drops on the ceiling.

3. As you do this, pause occasionally to visualize legions of white angels moving through your house on great waves of water, cleansing every corner, closet, and space.

Bless Yourself

You can do this quick blessing in the morning after you get dressed, or whenever you feel tired or stressed.

1. Wet your fingertips with angelic holy water.

2. Imagine that Gabriel and Hope are with you, pouring water over your head.

3. Touch your forehead with the holy water and repeat: "The angels renew my strength and hope now."

Angelic Food Blessing

Since remote antiquity, people have blessed and shared food to reaffirm our connection with others, the earth, and with Spirit.

Each tradition has its own approach to blessing food. Choose from the following options or make your own. You may enjoy putting your hands near or over your food as you mindfully repeat the blessing.

"We give thanks for this rich supply that fills our table and pours upon us always, equally blessing all beings, including (name a particular person or group you wish to bless), and guiding them to receive the rich good that flows for them, now."

"We give thanks for this table, this food, and all the rich blessings that fill our lives."

"Thank You, Beloved Mother-Father, for sending your angels to bless this food and all beings who gave something of themselves so it could manifest."

"We thank the angels who bless this meal and bring rich good to all beings now."

Gabriel and Hope Bless Your Space

Have on hand white flowers and a white candle.

1. Place the flowers in a vase with water.

2. Light the candle and walk all around your home, pausing frequently to touch the walls. Imagine that many white angels are with you, also holding candles and pausing alongside you to touch the walls.

3. As you do this, repeat: "I bless this space with the white light of the angels and with the energy of hope in my heart that I press into these walls now." Not only the word but also the emotional energy of the word "hope" is essential in this blessing. Each time you repeat the blessing and touch the walls, recall something that makes you feel hopeful or has made you hopeful in the past.

Flowers without Borders

Suiting their role as angels of purity, birth, and rebirth, Gabriel and Hope are the archangels of flowers. As mentioned at the beginning of this book, since I first came up with the idea of Angelic Intelligence in 2011, it was as though an invisible hand guided me to persistently notice and explore certain recurring themes. One of these themes was the importance of flowers. We're used to thinking of them as beautiful objects, but their energy has deep connections both to angels and humans. Let's see how their role in Angelic Intelligence is brought into relief.

Biologically speaking, plants transmute sunlight into food for the rest of the planet, and flowers are the reproductive organs of many plants. Flowers therefore have a key function in the chain of life on Earth.

In ancient cultures, flowers were considered sacred. They were a symbol of the divine feminine, associated with fertility, magical powers, and more, as we will see a bit further on.

Etched on the walls of Egyptian temples and in ruins around the world—from Tibet to Mexico to Iceland—is a symbol called the Flower of Life. It's a perfect circle that encloses a series of smaller circles interlaced in a symmetrical pattern that resembles a flower. Throughout this mandala, wherever two circles cross, they form an almond-like shape called the Vesica Piscis, symbol of the birth channel of the Great Mother. It's interesting to note that as living cells divide and multiply, they make a shape very similar to the Flower of Life. In sacred geometry, this symbol is considered a sort of map of the divine energy behind creation.

The connection between flowers, the sacred feminine, and creation recurs in myths worldwide. Manly Hall says that the ancient mystery traditions considered the lotus and the rose to be symbols of "the maternal generative mystery."[78] *Matripadma* (Mother Lotus) is the ancient Hindu name for the womb of nature.[79] Lakshmi, the most important Hindu goddess, is known to have been born from a lotus. Both she and Tara are depicted with a lotus aureole. In 2013, I visited an exhibit in the National Palace in downtown Mexico City. Organized by the prestigious Mexican Institute of Anthropology and History, it displayed a collection of ancient Mayan artifacts that had never been shown to the public. At the beginning of the exhibit, I noticed a small, glass case containing a figure of a calla lily. In the center of its petals was what looked like a little man. The identifying tag said, "The first Mayan god, being born from a flower."

In 2014, as I was preparing this book and teaching people to activate their light bodies and make mandalas with angels, flowers, and goddesses, I saw a headline in the news: "Experts Crack the Phaistos Disk!" A six-inch fired clay mandala, the disk was discovered in Crete in 1908, with an estimated age of four thousand years. Considered the oldest known sample of printing, it's covered with a series of symbols that are unlike any known languages. Numerous specialists had been working for more than a century to decipher its message. The news said that Dr. Gareth Owens, professor at the Technological Institute of Crete, and John Coleman of Oxford, together had cracked 50 percent of the code. It turns out that the disk is a hymn or prayer to a luminous mother goddess. On one side, she's described as pregnant. The central symbol on the other side is a flower. Gareth called the object "the Minoan bible," meaning

78. Manly P. Hall, *The Secret Teachings of All Ages* (New York: Penguin, 2003 reprint), 293.

79. Walker, *Woman's Dictionary*, 429.

that the goddess, the flower, and light were all central to the belief systems of ancient Crete.[80]

Besides their appearance in myth and symbol, flowers are featured in spiritual practices around the world. They can be found on the altars of most traditions. Nor is their role solely decorative. In the Hindu tradition, each chakra is thought to be an etheric lotus. One of the ways to activate them is to visualize them spinning. In the Yaki tradition, there's an energy sheath called the flower body. After devoting several months to interviewing Yaki *curanderos* (shamans) in northern Mexico, three anthropologists documented this belief in their book, *El Cuerpo Flor (The Flower Body)*. The Yakis say that the flower body is a "spiritual double"[81]—and also considered a sort of guardian presence or "angel"[82]—that imbues the bearer with healing gifts. Those born with it have certain physical traits and can astrally travel to heal from a distance, mainly in their sleep. They say that all Yakis once had a *cuerpo flor*, but now only those with a special mission are born with one, including musicians, dancers, midwives, and healers. (As the reader may recall from chapter 1, Xochiquetzal, goddess of flowers and the light body, is also from the Mexican tradition.)

Throughout Mexico, white flowers are used for cleansing and protection. Kept in a vase in your house, they are known to absorb envy or other negative thoughts people may send your way. Curan-

---

80. "Have researchers cracked the code of the 4,000-year-old Phaistos disc?" Ancient Origins website, October 26, 2014, https://www.ancient-origins.net /news-history-archaeology/have-researchers-cracked-code-4000-year-old- phaistos-disc-002256.

81. María Eugenia Olavarría, with Aguilar and Merino, *El Cuerpo Flor* (Mexico City: Miguel Ángel Porrúa and Universidad Autónoma Metropolitana, 2009), 72.

82. Ibid., 73.

deros clean their clients' energy by passing a large bunch of herbs and wildflowers in a sweeping motion over their bodies.

The archetype recurs in many places. In her book *The Wheel of Life,* Elizabeth Kubler-Ross describes a vision she had that was almost like a near-death experience: In an altered state of consciousness, she saw a sea of lotuses that turned into a single flower, and she was guided to move through this bloom into a field of light, bliss, and love beyond the physical plane. Once there, she heard the words *shanti nilaya.*[83] Kubler-Ross later learned that *shanti nilaya* is Tibetan for "definitive home of peace." In her book *Sacred Woman,* elder Queen Afua shares what is called a sacred lotus initiation, a spiritual rebirthing inspired in ancient African birth ceremonies.[84] These examples point to the role of blooms in spiritual magic and rebirth. A bit further on you'll find exercises to precipitate this connection.

Angel-Flower Cleansing

You don't need physical flowers for the following cleansing, which takes about nine minutes.

1. Imagine two white archangels before you, holding white lilies in their hands.

2. Repeat: "Gabriel and Hope, please cleanse me with your magical flowers."

3. Close your eyes and imagine that the angels pass their flowers over you, starting on your front side, from head to foot, and continuing with the same motion over your back and sides.

---

83. Elizabeth Kubler-Ross, *La Rueda de la Vida* (Barcelona, Spain: Ediciones Bergara, 2015), 297.

84. Queen Afua, *Sacred Woman* (New York: Random House, 2001), 372.

4. With your eyes still closed, "see" the angels put their hands above the crown of your head and send a shower of small, white flowers that fall gently over and around you, washing your entire aura.

5. Give thanks to the angels for their assistance.

Gabriel's Flowers

Gabriel relates to all flowers. White flowers, symbols of pure, new birth, have a special connection to him, in particular the lily and the white rose.

The Lily

The lily relates to Juno, the sometimes-virgin goddess; Eostre, Germanic goddess of spring (season of new growth); and dawn, hour of new beginnings. The lily's shape is similar to a trumpet and this flower is also related to good news. White flowers appear in the major arcana of the tarot in the Magician, the Fool, and the Hierophant cards, which are all related to magic and new beginnings.

Ask for Good News

Besides the exercises shared below, there is a simple way to invoke Lily's support:

1. Visualize a bouquet of white lilies in front of you, emitting gold dust and the sounds of a trumpet.

2. Choose one of the following invocations and repeat it three times:

   "Angels of lilies, please announce the good news I want to hear (name situation)."

*"Angels of lilies, please shower me with messages that
awaken my soul.*

"Angels of lilies, please fill my life with good news."

White Rose

The rose is second only to the lotus in sacred symbolism. Hall says,
"the rose and the lotus … symbolize primarily the maternal creative
mystery."[85] The rose has been related to Isis, Aphrodite, Venus, Juno,
Flora, and Cybele. Mary is called "Holy Rose," "Rose Garden," and
"Wreath of Roses." "Rose windows" are beautiful, stained glass mandalas that are put in the west, "feminine" side of churches, often
with Mary in the middle.

In chapter 5 we've seen this flower's relationship to ardor, love,
and self-esteem.

Roses are also related to the cycle of life and rebirth. During
Rosalia, a festival to honor the dead, Romans would throw rose hips
and buds on graves as a gift of new life. The roses depicted in the
Strength card of the tarot denotes this flower's connection with vital-
ity and will.

The white rose relates to sublime desire, spiritual passion, and
renewal.

Angelic Rosaries

Prayer beads and rosaries have been in use for many thousands of
years. The beads were sometimes made from rose wood or petals so
that the plant's energy would optimize the regenerative effects of
the user's prayers.

---

85. Hall, *Secret Teachings*, 293.

Call on Gabriel and Hope to bless your rosary. You can also make an angel rosary or mala of your own.

Make Your Rosary

Before gathering your materials, ask the angels to direct and facilitate this activity.

Have on hand:

- Depending on the length you want, 18, 27, or 36 rose-petal or rose wood beads with 1 mm holes. (These are easy to find online at reasonable prices.)

- A medal with a picture of Gabriel. Alternately, use a white bead that's somehow fancy or slightly bigger than the others (this bead could be of Gabriel's stone, danburite).

- A 1mm piece of nylon string, 1 to 2 feet long, depending on the length and number of beads you're planning on using. Alternately, you can use waxed cotton or hemp cord, although these options require silicone or clear nail polish to seal the tips of the string.

- My dear friend Diana Garibay, who makes personalized malas, suggests adding a tassel to the end to sweep away negative energies.

- Scissors.

1. Tie a knot on one of end of the string.

2. String the rose-petal beads one by one, tying a knot between each, pushing it tightly against the bead.

3. As you add each bead, repeat: "I bless this rosary with my love of angels and these beads are imbued with renewing power now."

4. After you string the rose beads, add the white bead or medal of Gabriel.

Rosary Blessing

Hold the rosary in your hands, imagining that two great, white archangels are with you, touching it also.

Repeat three times: "I thank the angels and flowers that have blessed this rosary with renewing powers!"

Choose from the many affirmations in this book to repeat as you use your rosary. You can also make special rosaries for the other archangels: use a medal of Zadkiel for a forgiveness rosary, Raphael for a healing rosary, Uriel for an abundance rosary, and so on.

Angelic Ceremony to Birth New Beginnings

There are times when we want to start over or try something different but feel somehow bound to the past. We might doubt our ability to pull it off, or think the old situation was our fate or karma. Maybe we're concerned about what someone will think of us, or we feel like we owe somebody something. Perhaps someone is manipulating us to feel that way.

The archangels of new birth bless our new beginnings and like the mother's body during birth, apply their magic to push us ahead on our new path. The following unique blessing integrates this boost. It also imbues your aura with the energy of flowers. You can use it anytime, although the new moon portal is particularly propitious (2 ½ days before and after the new moon). It's also fun to share with a confidant or group of trusted friends, taking turns enacting the angels or guiding one another through the portal.

Have on hand:

- two white flowers, preferably lily, lotus, or rose
- a fireplace or fireproof dish or receptacle where you can safely burn a paper
- matches or a lighter

- two 9-foot strips of white ribbon
- two sheets of white paper.

1. Lay out the ribbons in parallel lines about a yard apart to make a 9-foot path.
2. Set the flowers on the ribbons, at the halfway point.
3. Standing or sitting at one end of the path, on a white piece of paper, write the types of feelings, thoughts, and situations you would like to leave behind in your new phase.
4. Look ahead to the middle of the path. Imagine that Gabriel and Hope are standing on the ribbons where the flowers are.
5. Take a step ahead and ask that they shine their white light into the list you wrote, as you light in on fire and put it in the fireplace receptacle (if you do this with another person, they can burn it for you).
6. Walk toward the angels, stopping before them.
7. Imagine they are holding up a great white flower.
8. On another piece of paper, write how you would like to feel on your new path. Gabriel and Hope are connected to imagination and feelings, and the following examples are designed to align with their energy:

"I see myself feeling successful, joyous, and healthy."

"I imagine myself full of love and free from controlling attitudes."

"I visualize myself enjoying new and greater good than I've ever experienced before now."

"I wish to feel at peace with the past and confident about my future."

"I imagine myself free of remorse and doubts, happy with my spiritual and professional progress."

"I imagine myself totally renewed, financially success-ful, confident, free from toxic guilt, and living my full potential."

9. Roll the paper like a scroll. Holding it in your hand, step slowly through the angel-flower portal. As you walk, feel the great petals touching you, pressing all over your body, cleansing your aura, and pushing you ahead, as though you were being born through the flower.

10. Walk to the end of the path, feeling that the white light of the angels is radiating behind you.

11. Turn and repeat: "Thank you, Gabriel and Hope, thank you, Mother-Flower for cleansing my being and moving me forward in a new, higher experience now."

During the next four weeks after this ceremony, follow up by devot-ing a few minutes each day to visualizing that you're going through the flower as described above in step 9, and then reading your inten-tions. Alternately, follow up with the following mandala.

Gabriel's Mandala to Be Reborn to the Flower-Mother

The flowers and angels facilitate a spiritual rebirth. After clarifying the intention of this mandala, affirm: "Gabriel and Hope, please direct my angelic rebirth now."

Getting Ready

Before gathering your materials, take a moment to quiet your mind, focus on your intention of rebirth, and ask the angels, goddesses, and plant spirits to help you. Hold to your purpose as you put it together.

You will need:

- natural or hemp-colored paper or poster board; gold or silver pen, crayons, and/or paints

- depending on the size of your mandala, 20 to 30 small images of white lilies, roses, and lotuses

- 1 large (1½") image of a white lily

- 3 or more small (½") images of Archangels Gabriel and Hope (you can download, cut out, and paste; or if you prefer, draw the images onto the poster board)

- 3 or more small images of goddesses of Mary or Guadalupe-Tonantzin

- your favorite adhesive stick, paste, or glue.

1. Trace a large (10" or more) circle, and line it evenly with the images of white flowers.

2. Paste the large image of the lily in the middle, and the smaller images around the inside of the circle to taste.

3. Above your mandala, write: "White flowers of the planet, please send me your vibrations of renewal."

4. Below or to the side of your mandala, write: "Joyous, pure Mother, please purify my heart, mind, and light body, so that I may be born anew."

Center in Your Mandala

1. Repeat the flower invocation for 2 minutes, feeling as you do the energy of renewal that they send you.

2. Imagine that the angels are gathering around you and that they lift you up and direct you through the flower.

3. For about 2 minutes, feel the petals pressing on you, as though you were passing through the center of the flower like a birth channel.

4. Imagine that as you emerge from the flower, you find yourself coming into a realm of pure light where you are encircled by angels who receive you with love.

Ideally, use this mandala before going to bed each night for four weeks, and renew the practice yearly. If you're working with other mandalas, use them after this one.

More Ways to Connect with Flowers

- Keep a vase with white flowers in your space to absorb any negative thoughts others send your way.

- If you work as a healer, ask Gabriel to touch your client with his cleansing flower. Visualize that he does this as you apply your normal healing methods.

- Make a flower garden or plant flowers in your yard, or, for that matter, wherever you can. The planet needs their energy and the bees need them to pollinate and thrive. As the seeds go into the ground, imagine that white angels are touching and blessing them with abundant growth.

- Make a personal altar or prayer nook, or adapt your current altar. Integrate images of archangels: you may choose one or more you're especially connected to or currently working with, or use all seven. You can include pictures of goddesses or your personal spirit guides. You may also keep your rosary or prayer beads here. Include a vase of white flowers.

- Make a special nook for your positive ancestors or a loved one who has made her or his transition. Use pictures of them, and for positive energy include an orgonite and/or a piece of danburite or white quartz crystal and white flowers to send them light. (Because of their use at funerals, some researchers say that white flowers relate to death, but they actually promote rebirth.)

- Use a flower as a screensaver for your computer, tablet, or mobile phone. For cleansing, purity, and renewal, use a white flower. Or go through the chapters of this book and choose the flower most fitting for your current process or intention.

- Flowers are living, magical spirits. They're eager to be included and invoked. As you integrate them more consciously, you'll receive your own signs and guidance to enrich that collaboration. If you've begun to use some of the suggestions in this book, chances are you already have.

Letters to Gabriel

We can write to Gabriel so that we and our children may discover and walk our soul paths. Or we can ask for help in conceiving something new, whether it's a baby, a new mentality, or a new life. Write these letters on white paper or acquire a special notebook with white pages and soft, childlike colors on the outside.

I had been trying to conceive for a year and a half before I decided to visualize. I hadn't yet developed the angel mandalas but was using and teaching visualization techniques. Without telling anyone, I got bright pink poster board for the love vibration. On it, I pasted an image of Archangel Gabriel with a lily, color photographs of a pregnant woman, and a couple holding a baby. I also included a picture of a beautiful baby's room. I soon conceived my son. Now in his teens, he looks and acts like an angel.

You can make a mandala for this purpose. Use pink or cream-colored poster board, make a 12-inch circle of lilies, and include Archangel Gabriel and the rest of the images described in the previous paragraph. Like other mandalas for tangible manifestation, visualize with it three times daily for about six minutes each session. Radiate love to the baby and imagine that you can feel its softness, warmth, and weight in your arms. Keep this mandala secret.

Affirmation to Conceive and Bear a Child

Write it twelve or eighteen times daily in your letter or use it on your mandala.

> *"The angels bring me a perfect child, and I lovingly welcome it into my arms and life now."*

People who have near-death experiences often say they've seen a field of white light charged with bliss and love. We don't have to wait for transition from the physical to touch this power. By applying the keys in the present chapter, we can begin to drink now from a well that never runs dry. Like Gabriel, Hope, and their luminous colleagues, this blessed energy awaits our recognition, invocation, and the simple but amazing door of our intention: the intention to retrieve our original purity, the intention to resonate in hope, the intention to bring forth life, whether as a baby, a rose garden, or a new version of ourselves. This is the most important white candle we can light. Its flame will continue to glow, along with our flower connections in our rainbow body, completing a multicolored bridge to the Source.

CONCLUSION

When I first came up with the idea of Angelic Intelligence in 2011, I was excited about the archangels' connections with metaphysical principles I had been versed in from a young age. Connecting with the angels had been a wonderful adventure, increasing my love radiation, my openness to divine guidance, and my powers of manifestation. Our winged companions had helped me deepen my faith, and, in seemingly dire situations, made the difference to work miracles for me and those I helped. As I began to prepare this book and my course of the same name, I looked forward to sharing the connections with others.

What I discovered as I deepened my research turned out to be even more exciting. The archangels' roots in goddess traditions opened up a whole new world. It increased my confidence in my own spiritual powers and as a channel of these archetypal female energies, which are not only sweet, compassionate, and loving but also strong, empowering, and, when necessary, fierce. My female students have shared similar experiences of empowerment. In spiritual practice, self-confidence makes a tangible difference. The discovery of these pre-patriarchal roots also underscored my sense of connection to all life, a unity that was vital to ancient spiritual teachings that continues to shine in the subtle dimensions. And when guided by an invisible hand, I was led to understand the higher purpose of these ancient teachings: to awaken our angelic body, my new field took on a more heavenly and sublime meaning. Both women and men I've worked with note that this facet of Angelic Intelligence has lifted their entire spiritual experience to a higher level.

Since childhood I had been attracted to the topics of mind power, nature spirits, angels, and goddesses. Like a handful of loose gems, these once spontaneous, apparently disparate connections began to fall into place like stars in a constellation. In it, there are certainly more stars to be discovered. I have found some that I intend to share in future books. I'm sure that many applied readers will contribute to this rich, living field, and no doubt some already have before even reading this book. What's clear is that the forces we speak of are not disparate but belong to a light network that shines just beyond the threshold of our physical perception. As I've experienced myself and seen in others: when we invoke, connect, and fuse with these energies, our powers of manifestation, of healing, and of Angelic Intelligence increase continually. This is true for me, as it is for anyone, because we all have divine circuits waiting to be awakened, circuits that have been intuitively activated in me and in numerous participants of my groups, some of whom are even spontaneously guided to move their arms and hands during the healing sessions I facilitate. The angels activate these circuits, lifting us out of the patterns and energies of the world of appearances and fueling our angelic bodies to prepare us so that when we move to the beyond we may join the greater light community more readily.

This story is ancient, and although humanity's period of spiritual amnesia may have buried it for a time, it isn't finished. Every divine intention, every prayer, every thought, and every action of love and faith, every conscious connection with light beings, opens a new chapter of possibilities.

Since I started teaching Angelic Intelligence, humanity's need for solutions has become more evident than ever. What will happen with the planet? In every sphere of life, women and sensitive men are key players in defining outcomes with far-reaching effects. Does it serve us to doubt our power? Does it serve us to delay our calling as miracle workers? This is the time to use what you know.

Angels are among us. They guide us, supporting our intentions for the best and highest results. By the light of Infinite Good, they always open a way. This is the time to turn to them.

I tend to read my favorite books more than once. Often when I think I've got a certain title down, I end up learning something new. I hope this book may be like that for you. Most of all, I hope you take up the tools in its pages. They're inspired in the legacy of our magical ancestors. This is the time to walk your rainbow path.

PRONUNCIATION OF DEITY NAMES

Airmed—*AIR-mae-ith*

Anuket—*AN-oo-ket*

Aphrodite—*aff-row-DYE-teeArtha*—*ARTH-uh*

Astarte—*ah-STAR-tay*

Athena—*ah-THEEN-uh*

Artemis—*ARR-teh-miss*

Chac Chel—*shock-shell*

Chalchiuhtlicue—*chawl-chee-oot-LEEK-way*

Chicomecoatl—*cheeko-MAY-kwahttle*

Coatlicue—*KOHT-lee-cue*

Coventina—*cuh-ven-TEEN-uh*

Cybele—*sigh-bell*

Danu—*DAN-oo*

Demeter—*DEHM-me-ter*

Ertha—*earth-uh*

Haumea—*how-MAY-ah*

Hecate—*HEH-caught-tay*

Huitzilopochtli—*weet-see-luh-POACH-tuh-lee*

Innana—*in-AHNN-uh*

Isis—*EYE-sis*

Juno—*JUNE-oh*

Ixchel—*EE-shull*

Kuan Yin—*kwan-YIN*

Kukulkan—*coo-cool-KAHN*

Lakshmi—*LOCKSH-mee*

Ma'at—*mah-AT*

Matripadma—*mah-tree-PAHD-mah*

Ometeotl—*OH-mee-tee-oat-'l*

Osiris—*oh-SYE-rus*

Pachamana—*PAH-chah-mah-nah*

Palden Lhamo—*PAH-den LAM-oh*

Parnasavari—*par-nah-sha-vah-ree*

Quetzalcoatl—*ket-sahl-coh-AHT-'l*

Samhain—*SOW-en*

Sarasvati—*sar-uhs-VAHT-ee*

Sekhmet—*SEC-met*

Simhamukha—*sim-ha-MOOK-ah*

Takutzi Nakawe—*tah-KOOT-see nah-kah-WAY*

Tara—*TAIR-uh*

Tlazoteotl—*TLA-zo-tay-oat-'l*

Toci—*TOE-see*

Tonantzin—*tone-ahn-SEEN*

Urda—*oor-dah*

Urth—*oorth*

Vellamo—*VELL-am-oh*

Viracocha—*vee-rah-COE-cha*

Xochiquetzal—*SO-chee-ket-zal*

BIBLIOGRAPHY

Abadie, M.J. *The Everything Angels Book*. Holbrook, MA: Adams Media Corporation. 2000.

Aspra, Lucy. *A Manual of Angels*. Mexico City: The House of Angels, 2019.

———. *The Angels of Human Destiny, Vol. 1, Dying is Truly Living*. Mexico City: The House of Angels, 2005.

———. *The Angels of Human Destiny, Vol. 2, Who We Are and Where We're Going*. Mexico City: The House of Angels, 2005.

———. *The Sword of Heavenly Health,* Mexico City: The House of Angels, 2008.

Auset, Priestess Brandi. *The Goddess Guide: Exploring the Attributes and Correspondences of the Divine Feminine*. Woodbury, MN: Llewellyn, 2016.

Ayala, R. R. *Mitos y Leyendas de los Mayas*. Barcelona: Ediciones Brontes S. L., 2012.

Baldwin, William J. *Healing Lost Souls: Releasing Unwanted Spirits from Your Energy Body*. Charlottesville, VA: Hampton Roads, 2003.

Blofeld, John. *Bodhisattva of Compassion, The Mystical Tradition of Kuan Yin*. Boulder, CO: Shambala, 1978.

Braud, William. *Distant Mental Influence: Its Contributions to Science, Healing and Human Interactions*. Charlottesville, VA: Hampton Roads, 2003.

Cambell, Joseph. *Goddesses: Mystery of the Divine Feminine*. Edited by Safron Rossi. Novato, CA: New World Library, 2013.

Carroll, Cain, and Revital Carroll. *Mudras of India*. London: Singing Dragon, 2013.

Cowan, Eliot. *Plant Spirit Medicine*. Columbus, NC: Swan-Raven & Co., 1995.

Cross, Jerry, and Pauline Bondonno. *Knowing Yourself Inside Out for Self-Direction*. Berkeley, CA: Crystal Publications, 2011.

Cunningham, Scott. *Dreaming the Divine: Techniques for Sacred Sleep*. Woodbury, MN: Llewellyn, 2016.

Dale, Cyndi. *Energetic Boundaries*. Boulder, CO: SoundsTrue, 2011.

———. *The Subtle Body*. Boulder, CO: SoundsTrue, 2009.

Di Nucci, Hernán, *Diccionario de Mitología: Dioses, diosas y seres mitológicos de todo el mundo*. Mexico City: Océano, 2010.

Dossy, Larry. *Reinventing Medicine*. New York: HarperCollins, 1999.

Dowling, Levi H. *The Aquarian Gospel of Jesus the Christ*. New York: Penguin Group, 2009.

Durdin-Robertson, Lawrence. *The Year of the Goddess*. Wellingborough, UK: Thorsons Publishing Group, 1999.

Emoto, Masaru. *The Messages of Water*. New York: Atria Books, 2005.

Eisler, Rianne. *The Chalice and the Blade*. New York: HarperCollins, 1988.

Ferguson, Marilyn. *The Aquarian Conspiracy*. New York: Penguin, 1987.

Filmore, Charles. *The Twelve Powers of Man*. Eastford, CT: Martino Fine Books, 2013. Originally published 1930 by Unity School of Christianity (Kansas City, MO).

Foote, A. Lee. *Oral Exams: Preparing for and Passing Candidacy, Qualifying and Graduate Defenses*. Oxford, UK: Oxford University Press, 2016.

Garnier Malet, Jean-Pierre, and Lucile Garnier Malet. *El Doble ... ¿cómo funciona?* Spain: Editorial Reconocerse, 2003.

———. *El Doble Cuántico*. Madrid: Arkano Books, 2016.

———. *La Fuerza de lo Invisible.* Madrid: Arkano Books, 2017.

George, Demetra. *Asteroid Goddesses*. San Diego: ACS Publications, 1986.

Gerson, Michael D. *The Second Brain*. New York: HarperCollins, 1998.

Grant, Robert J. *Edgar Cayce on Angels, Archangels and Unseen Forces*. Virginia Beach, VA: A.R.E. Press, 2014.

Guiley, Rosemary Ann. *The Encyclopedia of Angels*. New York: Checkmark Books, 2004.

Hall, Manly P. *The Secret Teachings of All Ages*. New York: Penguin, 2003. Originally published 1928 by H. S. Crocker Co.

Hancock, Graham. *Supernatural: Meetings with the Ancient Teachers of Mankind*. Toronto: Doubleday Canada, 2005.

Harley, Gail M. *Emma Curtis Hopkins: Forgotten Founder of New Thought*. New York: Syracuse University Press, 2002.

Hoffman, Glynda-Lee. *The Secret Dowry of Eve: Woman's Role in the Development of Consciousness*. Rochester, VT: Inner Traditions, 2003.

Holmes, Ernest. *How to Change Your Life*. Deerfield, FL: Health Communications, Inc., 1999.

———. *How to Use the Science of Mind*. Los Angeles, CA: Science of Mind Publishing, 2002.

———. *Science of Mind*. New York: Penguin Putnam, 1998.

Hopkins, Emma Curtis. *Class Lessons 1888*. Compiled by Elizabeth C. Bogart. Chicago: Ministry of Truth International, 1990.

Hopkins, Emma Curtis. *High Mysticism*. Santa Monica, CA: De Vorss, 1977.

———. *Scientific Christian Mental Practice*. Santa Monica, CA: De Vorss, 1974.

Howard, Jane M. *Commune with the Angels: A Heavenly Handbook*. Virginia Beach, VA: A.R.E. Press, 1992.

Ireland Frey, Louise. *Freeing the Captives: The Emerging Therapy of Treating Spirit Attachment*. Charlottesville, VA: Hampton Roads, 2001.

James, G.M. George. *Stolen Legacy: The Egyptian Origin of Western Philosophy*. Ashland, OH: Library of Alexandria, 1989. Originally published 1954 by Philosophical Library (New York).

Kanigel, Robert. *The Man Who Knew Infinity: A Life of the Genius Ramanujan*. New York: Simon & Schuster, 1991.

Kerner, Nigel. *Grey Aliens and the Harvesting of Souls*. Rochester, VT: Bear & Co., 2010.

Kinsley, David. *Hindu Goddesses: Visions of the Divine Feminine in the Hindu Religious Tradition*. Berkeley, CA: University of California Press, 1986.

———. *The Goddesses' Mirror: Visions of the Divine from East and West*. Albany, NY: State University of New York Press, 1989.

Klausen, Brad. "Magical Egypt 2, Discovery 2." Video, 10:11, https://www.youtube.com/watch?v=HGWRWJH1mdk.

Douglas-Klotz, Neil. *Desert Wisdom: Sacred Middle Eastern Writings from the Goddess Through the Sufis*. San Francisco: HarperSanFrancisco, 1995.

Kubler-Ross, Elizabeth. *La Rueda de la Vida*. Barcelona, Spain: Ediciones Bergara, 2015.

———. *The Wheel of Life: A Memoir of Living and Dying*. New York: Touchstone, 1998.

Lanza, Robert, with Bob Berman. *Biocentrism: How Life and Consciousness are the Keys to Understanding the True Nature of the Universe*. Dallas: Benbella Books, 2009.

Lehner, Johanna, and Ernst Lehner. *Folklore and Symbolism of Flowers, Plants and Trees*. New York: Dover Publications, 2003.

Liberman, Jacob. *Light Medicine of the Future: How We Can Use It to Heal Ourselves NOW*. Rochester, VT: Bear & Co., 1991.

Lipton, Bruce. *Spontaneous Evolution*. Carlsbad, CA: Hay House, 2010.

———. *The Biology of Belief*. Carlsbad, CA: Hay House, 2016.

Llopis, José J. *Aztecas, Mayas e Incas*. Mexico City: Ediciones Daimon, 1980.

Lopez Luján, Leonardo. *Tlaltecuhtili*. Mexico City: Instituto Nacional de Antropología e Historia, 2010.

MacDougall, Mary Katherine. *Be Healthy, Now!* Unity Village, MO: Unity Books, 1994.

Maclean, Dorothy. *To Hear the Angels Sing.* Hudson, NY: Lindisfarne Press, 1990.

Mancuso, Stefano. *Brilliant Green: The Surprising History and Science of Plant Intelligence.* Washington, D.C.: Island Press, 2005.

McFadden, Steven. *Legend of the Rainbow Warriors.* Bloomington, IN: iUniverse Publishers, 2005.

McTaggart, Lynne. *The Field: The Quest for the Secret Force of the Universe.* New York: HarperCollins, 2002.

Melchizedek, Drunvalo. *El Secreto Ancestral de la Flor de la Vida.* Madrid: Arkano Books, 2013.

Menard, Louis, *Los Libros de Hermes Trismegisto.* Bogotá, Colombia: Editorial Solar, 1995.

Miller, Carol. *Ancestral, La Sorprendente relación entre las antiguas civilizaciones de Asia y América.* Mexico City: Planeta, 2015.

Miller, Ruth. *Unveiling Your Hidden Power: Emma Curtis Hopkins Metaphysics for the 21st Century.* Beaverton, OR: WiseWoman Press, 2005.

Mishlove, Jeffrey. *The Roots of Consciousness.* Tulsa, OK: Council Oaks Books, 1993.

Montalk. *Fringe Knowledge for Beginners.* montalk.net, 2012. Kindle.

Montgomery, Pam. *Plant Spirit Healing.* Rochester, VT: Bear & Co., 2008.

Mullin, Glen, trans. *Meditations on the Lower Tantra: From the Collected Works of the Previous Dalai Lama.* Dharamasala, Tibet: Library of Tibetan Works and Archives, 1983.

Musaios. *The Lion Path: The Big Picture and What It Means to You.* Sardis, Canada: House of Horus, 1996.

Musès, Charles. *Grail Most Ancient: Advanced Guide for the Lion Path.* Sardis, Canada: House of Horus, 1993.

Musès, Charles. *The Lion's Path.* Berkeley, CA: Golden Scepter, 1988.

———. In *All Her Names: Explorations of the Feminine in Divinity,* edited by Joseph Campbell. San Francisco: HarperCollins, 1991.

Norbu, Namkhai. *Rainbow Body: The Life and Realization of a Tibetan Yogin, Togden Ugyen Tendzin.* Berkeley, CA: North Atlantic Books, 2012.

Ober, Clinton, Steven Sinatra, and Martin Zucker. *Earthing: The Most Important Health Discovery Ever.* Laguna Beach, CA: Basic Health Publications, 2010.

Olavarría, María Eugenia, Cristina Aguilar, and Érica Merino. "El Cuerpo Flor: Etnografía de una noción yoeme" in *Journal de la Société des américanistes* 98, 1 (2012): 206–210.

Paddison, Sara. *The Hidden Power of the Heart.* Boulder, CO: Planetary Publications, 1998.

Page, Christine. *2012 and the Galactic Center: The Return of the Great Mother.* Rochester, VT: Bear & Co., 2008.

Palmer, Clara. *You Can Be Healed.* Unity Village, MO: Unity Books, 1950. Originally published 1937 by Unity School of Christianity (Kansas City, MO).

Pallardy, Pierre. *Gut Instinct: What Your Stomach is Trying to Tell You.* London: Rodale International, 2011.

Pennick, Nigel. *The Pagan Book of Days: A Guide to the Festivals, Traditions, and Sacred Days of the Year.* Rochester, VT: Inner Traditions, 2001.

Pomeroy, Crystal. *Los Pergaminos de la abundancia.* Mexico City: Alquimia Science Project, 2008.

———. *The Spiritual Magic in Our Daily Bread.* Mexico City: El Buscador, 2011.

Pseudo-Dionysius the Areopagite. *Celestial Hierarchy.* Whitefish, MT: Kessinger Publishing, 2004. First published in English (from original Greek ca. 5 CE) as *De Coelesti Hierarchia* in 1935 by Shrine of Wisdom.

Ponder, Catherine. *The Healing Secrets of the Ages.* Santa Monica, CA: De Vorss & Co., 1985. Originally published 1967 by Parker Publishing Company.

———. *The Prospering Power of Love.* Santa Monica, CA: De Vorss & Co., 2006. Originally published 1966 by Unity Books.

Queen Afua. *Sacred Woman: A Guide to Healing the Feminine Mind, Body, and Spirit.* New York: Random House, 2001.

Raven, Hazel. *The Angel Bible: The Definitive Guide to Angel Wisdom.* London: Octopus Publishing, 2006.

Randolph Price, John. *The Love Book.* Carlsbad, CA: Hay House, 1988.

Richardson, Tanya Carroll. *Angel Insights: Inspiring Messages From and Ways to Connect With Your Spiritual Guardians.* Woodbury, MN: Llewellyn Worldwide, 2018.

Roob, Alexander. *Alchemy & Mysticism.* Koln, Germany: Benedikt Taschen Verla, 1997.

Rose, Sharron. *The Path of the Priestess: A Guidebook for Awakening the Divine Feminine.* Rochester, VT: Inner Traditions, 2002.

Rosenblum, Bruce, and Fred Kuttner. *Quantum Enigma: Physics Encounters Consciousness*. New York: Oxford University Press, 2011.

Sagan, Samuel. *Entity Possession: Freeing the Energy Body of Negative Influences*. Rochester, VT: Inner Traditions, 1997.

Shaw, Miranda Eberle. *Buddhist Goddesses of India*. Princeton, NJ: Princeton University Press, 2006.

Shelley, Beatrice. *Diccionario de Flores*. Barcelona: Grupo Océano, 2010.

Stocker, Ricardo Horacio. *Our Compassionate Kosmos: Awakening to the Presence of Celestial Love*. Bloomington, IN: Balboa Press, 2015.

Stone, Merlin. *Ancient Mirrors of Womanhood: A Treasury of Goddess and Heroine Lore from Around the World*. Boston: Beacon Press, 1990.

———. *When God Was a Woman*. Reprint, New York: Harcourt, 2006. Originally published as *The Paradise Papers: The Suppression of Women's Rites* in 1976 by Virago.

Tate, Jessica, *El Mensaje de las Flores*. Barcelona: Ediciones Brontes, 2012.

Taylor, Jeremy. *The Wisdom of Your Dreams: Using Dreams to Tap Into Your Unconscious and Transform Your Life*. New York: Penguin, 2009.

Taylor, Terry Lynn. *Guardians of Hope: The Angels' Guide to Personal Growth*. Tiburon, CA: HJ Kramer, 1992.

Tedlock, Barbara. *The Woman in the Shaman's Body: Reclaiming the Feminine in Religion and Medicine*. New York: Bantam Books, 2005.

Tiso, Francis V. *Rainbow Body and Resurrection: Spiritual Attainment, the Dissolution of the Material Body, and the Case of Khenpo A Chö.* Berkeley, CA: North Atlantic Books, 2016.

Torkildson, Maura McCarley. *The Inner Tree: Discovering the Roots of Your Intuition.* Asheville, NC: Citrine Publishing, 2018.

Trobe, Kala. *Invoke the Goddess: Visualizations of Hindu, Greek, and Egyptian Deities.* St. Paul, MN: Llewellyn Worldwide, 2000.

Vaughan-Lee, Llewellyn, ed. *Spiritual Ecology: The Cry of the Earth.* Point Reyes Station, CA: The Golden Sufi Center, 2013.

Walker, Joseph M. *Seres Fabulosos de la Mitología.* Barcelona: Ediciones Brontes, 2012.

Walker, Barbara G. *Man Made God: A Collection of Essays.* Seattle: Stellar House Publishing, 2010.

———. *The Woman's Dictionary of Symbols and Sacred Objects.* New York: HarperCollins, 1988.

———. *The Woman's Encyclopedia of Myths and Secrets.* New York: HarperCollins, 1983.

Wohlleben, Peter. *The Hidden Life of Trees: What They Feel, How They Communicate—Discoveries from a Secret World.* Vancouver: Greystone Books, 2016.

Yeshe, Lama Thubten. *Introduction to Tantra: The Transformation of Desire.* Boston: Wisdom Publications, 2001.

Additional Books for Dream Interpretation

Dreaming the Divine: Techniques for Sacred Sleep, by Scott Cunningham. Llewellyn, 2016. Originally published 1985 as *Sacred Sleep: Dreams & the Divine* by Llewellyn.

Dreams: Your Magic Mirror, by Elsie Sechrist. A.R.E. Press, 2005.

Inner Work: Using Dreams and Active Imagination for Personal Growth, by Robert A. Johnson. Harper & Row, 2001.

Llewellyn's Complete Dictionary of Dreams: Over 1,000 Dream Symbols and Their Universal Meanings, by Dr. Michael Lennox. Llewellyn, 2015.

Llewellyn's Little Book of Dreams, by Dr. Michael Lennox. Llewellyn, 2017.

The Dream Book: Symbols for Self-Understanding by Betty Bethards. New Century Publishers, 2001.

Web References:

SAND. "The Secrets of Ramanujan's Garden." https://www .scienceandnonduality.com/article/the-secrets-of -ramanujans-garden.(No date.)

Pomeroy, Crystal. "Mayan Metaphysics for 2012." Maya del Mar's Daykeeper Journal. https://daykeeperjournal.com/2012/01 /mayan-metaphysics-2012/. (No date.)

Inside Mexico website. "Leyenda de Coatlicue y Coyolxauhqui." https://www.inside-mexico.com/leyenda-de-coatlicue -y-coyolxauhqui/. Posted February 2, 2015.

Lipton, Bruce. "What are the volts of electricity in your human body?!" Bruce Lipton's website. https://www.brucelipton.com /blog/what-are-the-volts-electricity-your-human-body. Posted May 20, 2019.

Jones, Ryan. "Brain Battery." Knowingneurons.com. https://knowingneurons.com/2012/12/14/brain-battery/. Posted December 14, 2012.

Labozzetta, Chandell. "Your Unconscious Mind Does Not Process Negatives: Replace Don't ... with What You WANT." LifePuzzle website. https://lifepuzzle.com.au/your-unconscious-mind -does-not-process-negatives-replace-dont-with-what-you-want. Posted February 7, 2017.

Sherburne-Michigan, Morgan. "Finally, the Mysterious First Part of Photosynthesis Comes Into View." Futurity.org. https:// www.futurity.org/photosynthesis-energy-conversion-1711092/. Posted March 23, 2018.

Scott, Martin. "The Miraculous Springs of Fatima." The American Society for the Defense of Tradition, Family and Property web-site. https://www.tfp.org/miraculous-springs-fatima/. Posted November 7, 2016.

Petit, Jean-Pierre. "Jacques Benveniste and the 'memory of water.'" Q-mag.org. https://q-mag.org/jacques-benveniste-and-the -memory-of-water.html. (No date.)

"Dr. Masaru Emoto and Water Consciousness: New frontiers in mind-body wellness." The Wellness Enterprise website. https:// thewellnessenterprise.com/emoto/. (No date.)

Stromberg, Joseph. "The Microscopic Structures of Dried Human Tears." *Smithsonian* magazine website. https://www.smithso-nianmag.com/science-nature/the-microscopic-structures-of -dried-human-tears-180947766/. Posted November 19, 2013.

Holloway, April. "Have researchers cracked the code of the 4,000-year-old Phaistos Disc?" Ancient Origins website. https:// www.ancient-origins.net/news-history-archaeology/have -researchers-cracked-code-4000-year-old-phaistos-disc-002256.

Updated October 26, 2014.

The reader will find guided meditations and videos with angelic mudras and other tools in this book at the author's website, www. crystalpomeroy.com. Follow the author by her name on Facebook and YouTube, and on Instagram at crystal_clearalways.

To Write to the Author

If you wish to contact the author or would like more information about this book, please write to the author in care of Llewellyn Worldwide Ltd. and we will forward your request. Both the author and publisher appreciate hearing from you and learning of your enjoyment of this book and how it has helped you. Llewellyn Worldwide Ltd. cannot guarantee that every letter written to the author can be answered, but all will be forwarded. Please write to:

Crystal Pomeroy
℅ Llewellyn Worldwide
2143 Wooddale Drive
Woodbury, MN 55125-2989

Please enclose a self-addressed stamped envelope for reply,
or $1.00 to cover costs. If outside the U.S.A., enclose
an international postal reply coupon.

Many of Llewellyn's authors have websites with additional information and resources. For more information, please visit our website at http://www.llewellyn.com.